The Post-Soviet Wars

The Post-Soviet Wars

Rebellion, Ethnic Conflict, and Nationhood in the Caucasus

Christoph Zürcher

NEW YORK UNIVERSITY PRESS
New York and London

NEW YORK UNIVERSITY PRESS
New York and London
www.nyupress.org

First published in paperback in 2009.

Library of Congress Cataloging-in-Publication Data
Zürcher, Christoph.
The post-Soviet wars : rebellion, ethnic conflict, and nationhood in the Caucasus / Christoph Zürcher.
p. cm.
Includes bibliographical references and index.
ISBN-13: 978-0-8147-9724-2 (paper : alk. paper)
ISBN-10: 0-8147-9724-5 (paper : alk. paper)
ISBN-13: 978-0-8147-9709-9 (cloth : alk. paper)
ISBN-10: 0-8147-9709-1 (cloth : alk. paper)
1. Ethnic conflict—Caucasus—Case studies. 2. Caucasus—Ethnic relations—History—20th century. 3. Caucasus—Politics and government—20th century. 4. Political violence—Caucasus—Case studies. I. Title. II. Title: Rebellion, ethnic conflict, and nationhood in the Caucasus.
DK509.Z87 2007
947.5'086—dc22 2007023003

New York University Press books are printed on acid-free paper, and their binding materials are chosen for strength and durability.

Manufactured in the United States of America
c 10 9 8 7 6 5 4 3 2 1
p 10 9 8 7 6 5 4 3 2 1

To Anna, Max, and Carla

Contents

Preface

This book examines the causes of internal wars in the aftermath of the Soviet Union. Between 1988 and 1997, there were seven internal wars on the territory of the former Soviet Union. Five of them are examined in this book: the war between Armenians and Azerbaijanis over the territory of Nagorny-Karabakh, the wars between Georgia and its breakaway regions of Abkhazia and South Ossetia, the civil war within Georgia, and Russia's war in breakaway Chechnya.

Every case of war is distinct and follows its specific trajectory shaped by a unique confluence of grievances, perceptions, and, above all, opportunities. But all cases of war covered in this book also subscribe to a common "script," which is clearly shaped by the unique historical structures of the Soviet system—and by a historically unique event, the collapse of the Soviet Empire. Crucial elements of this script are the collapse of the Soviet system, which increased the incentives and opportunities for nationalist elites to capture the state and for nationalist secession; the institutional legacy of Soviet ethnofederalism, which predetermined ethnic cleavages; the lack of state capacities in the newly emerging states, which led to serious commitment problems; the weakness of the elites in the newly independent states, which led them to tolerate or even actively sponsor entrepreneurs of violence; and their failure to reimpose state control over entrepreneurs of violence, which derailed the consolidation of statehood and paved the way for new waves of violence.

The analysis of idiosyncratic features of individual cases of war does not, in the end, make the study of post-Soviet wars relevant, nor does the attempt to contribute to a specific theory of post-Soviet wars, although both are important endeavors in their own right. The study of post-Soviet wars is justified in bringing this important subclass of cases of war to the attention of theorists of internal wars. Hence, the guiding questions that this book seeks to answer are the following: How well are existing theories equipped to explain the onset and trajectories of post-Soviet wars? And, vice versa, how can the study of post-Soviet wars contribute to general theory?

The wars in the former Soviet Union and in former Yugoslavia account for roughly one-third of all internal war since 1989 and for two-thirds of all wars within Europe since 1945. If one accepts that the wars in the former Soviet Union and former Yugoslavia have many similarities, then the sample presented in this book is sufficiently large to make a significant contribution to theories of internal wars. Consequently, an important objective of this book is to help organize a discussion between general theories of internal wars and the lessons that the study of war and peace in the post-Soviet space offers. There is ample material for doing so. Perhaps the most surprising findings emerging from this study are that post-Soviet wars do not support two of the statistically best established claims of general conflict theory: the association between mountainous terrain and the advent of internal war, and the association between a low level of economic development and the advent of war. Caucasian wars emerged in societies that were not poor, neither within the Soviet Union nor on a global average. They emerged in mountainous terrain, but the now common assumption that mountains facilitate the military resistance of rebels is not supported.

The study of post-Soviet wars also offers valuable insights into the causal mechanisms that link newly independent states, state weakness, and the occurrence of internal wars. All Caucasian polities suffered from a sudden loss of state capacities, but some were able to reconfigure statehood and avoid violence. As I argue in this book, the explanation for success or failure is to be found in the cleavage structures of elites and in the degree of internal fragmentation of the new nationalist elites. Ethnic demography is often said to be among the most salient risk factors making societies prone to internal violence. The cases in this book support the importance of ethnic demography, but they also offer insights as to the circumstances under which ethnic demography increases the risk of internal wars and when it does not. Last, the study of post-Soviet wars holds unexpected lessons with regard to the financing (and, hence, the feasibility) of rebel organizations. Rebel movements in the Caucasus financed themselves by various means, and the support of the population in what were, in the beginning, popular wars, played a significant role. But all organizers of violence actually accumulated their start-up capital in the shadow and criminal economies of the Soviet Union.

I developed these arguments over several years. During this time, I was blessed with many sharp-eyed, thoughtful, and supportive friends and colleagues, most of whom offered their comments and advice for this project in its various stages. Earlier drafts of this book immensely profited by the comments of Andrea Genest. For their support, I am grateful to Holm Sundhaussen, Thomas Risse, and the late Georg Elwert at the Free University of Berlin. Graham Stack translated an earlier version of this book into English, and Erica Richardson did the style and language editing of the final manuscript. I am most grateful to both. In the Caucasus, the help and support of Gayane Novikova, Arif Yunusof, Gaga Nizheradze, and Armine Alexanian is gratefully acknowledged. They were the most knowledgeable colleagues and gate-openers one could imagine. Without the help of Alexander Orlov, travels to Chechnya would have been much harder and my insights much smaller. I owe a debt of gratitude to Paul Collier and Nicholas Sambanis; my own research has benefited much from collaborating with them within the World Bank's research project on the economics of civil wars, crime, and violence. Pavel Baev, Georgi Derluguian, Ron Suny, Gail Lapidus, and Jonathan Wheatley have all at various stages generously shared their impressive knowledge of the Caucasus with me.

I gratefully acknowledge financial assistance from the Heinrich Böll Foundation, Berlin, which sponsored an initial workshop on the topic in 1999. Much of the subsequent research for this book was made possible by a generous grant from the Volkswagen-Stiftung. This book reached the final stage of completion at Stanford's Center for Democracy, Development and the Rule of Law, and I thank Steve Krasner, Gerhard Casper, Thomas Risse, and Kathryn Stoner-Weiss for making this possible. The Alexander von Humboldt Foundation generously supported my stay at Stanford with a Fedeor-Lynen grant. I am deeply grateful to CDDRL's staff and faculty for providing the most inspiring and productive atmosphere one can possibly imagine. At Stanford, Amichai Magen was the best of friends, and our occasional skiing and the many espressos kept me on track while finishing the manuscript.

Finally, this book would never have been written without the support of friends and family. First and foremost, I thank my parents for their support and encouragement over the years. Jan Koehler has been an exceptional colleague and an exceptional friend. Many of the ideas expressed here have been shaped by year-long discussions, from which I have enormously benefited. But my greatest appreciation goes to my wife, Anna, and our two children, Max and Carla. For all that they mean to me—the book is dedicated to them.

1 Introduction

War and Peace in the Caucasus

This book is about war and peace in the Caucasus. It is not the first written on this topic, but it is not yet another variation of a theme popularized by Russian writers of the 19th century. Many writers and scholars—then and now—depict the Caucasus as caught in a never-ending epic struggle between mountain dwellers and Cossacks, Christians, and Russians, taking place in the borderlands of empires, and being fueled by a mountainous topography, as well as by deeply rooted cultural beliefs. In contrast, the accounts given in this book of war and war avoidance in the Caucasus in the aftermath of the Soviet Union are informed by recent developments in conflict research. Mountains, culture, and collectively held narratives about the past are still important, but so are the motivations and opportunities of elites and counterelites, of politicians, entrepreneurs, and warlords. These opportunities have been shaped less by culture and geography than by political and economic institutions, especially by the collapse of these institutions in the aftermath of the Soviet Union.

In August 1991, after half a decade of creeping erosion, the Soviet Union dramatically imploded, and the Caucasus region found itself being transformed from an imperial periphery to a periphery without a center. From this point on, the societies of the Caucasus have been treading the path of state building, at different speeds, and with different successes and contrasting goals. This is not a task that Caucasian societies sought out for themselves. For both elites and the population, for most of the 1980s, ideas of national independence were largely unthinkable and, arguably, for many also undesirable. It was the collapse of the Soviet Union that not only enabled but also forced these societies to replace crumbling Soviet institutions with a new set of institutions, suited to new modes of governance. None of the former Soviet republics has been in a position to opt out of this reconstruction of regime and statehood.

Regime change and state building are necessarily highly conflictive processes. The emerging post-Soviet Caucasian polities were open to violent conflicts because they were caught in power struggles between old and new elites, were engaged by mobilizing ethnic groups, were seriously restricted in their ability to provide public goods, and lacked an established monopoly on the legitimate means of violence. Some of the Caucasian societies evaded violent escalation, while others did not. In this book, I seek to explain both outcomes.

Unlike other state collapses in history—from the fall of the Roman Empire to the fall of Yugoslavia—the collapse of the Soviet Union and subsequent regime change in the successor states took place surprisingly peacefully.[1] There were indeed numerous small, armed conflicts, which generally failed to gain the attention of an international or even the Russian public, but large-scale armed conflicts were rare.[2] However, the Caucasus became the exception: between 1988 and 2005, there were five major cases of internal wars in the Caucasus.[3] The first war (1988–1994) was between Armenians and Azerbaijanis over the territory of Nagorny-Karabakh, which has an Armenian majority and was an autonomous territory within the Soviet Republic of Azerbaijan. The demand of the Karabakh Armenians to be annexed to the neighboring Soviet Republic of Armenia led to a forced exchange of populations and to a bitter war between the Karabakh Armenians and Azerbaijanis. The status of Karabakh has never been fully settled. Georgia, a multiethnic republic in the South Caucasus, became the theater of three more wars between 1989 and 1993. These were the war over the status of the breakaway region of South Ossetia, the civil war for power in Tbilisi, and the war over the status of the breakaway region of Abkhazia. The fifth war was fought in and about Chechnya. In 1991, Chechnya declared its independence from Russia. Since then, Russia has twice attempted by military means (in 1994–1996 and from 1999 on) to bring the separatist republic under its control.

However, there are also a number of potential hotbeds in the Caucasus that have not escalated into war. This is especially true for the republics neighboring Chechnya in the North Caucasus—Dagestan, Ingushetia, Kabardino-Balkaria, and Karachai-Cherkessia—all of which were seen by many experts as highly prone to conflict, but, nevertheless, all of which have avoided spiraling into internal violence. By the same token, of the three autonomous regions within Georgia, two have sought to break away, whereas the third, Ajaria, has not, thereby avoiding the fate of violent conflict within its borders. Thus, it is not only the violent conflicts that demand explanation; the cases where violence has been avoided against all odds are just as deserving.

Explaining Post-Soviet Wars

Choosing to organize violence is both extremely risky and extremely costly, and, for the good of society, it is an extremely rare strategy. In the context of rapid social change, however, and especially when this change culminates in state collapse, the threshold for violence falls, and a window for violent opportunities opens up. Organized violence may then become a strategy that incumbent elites apply to secure the survival of their regime. Likewise, elites challenging incumbents may choose violent strategies either to capture the state or to break away from the state and establish territorial independence. In the course of violent conflict, both sides may find that organized violence can generate profits from looting, racketeering, and smuggling.

As the case studies about the wars in the Caucasus show, organizers of violence typically meandered back and forth between politically motivated and economically motivated violence. In both cases, they framed their actions as a struggle in the name of the nation. During this period, a new type of violent political entrepreneur evolved: the patriot-businessman. In the early 1990s, patriot-businessmen took center stage in most of the Caucasian polities. They combined military skills, often earned in the Soviet army or in the Soviet underworld, with a sharp instinct for the business opportunities that the collapse of the Soviet Union provided, and they framed their activities as a patriotic struggle for the nation's benefit. The complex relations between political violence, economic activities, and the seductive power of nationalism (embodied in the figure of the patriot-businessman) is a recurring theme in this book. When the period of state weakness and internal strife came to an end by the mid 1990s (with the notable exception of Chechnya), the patriot-businessman departed, leaving the field to other, more familiar, actors such as presidents, prime ministers, and terrorists.

The trajectories of post-Soviet wars were decisively shaped by the political and cultural institutions that the Soviet Union had established and by the sudden collapse of the Soviet state. As many scholars have pointed out, the Soviet system of ethnofederalism that linked a territory to an ethnically defined titular group (e.g., Azerbaijan to the Azerbaijanis), historic grievances between various ethnic groups, and the opportunities and fears that arise when a state collapses are powerful factors that help explain the onset of internal wars. As such, they are important elements of a theory of post-Soviet wars.

In this book, I aim to take the study of post-Soviet wars one step further: the objective is to apply general theories of internal wars to an important subset of cases and, vice versa, to make these cases available to those interested in testing and refining existing theories. Ultimately, this book is about bringing the study of post-Soviet wars back into the realm of conflict theory.

In recent years, theories of internal wars have made impressive progress. Often at the forefront were quantitative, large-*n* studies that seek to systematically identify those factors that make societies in general more prone to violence.[4] The findings from recent quantitative literature point to six factors that increase a society's risk of internal war:

First, one of the statistically most robust findings suggests that a low level of economic development makes a society considerably more prone to conflict. Poor societies more often experience internal wars than rich societies do.

Second, state weakness and state collapse increase the risk of internal wars. Hence, states are at risk when they are newly independent and have not yet developed stable and efficient institutions, and they are at risk when these institutions crumble or fall because of exogenous shocks or internal crisis.

Third, the organization of sustained violence depends on financing. Organizing war requires significant investments in logistics and manpower. A protest movement that cannot secure enough funding will not transform into a rebellion. Hence, among the most important factors that increase the risk of internal wars are opportunities for financing.

Fourth, war breeds war. Societies that have experienced conflict in the last five years face a high risk of slipping back into violence.

Fifth, a complex ethnic geography is seen as increasing the risk of internal wars. Even though an impressive body of academic research shows that ethnicity per se is not a threat to internal stability, statistically, societies in which one ethnic group forms a potentially dominant majority seem to be more at risk than either very homogenous or very heterogeneous societies.[5] And once a society has become unstable, ethnicity does play a prominent part in shaping the dynamics of violence. In 51 percent of all internal wars since World War II, at least one party to the conflict recruited mainly along ethnic lines; in 18 percent of all wars, recruiting was also done at least partly along ethnic lines. Only roughly one-third (31 percent) of all wars cannot be labeled ethnic wars.[6]

Sixth, the statistical data indicate that mountainous terrain increases the risk of conflict, and wars tend to be longer when they are fought in mountainous countries.

To discuss the applicability of these predictions to post-Soviet conditions, to test their viability, and to shed light on causal relations beyond simple correlation, case studies on war and war avoidance are presented in chapters 4 to 7. These case studies cover the wars in Chechnya, in Georgia, and in Nagorny-Karabakh, as well as the cases of war avoidance in Dagestan and Ajaria.

Case studies are instrumental in detecting the causal mechanisms that link factors to outcomes. They uncover the transmission belts that link, for example, ethnic composition, state weakness, and terrain to the emergence of internal war. Case studies also serve to identify the conjunctural effects of factors that are not easily captured by statistical approaches, and they help in identifying missing factors. Finally, case studies also help trace the dynamics of conflict and pinpoint how violence induced change in a specific environment. Focusing on such processes means moving beyond the snapshots that statistical analysis provides of societies under stress.

From the factors that conflict theory identifies as being among the prime suspects for causing internal war, state weakness, mountainous terrain, and a complex ethnic geography clearly apply to all cases discussed in this book. Yet there is no specific link between any of these factors and the onset of war. After all, Dagestan and Ajaria avoided war. And where war broke out, the causal chain that links these factors to the emergence of sustained organized violence is often more complex and tangled than a simple statistical correlation would suggest. Other factors apply to only some cases or to none at all. For example, Chechnya,

Azerbaijan, and Dagestan possessed significant natural resources, in all cases oil. But, as the case studies show, Dagestan avoided war. In Chechnya, revenues from illegal and decentralized oil extraction doubtless contributed to the prolongation of the war, but a direct causal connection between having oil and the start of organized violence cannot be established. In Azerbaijan, as well, there was no causality between the outbreak of conflict and the presence of oil. There is even a negative correlation between oil reserves and length of war. Because Azerbaijani strongmen gave priority to investment in the power struggle in Baku rather than the war over Karabakh, the Azerbaijani front was weakened, leading to the battleground victory of the Armenians.

This mixed evidence does not devalue the general argument that the organization of violence crucially depends on opportunities for financing. However, evidence from the post-Soviet wars suggests that it need not be the extraction of natural resources that fuels war. Profits accumulated in the shadow and criminal economies proved to be the single most important source of revenues for the various rebel movements.

Evidence from the case studies also means reconsidering and refining other assumptions: Caucasian wars emerged in societies that were not particularly poor, neither within the Soviet Union nor compared with a global average, and it was not the poorer groups that sought to secede. What triggered rebellions, among other factors, was that some groups feared future economic losses. The fear of losing a potential future was a much more powerful factor than the desire to change the present. Hence, neither a general low level of development nor an uneven distribution of wealth among ethnic groups accounts for the onset of war.

Similarly, the fact that all wars emerged in mountainous terrain does not mean that there is a straightforward causal link between territory and the onset of war. Most decisive battles took place on the plains, and mostly in an urban environment. In Karabakh, the rebels initially had the mountainous terrain against them, as did the Ossets in the conflict with the Georgians.

Furthermore, no rebel movement had its origins in rural elites opposing urban elites. On the contrary, all rebel movements were initiated and led by the provincial urban intelligentsia, which formed alliances with entrepreneurs of violence with a background in the Soviet shadow economy. Certainly, "mountains" played a role, but the causal chain is much more complex than the classic argument that mountainous terrain militarily favors rebels over governments would suggest. Mountains work through what French historian Fernand Braudel has called the "longue durée"—that is by shaping long-term historical structures, not by triggering events. Over the centuries, mountainous terrain made it more difficult for the Tsarist and the Soviet central state to culturally and socially penetrate the remote mountainous regions; hence, mountainous regions remained peripheral, only loosely connected to the administrative center of the imperial power. A weakening of the central power—Moscow—then led to centrifugal reactions in such peripheral regions. Once centrifugal tensions condensed under the influence of many other factors and processes to crisis and finally rebellion, remote mountainous regions may have helped overcome recruitment problems. Many of the fighting units in Chechnya, Abkhazia, Ossetia, and Karabakh were filled by rural youth, recruited on the basis of village communities and family ties.

Whatever specific conjunctures of factors worked in the cases discussed here, it becomes clear from the case studies that there is no causal link between risk factors and organized violence. This is because, first, the impact of risk factors is embedded in domestic structures that can neutralize or exacerbate their effect. Second, organizers of violence, notwithstanding their motivations and objectives, always have massive difficulties to overcome. They must recruit members to join the rebellion; they must sustain the rebellion by providing internal cohesion, organizational structure, and discipline; and they must finance the logistics of organized violence. In short, they must overcome considerable collective action problems, which is usually not possible without gaining access to considerable resources and without making use of social capital available within a group. Hence, the case studies in this book also focus on domestic structures and how they interacted with the general predictions of conflict theory. By tracing the processes that led, in some cases, from risk to violence and, in other cases, from risk to regained stability, it is possible to construct a "script" of post-Soviet wars that is both specific enough to do justice to the individual cases and general enough to speak to conflict theory.

Such a script highlights the following points. Both the conjunction of a specific ethnic demography institutionalized by the Soviet Union and the weakness of the central state account for an atypically high risk of conflict in the Caucasus. The collapse of the Soviet Union dramatically increased nationalist elites' opportunities for capturing or secession from the state, but their weakness also meant that the new states were challenged by commitment problems on a massive scale. This added up to a breeding ground for the organization of violence, and, in five cases, groups capable of waging war emerged.

Clearly, state weakness emerges as the single most important factor. It was the collapse of the Soviet structures that opened up windows of opportunity for nationalist elites to pursue state-capture strategies. State weakness also explains other striking Caucasian peculiarities. The weakness of the new states led to a blurring of the boundary between private, entrepreneurial violence and state, or at least state-funded, organized violence. Both the "rebels" and the "states" employed private groups with the capacity for violence, which were fighting in the name of the state or the nation, but motivated additionally, or even mostly, by private profit. In all conflicts, alongside the nominally "state" troops (themselves, in fact, often the armed retinues of private violent entrepreneurs), volunteer militias, self-defense units, part-time fighters, weekend soldiers, and various mercenary groups also had roles. It is a notable peculiarity that neither Russia, nor Georgia, nor Azerbaijan was able to win its war against secessionist regions. Karabakh, South Ossetia, and Abkhazia are today de facto independent states, and so was Chechnya until the second Russian invasion of 1999.

Admittedly, none of these quasi-states have reached the status of being an internationally recognized sovereign state, and none of the conflicts have been resolved by a formal peace treaty. However, the military victory of "rebels" over "their" government is a rare event, since the government, as a rule, has far more resources at its disposal than do the rebels. In the Caucasus, the success of the rebels can be explained by the weakness of the respective states they were challenging. Georgia and Azerbaijan were new states, having to construct their organizational capacities almost from scratch and lacking the resources necessary for waging an efficient war. The newly thrown-together armies were poorly trained and lacked any motivation to fight a dangerous war over peripheral regions. Additionally, almost all the new states were plagued by protracted internal power struggles and a high level of corruption. In this respect, the "governments" were just as poorly prepared for a war as the "rebels," since both sides had yet to develop the necessary capacity for violence. Consequently, violent conflicts in the Caucasus would be better characterized as a war between two start-up firms than as a war between state and rebels. In Karabakh, South Ossetia, and Abkhazia, the secessionist "firms" proved to be more efficient organizers of violence than the state firms that they challenged.

There is another consequential aspect of state weakness. The last years of the Soviet Union were not simply marked by a creeping loss of legitimacy, dwindling administrative capacities, and, ultimately, the loss of the monopoly over the means of violence. These years were also marked by booming opportunities in the shadow and criminal economies. As the case studies show, all successful organizers of violence had access to profits generated in the Soviet shadow economy, or at least they formed coalitions with shadow entrepreneurs. It was a peculiarity of the Soviet Caucasus that much of this profit was allocated to the nationalist cause, but the general lesson remains valid: state weakness opens up opportunities in the shadow and the criminal economies, the profits of which may turn into a source of funding for rebel organizations. In the cases reported in this book, this source proved to be more important than the sources which, in the literature, are primarily associated with funding rebel activities, such as exploitation of oil, timber, gemstones, and narcotics.[7]

Despite the pervasiveness of state weakness, however, not all polities in the Caucasus spiraled to war. Whether a polity sailed through the storms of state weakness by and large unharmed or perished in it depended to a large extent on the cleavage structure of elites. A close reading of the cases of war and war avoidance in the Caucasus reveals that the successful recovering of statehood after the shock of the Soviet collapse is attributable to three factors: a high level of elite continuity, the capability of new elites to form coalitions with significant parts of the old *nomenklatura* (administrative classes), and the degree of internal fractionalization of new elites. These factors, in turn, were shaped by highly idiosyncratic social and cultural constellations, which can be described, as is done in the case studies, but which resist any further generalization.

Chapter Organization

This book is structured as follows. Chapter 2 sets the stage for the subsequent narratives of war and war avoidance in the Caucasus. I start with a brief discussion of the concepts of nation, state, and conflict and then examine how these, historically, have been institutionalized in the Caucasus. I argue that the Soviet institutionalization of ethnicity and statehood in the Caucasus, which served for more than 50 years as an instrument for the control of national aspirations, was suddenly turned into a "subversive institution" through the weakening of Soviet hierarchies and thus encouraged secessionism. In chapter 3, I provide a framework for the analysis of violent conflict, developing it with reference to general theories of conflict research. Specifically, I mine theories of internal wars for propositions to explain the onset of war, and I discuss their applicability in the post-Soviet context. Based on the discussion in the preceding chapter, in chapters 4, 5, 6, and 7, I present studies of Chechnya, Georgia, and Karabakh as cases of war and of Dagestan and Ajaria as cases of war avoidance. Finally, in chapter 8, I summarize the main findings of the book.

2

Setting the Stage
The Past, the Nation, and the State

"Forget the Nation!"[1]

This chapter describes the stage on which the drama of the Caucasian wars took place.[2] The focus is on two concepts that are crucial for an understanding of events: the "nation" and the "state." Most of the collective action described in this book, and almost all the discourse accompanying it, centers on these concepts, both of which are still the subject of heated debates in the literature. First, I describe the process by which state and nation became institutionalized in the Caucasus, as a result of the interplay between the commanding geography of the Caucasus region and history. I argue that the Soviet Union, the latest and most powerful of all the empires that have tried to incorporate the Caucasus, promoted an institutionalization of nation and state, which, after the Soviet Union collapsed, determined where and how violence emerged in the name of these concepts. By focusing on the process of "institutionalization," I give a clear position in the debate on the substance of nation and ethnicity. The nation is understood as coming to life only as a result of political institutions. When it comes to life, nation does so as a powerful symbol around which collective action is organized, not as an actor in its own right. Second, I briefly discuss nation and state as concepts and how they are used in this book.

The Past

The geographical position and structure of the Caucasus explains two of the most notable peculiarities of the region: the late and weak formation of statehood, and the ethnocultural complexity of the region. In the

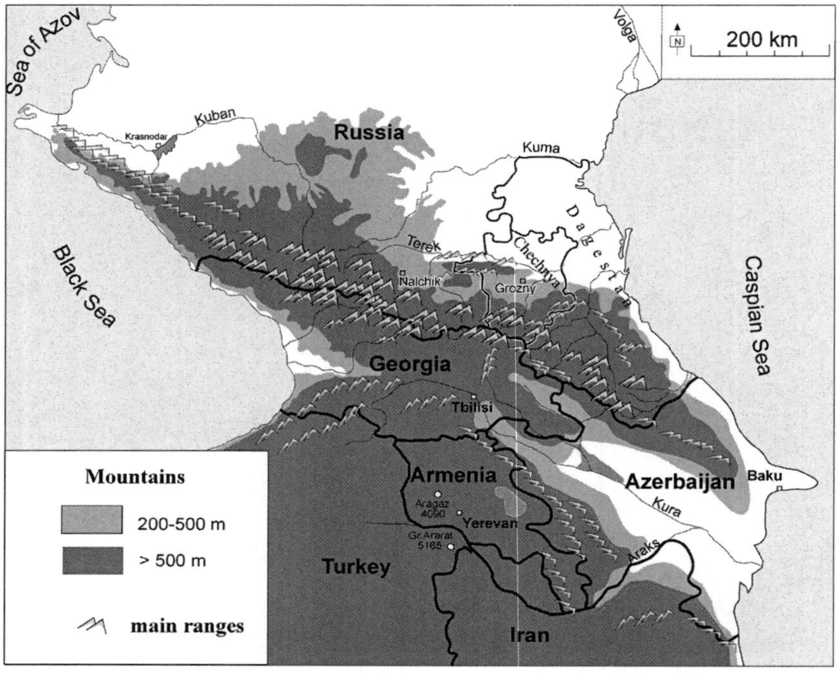

Caucasus, history starts with geography. The double range of the Caucasus Mountains acts as one of the geographical boundaries between Europe and Asia. It stretches over 1,100 km from the Taman Peninsula on the Black Sea around to the Aspheron Peninsula on the Caspian Sea. The mountain ranges run parallel to each other, separated by between 10 and 15 km. The northern range is higher, on average 3,600 m, and its highest peak, Elbrus, soars to 5,593 m.

The Caucasus forms a mountain barrier which is, on average, 160 km across. In the north, the mountains run out into a plain, bordered by the Terek and Kuban Rivers. Beyond them, the Russian steppe begins. The North Caucasus is usually subdivided into three parts. The western part stretches from Elbrus to the Black Sea. The eastern part is bordered by the Caspian Sea in the east and the Terek River in the west. Dagestan, Chechnya, and Ingushetia are in this part of the North Caucasus, and this was the core of the mountain dwellers' resistance to Tsarist Russia, the Soviet Union, and, currently, the Russian Federation (RF). The central part of the North Caucasus is the highest part of the mountain range. The Ossets, Kabardins, and Balkars, among others, live here.

The Caucasus is located at the margins of three expanses—the Russian steppe to the north, the Persian hill country to the southeast, and the Anatolian uplands to the southwest—all of which were incorporated into the empires of various dynasties in different historical periods. The history of the Caucasus has always been the history of empires competing for both influence and territorial rule. Situated at the peripheries of empires, statehood in the Caucasus was established in most historical periods only as a shadow of these empires, either as a governed province or ruled indirectly though local elites. Thus the Caucasus owes its multifaceted cultural landscape to its geographical position, but the underdevelopment of the sociocultural and socioeconomic structures on which statehood is constructed have also been geographically and historically conditioned.

The North Caucasus was better protected than the South Caucasus from the gravitational pull of empires by its mountain range. However, while this geological constellation hindered conquest by external powers and long impeded colonization—that is, the establishment of foreign statehood—it also impeded the indigenous formation of statehood.

Before the 19th century, the mountainous, inaccessible, and impoverished North Caucasus avoided the rule of external powers. The difficult terrain impeded the establishment of direct control, and the harsh natural conditions made for easier defense against an invading army. This made any potential conquest very costly, with very little reward for conquerors, since the mountainous region had no riches to speak of. These factors increased the costs of conquest while hindering the establishment of a local hegemon. No central power could maintain control over the inaccessible mountain valleys. Geography isolated the North Caucasus from external powers, but it hindered the establishment of a central political instance and molded a shared cultural value system of the mountain dwellers. Regardless of the ethnic, religious, and linguistic differences, a value system developed, based on independence, physical strength, courage, self-sufficiency, and high individual ideas of honor and demanding strict loyalty to family and clan. This canon of values struck roots in the North Caucasus and proved resistant to the numerous cultural deposits left by various empires over the course of time.

The first invaders to bestow a crucial cultural good were the Arabs. In 642, Arabian armies reached the area of Derbent in contemporary

Dagestan and named it Bab al-Abwab, the "gate of gates," in recognition of its strategic significance. The Arabs could not establish themselves in Dagestan or the southern Volga area. They nevertheless left behind Islam as their legacy, which then, over the course of decades, spread gradually into Chechnya and Ingushetia. In the 13th century, Islam was carried further west by the next wave of invaders, the Mongols. By the 17th century, the North Caucasus was, at least superficially, "Islamized," although a centralized, institutionalized polity had not been assembled anywhere. Only in the eastern part of the North Caucasus, in contemporary Dagestan, had several small and unstable principalities been established.

Their neighbors, the Vainakh tribes (i.e., the Chechens and the Ingush) lived in egalitarian and decentralized societies. The most important sociopolitical organizational unit here was the *teip*—a term for a union of several extended families, or a "clan." Councils of elders conferred over important decisions.[3] Both institutions, the *teip* structures and councils of elders, resisted 50 years of forced Soviet secularization and modernization, functioning in parallel to official Soviet structures, which were never able to dislodge these traditional mechanisms of self-regulation. After 1991, when the Chechens embarked on the construction of their own statehood, this headless social organization proved ideally suited to the organization of a guerrilla war; but it was unsuitable for the construction of a depersonalized, modern statehood.[4]

This dilemma is a constant in the history of the North Caucasus: the same mechanisms that gave the North Caucasian societies high organizational capacity against internal and external colonization also hindered state building. To circumvent this dilemma, the leaders of separatist resistance in the North Caucasus have sought to offer society a new, superior framework for loyalty. One such framework was and is provided by Islam, which has always competed in the Caucasus with traditional values and behavioral codices. While the traditional value codex, known in the Caucasus as *adat* (Arabic for tradition) held that the *teip* was the chief reference point for loyalty, honor, shame, and collective responsibility, Islam liberated the individual from the collective and emphasized the responsibility of the individual before the religion-based law (Sharia). Islamization always implied relegation of the locally rooted *adat* and promotion of the universalistic Sharia, superseding particular loyalties.[5] Armed separatism against the Russian state in the North Caucasus, from the uprisings led by Imam Shamil and Sheikh

Mansur in the 19th century up to the contemporary Chechen war, led by field commanders such as Aslan Maskhadov and Shamil Basayev, goes hand in hand with a strengthened Islamization, which is often falsely portrayed merely as "radicalization" and "fundamentalism." That Islamization constitutes a culturally conditioned attempt at unifying the Chechen population, by larger bonds than those the extended family or clan could provide, is often overlooked. Therefore, Islamization can also be seen as an attempt to build the base for statehood. However, this attempt failed in the 19th century, and it failed again in the 20th and early 21st centuries, as the case study on Chechnya in this book shows.

Geographical and historical conditions also hampered state and nation formation to the south of the mountains, in contemporary Armenia, Georgia, and Azerbaijan, although history ran a different course to the south of the mountains than it did to the north.

The South Caucasus, even more than the North, was a transit region, shaped by invasions, migration, and retreats to the safe havens of the mountain valleys. Each movement deposited cultural sediment, changed or created new cultural formations ("ethnies"), and blurred borders again. The political map inscribed on the South Caucasus by the Soviet Union coupled territory and nations for the first time. This Soviet, modernist ordering distracted from the peculiar Caucasian cultural landscape, shaped by constant migrations and melanges, which had engendered a unique multiethnic, multilingual, highly differentiated and specifically Caucasian culture that was common to all the inhabitants of the region. In such a cultural landscape, geographic proximity was more important in defining culture and for relations between the inhabitants than were abstract ideas about ethnicity or ideological conceptions of the "nation."[6]

In some respects, this remarkable cultural landscape is similar to that of the Balkans. A largely shared everyday culture unites the groups, whose referent for loyalty and identity was informed more by religion, locality, and kinship than by the concept of the nation. This does not mean that nations or ethnic groups are absent as mythological reference points. On the contrary, the members of these "old" nations are constantly separating and differentiating themselves from others with the help of numerous ethnic stereotypes and myths, and, precisely due to the daily culture they share, they indulge in a narcissism of minor difference.[7] Nation and ethnicity, however, exist in the Caucasus as in the

Balkans above all as myth because history and geography have long prevented the institutionalization of the nation.

While in the North Caucasus, geography walled off the area from imperial claims—although not from cultural influences—geography also exposed the South Caucasus (today comprising Armenia, Georgia, and Azerbaijan) to the cultural and political influence of rival empires. As this intensified cultural interaction, it also regularly stalled the process of state building. Armenians and Georgians repeatedly produced dynasties that came to exercise a relatively high level of sovereignty, and at times they controlled territories that were significantly larger than the contemporary states. Historical experience was molded by their geographical location on the fringes of competing empires. The relative strength or weakness of competitors determined the freedom to maneuver that local dynasties had and the territorial scope of their dominion.

In the 18th century, a new player stepped onto the political stage of the Caucasus: the Russian Empire. After two short-lived periods of Russian rule in the South Caucasus under Ivan the Terrible and 200 years later under Peter the Great, the Tsarist Empire got seriously involved in empire building in the Caucasus in 1783. Irakli II, ruler of Georgia, entered into a military alliance with Russia to shore up his teetering empire against the Persians. Hardly a generation later, in 1801, Alexander I annexed east Georgia. Piece by piece, Russia began to dislodge the Persians from the southeast and the Ottomans from the southwest of the Caucasus, which belonged entirely to the Tsarist Empire just 20 years later.

After the new possessions in the South Caucasus were secured, Russia embarked on the "pacification" of the mountainous North Caucasus, to gain a secure land link to the newly annexed territories. At the start of the 19th century, the eastern and western parts of the North Caucasus were war zones and remained so for half a century. In the central part of the North Caucasus, Russia found allies in the Christian Ossets, Kabardins, and Karachai, who either allied themselves with the Russians or at least did not offer violent resistance to Russian expansion.

The epic struggles in the North Caucasus through the 19th century—to which Pushkin, Lermontov, and Tolstoy erected literary monuments, and in the tradition of which the Chechen rebels of today see themselves—took place in the east, in the territories of contemporary Dagestan, Chechnya, and Ingushetia. Unlike previous attacks in the mountainous remoteness of the North Caucasus, the Russian empire under the Romanovs was no longer merely pursuing formal sovereignty or tribute payments. This Russian expansion into the North Caucasus was an internal colonization and was accompanied by the migration of Slavic settlers and attempts at forced conversion to Christianity.

The mountain dwellers reacted to this fundamental threat to their political, demographic, and religious-cultural life with repeated attempts to coordinate their defense. The bond, which was to hold together the locally rooted, often ethnolinguistically diverse groups and clans, was first and foremost their shared religion. Islam became the social putty that served as a surrogate for central organization and for the absence of any common national sentiment, so the military and cultural defense came to be organized in the name of Islam. Religious warlords became the exponents and organizers of resistance against Imperial Russia. The first in a long line of such leaders was the Chechen Sheikh Mansur (1748–1794); the most successful and famous was and is Imam Shamil, whose heroic resistance lasted 25 years (1834–1859).

In 1859, the wars in the North Caucasus ended. In the east and in the west, the Russian policies of scorched earth, deportation, and merciless reprisals against whole villages finally broke the resistance. Half a million Cherkessians went into exile in Ottoman Turkey; thousands of Chechens emigrated to Jordan and Syria. The Tsarist Empire became the first great power to bring the entire Caucasus under its rule for an extended period of time. However, the inner colonization of the North Caucasus remained incomplete at the end of Tsarist Russia. The regions were a constant source of unrest, and the mountain dwellers sporadically rebelled against Russian rule. The rebellions of 1877, in the wake of the Russo-Turkish Wars, and the unrest of 1905 could only be suppressed with great effort and with great losses on both sides.

In the last quarter of the 19th century, the national awakening that was spreading throughout the Russian Empire reached the ethnic groups of the South Caucasus. In the ethnically ragged margins of the empire—the Baltic, Central Asia, and the Caucasus—the emerging national question was overlaid by the question of how the Tsarist autocracy could be transformed into a constitutional regime and was undercut by the social tensions that were manifesting themselves powerfully in the industrializing societies of the empire. While the Russian countryside increasingly came under the influence of social revolutionary movements, socialist ideas won a foothold in the urban centers of the South Caucasus. In the oil and tobacco industry in Batumi and the factories of Tbilisi, the Georgian branch of Russian social democracy rose to become the dominant force on the political stage, as it did in the Azeri oil boom city of Baku. The social question, however, was becoming increasingly intertwined with the national question.

Each of the three large South Caucasian groups handled the national question in a very different manner. The Armenians within Tsarist Russia maintained a pro-Russian stance. For them, Russia counted as a natural ally against the Islamic Ottomans. Russian Armenians were significantly better off in economic and cultural terms than the Armenians who lived in the six provinces of the eastern Ottoman Empire. While the Armenians in the Ottoman provinces competed for scarce land with Kurds, and with the numerous refugees and émigrés from the North Caucasus, after it was conquered by Russia, the Armenian population in Russia benefited from an economic upswing. Most merchants in the Caucasus were Armenians; in Tbilisi, trade and retail were in their hands, and they constituted the middle class; and in the Batumi and Baku oil industry, the majority of the qualified workers were Armenians. For these reasons, most of the national energy of the Armenians was focused on relations in the Ottoman Empire. The threat to Armenians in the Ottoman Empire "immunized" the Armenians in Russia against the wish for independence and a nation-state, and, compared with conditions and prospects in the Ottoman Empire, cultural autonomy within Russia seemed to be the preferable, and more European, option for Armenians.[8] In 1890, the Armenian Revolutionary Union (Dashnaktsutiun) was founded. The Dashnaktsutiun program united political demands (such as freedom of the press, the right to public assembly, an eight-hour day and minimum wage), with the demand for internal autonomy for Armenians in the Ottoman and Russian Empires. At the turn of the 20th century, the Dashnaktsutiun was the strongest political force among the Armenians in the Ottoman Empire, in what is now Armenia, and among the Armenian communities in Tbilisi and Baku.

The last quarter of the 19th century also witnessed a hesitant awakening of the national agenda among the Georgians. Georgian culture was discussed within the urban intelligentsia in Tbilisi, and the call for greater cultural autonomy for Georgians within the framework of the Russian Empire was heard, if not throughout the country, then at least in the cafes of the capital. However, due to social circumstances, the national question in Georgia was clearly overshadowed by the social question. In Georgia, the Armenians constituted the middle class, and the natural upper class, the Georgian nobility, had long been integrated into the Russian service nobility. Therefore, the Georgian national movement lacked a real social basis because the workers and the rural population were drawn toward social democratic ideas more than toward national projects.

In neighboring Azerbaijan, a national consciousness began to form for the first time around the end of the 19th century. As with any collective identity, Azerbaijani national consciousness emerged in relation to the national awakenings in surrounding regions. The Muslim Azeri marked themselves off from their Georgian and Armenian neighbors through religion. Membership of Islam thus formed the core of the emerging Azerbaijani collective identity. However, there were two further options to build a specific Azerbaijani cultural identity beyond the religious difference—namely, Turkic identity through the language, or the proximity to Persian culture through both the Iranian element in the ethnogenesis of the Azerbaijani and the shared Shiite religion. The Young Turk revolution and subsequent modernization successes in Turkey were considerable attractions and strengthened the Pan-Turkic component of Azerbaijani national identity. As a consequence, the Azerbaijani self-conception as Caucasian Muslims in the Tsarist Empire was increasingly complemented and strengthened by an Azerbaijani-Turkic identity, nurtured and preached by the Freedom Movement (Musavat Party) in particular. Immediately before the First World War, the Musavat became the strongest political force among the Azerbaijani.

Azerbaijan was the least industrialized province of the South Caucasus, with a clear split between the rural areas and the metropolis of Baku, which, thanks to oil, had become a boomtown by the 1870s. At the beginning of the 20th century, more oil was produced in Baku than in the United States of America, and the city grew apace. However, the local Muslim population profited least from this: the investment came from Europe, and the manpower from Russia and Armenia. Baku did burgeon into a multiethnic metropolis, but the different ethnic communities lived apart, and social stratification along ethnic lines was sharp. This superimposing of ethnic and social borders generated conflict potential, which was realized for the first time in the revolutionary year of 1905. For three days, the mob looted Armenian neighborhoods in Baku, burned down houses, and set fire to oil fields owned by Armenians. The

Tsarist police let the mob run riot, just as, more than 80 years later, Soviet security forces, failed to intervene and stop the pogroms against Armenians in Sumgait (1988) and Baku (1990). The interethnic violence spread to most areas where Armenians and Azerbaijani lived next door to each other and only receded after some months. There were estimated to have been several thousand victims of the interethnic violence. In the revolutionary year of 1905, but again in 1917 and 1989, state weakness and looming anarchy led to bloody clashes between Armenians and Azerbaijanis. It is a pattern of events that has repeated itself in Caucasian history.

On the eve of the First World War, each of the three largest ethnic groups in the South Caucasus had their own political movements. But none—neither the Georgian followers of Russian social democracy nor the Armenian Dashnaktsutiun nor the Musavat in Azerbaijan—demanded independence from Russia and the founding of a sovereign nation-state. The Armenians regarded Russia as a protector power against the Turks and opted for an Armenia within the framework of a liberal Russia. The Georgian socialists were not a national movement and recruited members from among Georgian, Russian, and Armenian workers. Their program only had national implications inasmuch as the freedom they strove for was to benefit all peoples of the Russian Empire equally. The Azerbaijani, who were able to pin their national identity to several masts, and hence had various options available to them, looked to a future as either Caucasian Muslims in a reformed Russia or, in the wake of the Young Turk cultural hegemonic claims, eventually as part of a large Turkic family in a newly constructed Turkic multinational state.

At the beginning of the 20th century, the concept of an independent sovereign nation-state was not yet deeply rooted in society. The national question had indeed been raised, but "nation" as a reference point denoting the first step toward a desired political and territorial order was by no means uncontested in the sociocultural landscape of the Caucasus. As was typical of late industrializing societies, social consciousness and ethnic consciousness were superimposed and often antagonistic lines of force, complemented in the Caucasus by the gravitational tug of religious difference on the one hand and imperial great power politics on the other. Therefore, when the Russian Revolution set free its centripetal forces throughout the Tsarist Empire, the Caucasus neither fragmented neatly into nation-states nor joined together as a united Caucasus. On the basis of its complex internal structure and its geopolitical position on the fringes of empires, the region split apart messily, until it was again united by and under the Soviet authorities in 1923.

The First World War, the end of the Russian Empire, and the confusion of the Russian Revolution showed yet again, and with disastrous consequences, the extent to which the Caucasus was enmeshed in the games of great powers. Between 1914 and 1923, the societies of the Caucasus experienced a collective disaster, initially as a pawn of the great powers but then, after the collapse of the Russian Empire in 1917 and of the Ottoman Empire in 1918, as a power vacuum. As the region was released, for a short historical moment, from the grip of empires, centrifugal social and cultural forces were also released. Escalating ethnic violence, failed state founding, and the genocide of Armenians in Turkey were the disastrous results of those years.

In 1917, the February Revolution put an end to autocracy in Russia, and the peoples of the North Caucasus presented the provisional government with the proclamation of the Union of Caucasian Mountain Peoples, creating the North Caucasian Republic. More than 500 delegates took part in the founding convention, which was held in the municipal theater of Vladikavkaz in Ossetia, and drew up a constitution for the new republic. The North Caucasian Republic was to have a bicameral parliament. The lower house would be comprised of the people's deputies, while the upper house would be constituted by two delegates from each nation. The republic was to be ruled by an executive committee.

The North Caucasian Republic was not initially conceived of as an independent state as much as a political union, representing the interests of the North Caucasus in a new Russia. However, when the Bolsheviks seized power in Petersburg and Moscow in October 1917, the North Caucasian Republic moved away from this option, and in December 1918, independence was declared.

The Russian civil war opened a new line of conflict, which was reproduced in the Caucasus. The North Caucasian Republic was trapped between the lines of the advancing Red and White Armies. Officially, the North Caucasian Republic resisted the armies of the White General Denikin, but a considerable proportion of the military command was won over by the general's offers, and they assumed administrative tasks in the Whites' sphere of influence. Then, in 1920, the 11th Red Army reached Dagestan and brought with it not only military superiority but also the promise of national self-determination. In accordance with Lenin's tactics of wooing the nationalities over to the side of the revolution, the Council of People's Commissars had already sent an appeal to all Muslims of Russia promising them cultural, religious, and national self-determination in a new state in 1917. The People's Commissar responsible for nationality questions, Stalin, negotiated a compromise with the North Caucasian Republic, on the basis of which, in 1921, the Autonomous Soviet Socialist Republic (ASSR) of Dagestan and an autonomous mountain republic (Gorskaya ASSR) were instituted. The Caucasians received rights to autonomy and a legal system based on the Sharia. Setting up these autonomous republics was undoubtedly a temporary tactical compromise, which clearly shows that the still weak Soviet state was capable of great flexibility in building up a system of informal rule and integrating local institutions. However, the autonomous mountain republic survived only five years before it was dissolved, and local mechanisms of self-regulation were soon replaced by the official institutions of the Soviet state.

As was the case in the North, in the South Caucasus, the influential political groups were not in favor of independence from Russia at the beginning of 1917, but after the October Revolution, none of them recognized the Bolshevik regime. Thus, after the evacuation of the demoralized Tsarist Russian troops from the Caucasus and the ensuing power vacuum, the South Caucasus, although ill prepared, quite unexpectedly found itself to be de facto independent. For a very short historical moment, the societies of the South Caucasus experimented with a Transcaucasian Federal Democratic Republic. However, it quickly became clear that the internal contradictions of the South Caucasus would not permit the formation of a common state. In May 1918, the Transcaucasian Federal Democratic Republic came to an early end and collapsed into three parts. Georgia was first to declare its independence, followed by Azerbaijan and Armenia. The Caucasian May was short-lived, however. It endured only until Bolshevik Russia had gathered enough strength to bring the region under its control. The Russian advance was facilitated by the Turkish and Central Powers' retreat, and the Allies' lack of interest in filling the power vacuum by intervention. In April 1920, the 11th Red Army under Sergo Ordzhonikidze reached the South Caucasus. After an ultimatum, the government in Azerbaijan was the first to capitulate. Armenia followed without any pressure, as the Red Army was as welcome a protector against the Turks as had been the Tsarist army. Finally, Georgia was incorporated into the Soviet state in 1921.

Soviet Power

Tsarist Russia was the first empire to bring the entire Caucasus under its rule for an extended period of time. Its successor state, the Soviet Union, not only integrated the Caucasus into a single state but also subjected the entire territory to a highly centralized bureaucratic structure. By the mid 1920s, the Soviet Union had consolidated its control of the region, and in the following ten years it became the most powerful cartographer the region had ever seen. A new political map was imposed on the region. The new map was based on the territorialization of ethnicity: administrative units with a defined titular nation were created and slotted into the strict hierarchy of Soviet ethnofederalism.

Soviet ethnofederalism and, indeed, the history of the Soviet Union were the result of massively ideological and often utopian politics on

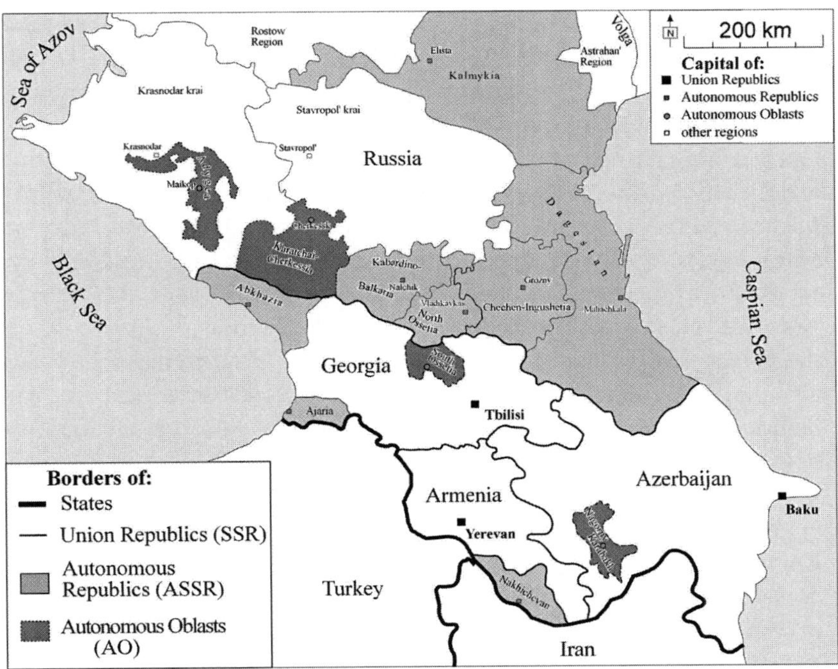

the one hand and tactical concessions to the realities of one of Europe's more industrially backward regions on the other. In addition, there was a sizeable dose of simulation politics, which was meant to heighten the internal and external acceptance of the new revolutionary state.

Fundamentally, Soviet ethnofederalism can be viewed as the solution to the three main tasks confronting the Bolshevik state founders, who had inherited the legacy of the multiethnic Tsarist Empire. The first task was the organization of territorial authority. To rule over an area—the job of any modern territorial state, but especially one as centralized as the Soviet Union—it must first be divided up into administrative units subordinated to a central hierarchy. The second task was to bind the nations, which had been "awakened" by war, revolution, and state collapse, into a common state. The force of nationalism, which the Bolsheviks so successfully instrumentalized against the Tsarist regime, was to be reined in once more. The third challenge stemmed from the need to win internal and external legitimacy for the new Soviet state, and this could only be done by granting at least de jure substantial rights to the nations, which the Soviet Union claimed to have freed from Tsarist oppression.

Soviet ethnofederalism—centralist in content, federal in form—was the solution to these tasks. All important regulative tasks were centralized and assigned to the authority of the federal center. The Communist Party of the Soviet Union (CPSU) was installed as the main instrument of rule, and its dominant position was anchored in the constitution. From then on, the party permeated state structures on all levels, from the center in Moscow, to the soviets (parliaments) of the new union and autonomous republics, down to the collective farms (*kolkhozi* and *sovkhozi*) in the rural regions of the new empire. Despite this de facto supercentralism, the Soviet Union was constructed as a federation, and the fiction that it was the voluntary unification of sovereign nations was also maintained in the constitution. The new Soviet state was an asymmetrical federation, comprising ethnoterritorial units. Each unit was delegated a certain amount of autonomy and privileges, which differed according to the status of the unit.

At the top of the hierarchy were the union republics (Soviet Socialist Republics, or SSRs), which together constituted the Union of Soviet Socialist Republics (USSR). After the annexation of the Baltic states in 1939, the Soviet Union was composed of 15 union republics. Union republics had borders to foreign states and usually had a numerically significant non-Russian native titular nation. According to Soviet doctrine and the tradition of "scientific Marxism," only those ethnic groups deemed culturally progressive nations, from a Soviet point of view, were awarded a union republic. On the basis of these qualification criteria (international borders, significant non-Russian population, and sufficient sociocultural development), Armenians, Georgians, and Azerbaijanis all received their own union republics.

Autonomous republics (Autonomous Soviet Socialist Republics, or ASSRs) took second place in the hierarchy of Soviet ethnofederalism. These were subunits of the union republics and were awarded to those ethnic groups that did not inhabit strategically important border regions and that were numerically smaller than the titular nations of the union republics. Autonomous oblasts (AOs; also called autonomous regions) were the third tier within a union republic for numerically small ethnic groups that had a relatively compact area of settlement. Finally, autonomous okrugs (also called autonomous units) were the fourth and smallest tier, and they were assigned to small ethnic groups with a compact area of settlement within an oblast. Apart from the right to cultural autonomy, autonomous okrugs had no privileges.

There were also the nonnationally defined territories, the oblasts and the krais. Oblasts were the basic administrative unit of the union republics. The title *krai* was given to a territory of historical strategic significance—for instance, the border regions of Stavropol' and Krasnodar on the border to the North Caucasus, and Krasnoyarsk and Khabarovsk in the Far East with a border to China. Functionally, however, there was no difference between an oblast and a krai.

Three of the four ethnoterritorial units (the union republics, the autonomous republics, and the autonomous oblasts) had attributes of sovereignty.[9] The union republics were described in the constitution as sovereign states, and they had borders, along with their own governments, legislatures, constitutions, and judiciaries; they had their own armed troops and the right to entertain direct relations to foreign powers. Union republics also possessed the right, according to the Soviet constitution, of secession from the union.

According to the constitution, autonomous republics were "national states" and not "sovereign states" like the union republics. The cultural rights of an ASSR were far more restricted than those of a union republic. In an ASSR, as a rule, school and university education was only available in Russian. Nevertheless, the ASSRs had the possibility of forming their own cadres, and, according to an informal but ubiquitous rule, members of the titular nation of an ASSR were allocated a disproportionately large number of cadre positions and university places. This positive discrimination adhered to the Soviet drive for the incorporation of national elites. ASSRs were subjects of union republics. As national, but not sovereign, states, they did not have the right of secession either from the Soviet Union or from the union republic to which they were subject.

Autonomous oblasts had far fewer attributes and institutions of national sovereignty than the ASSRs. They were only accorded a few privileges in the realm of cultural self-administration, which did not go as far as those of the ASSRs. AOs did not have their own universities or media, nor was there a regional bureaucracy, which could have molded and defended distinct national interests.

By 1924, the entire Caucasus had been incorporated into the Soviet Union, and the new political map of the region, based on the principles of ethnofederalism outlined above, was superimposed onto the region by Soviet cartographers. In the North Caucasus, ASSRs and AOs were set up for the larger ethnic groups and assigned to the Russian Union Republic. In the South Caucasus, union republics were instituted for the Georgians, Armenians, and Azerbaijanis. The principle of ethnic representation was combined with the "divide and rule" principle, which was important for establishing central power. Each ethnoterritorial unit was inhabited by a range of ethnic groups. The titular nations enjoyed some privileges, but they were always confronted with the possible ambitions of the nontitular groups. Inevitably, this led to the self-limitation of the titular nation and impeded collective action, but it also gave the center the possibility of playing groups off against one other. In all three South Caucasian union republics, "foreign" autonomous republics or autonomous oblasts were instituted as counterweights to any possible nationalist politics on the part of the respective union republic. In the north of the Soviet Republic of Georgia, the Ossets gained an AO (the South Ossetian Autonomous Oblast); in the northwest the Abkhazian ASSR and in the west the Ajarian ASSR were instituted. The Azerbaijan SSR acquired an exclave in Armenia (the Nakhichevan ASSR), inhabited almost exclusively by Azerbaijanis. On the other side, Nagorny-Karabakh, populated almost exclusively by Armenians, was made into an AO inside the Azerbaijan SSR.

Soviet ethnofederalism also shaped the North Caucasus. In the northeast, the Dagestan ASSR was created. In view of the numerous ethnic groups living here, no titular nation was established.[10] A common ASSR was awarded to the closely related Chechens and Ingush. The Kabardins and Balkars, which are not related to each other (the former belonging linguistically to the Caucasian languages, the latter to the Altaic languages) were also given a common autonomous republic, the Kabardino-Balkarian ASSR. Similarly, the Caucasian Cherkessia and the Altaic Karachai shared the Karachai-Cherkessian ASSR. The mainly Christian Ossets were divided. Those living on the north side of the Caucasus Mountains received their own ASSR. The Ossetian settlements in the South Caucasus, however, were assigned to the Georgian SSR as an AO.

The proportion of the titular nations in the ethnoterritorial units of the North Caucasus varied considerably, from a mere 22 percent of the Adygian in the Adygian AO up to 73 percent Chechens in the Chechen-Ingushetian ASSR. However, with the exception of Adygeya and of Dagestan, where there was no titular nation, the titular nations constituted the relative majority. In the South Caucasus, the proportion of the titular nation in all three union republics was relatively large. In Armenia, the most ethnically homogenous union republic, Armenians made up 92 percent of the population, in Georgia the titular nation accounted for 70 percent, and in Azerbaijan 82 percent.

The system of Soviet ethnofederalism emerged mainly between 1922 and 1924, although the new constitution of 1936, introduced under Stalin, brought with it some small changes in the administrative borders. From 1936 until the end of the Soviet Union, the state structure remained essentially unchanged, with the exception of some temporary changes in the aftermath of the Stalinist deportations. In 1943, the Stalinist totalitarian machine hit the North Caucasus with its full brutal force. Entire ethnic groups (Koreans, Germans, Tatars, Kalmyks, Karachai, Balkars, Ingush, and Chechens) were deported. The deportation of Chechens and Ingush began on February 23, 1944, and took only a few days to be completed. In July 1944, Lavrenty Beria reported to the Kremlin that in February and March 1944, some 602,123 residents of the North Caucasus were moved to the Kazakh and Kyrgyz SSRs, including 496,460 Chechens and Ingush, 68,327 Karachai, and 37,406 Balkars.[11] The Stalinist mass deportations of the Chechens, the Ingush, and the Balkars necessitated temporary border changes, since, in some cases, the entire titular nation of a territory had been deported. However, the autonomous territories of those peoples who had fallen victim to the deportations were restored subsequent to their rehabilitation and the return of survivors after 1956.

Tables 2.1 and 2.2 show the ethnic composition in North and South Caucasus in 1989.

TABLE 2.1
Ethnic Composition of SSRs, ASSRs, and AOs in the North Caucasus, 1989

Administrative Unit	*Status*	*Population*	*Proportion of Titular Nation (%)*	*Largest Nontitular Groups (%)*
Adygea	Founded on July 27, 1922, as Adygian-Cherkessian AO within Krasnodar krai (region). In 1928 became the Adygian AO.	432,064	Adygian, 22	Russians, 66
Chechnya	Founded as Chechen AO within the RSFSR on November 30, 1922. On January 15, 1934, combined with the Ingushetian AO to form the AO of the Chechens and Ingushetians. Raised in status to the Chechen-Ingushetian ASSR on December 5, 1936. Dissolved after the mass deportation of Chechens and Ingushetians on March 7, 1944. Restored as an ASSR on January 9, 1957. In 1990, Chechnya broke away and declared independence. Ingushetia remained an autonomous republic within the RF.	836,000	Chechens, 73	Russians, 27
Dagestan	Founded on January 20, 1921, within the RSFSR. In 1991, became an autonomous republic within the RF	1,802,188	No titular group ["Dagestani" refers to all residents of the area]	Avars, 8 Dargins, 16 Kumyks, 13 Russians, 9 Lezgins, 11 Tabasarans, 4 Nogai, 2 Rutulers, 1 Agulers, 1
Ingushetia	Founded as the Ingushetian AO within the RSFSR on July 7, 1924. On January 15, 1934, combined with the Chechen AO. Raised to Chechen-	193,000	Ingush, 70	Russians, 18 Chechens, 6

TABLE 2.1 (*continued*)

Administrative Unit	*Status*	*Population*	*Proportion of Titular Nation (%)*	*Largest Nontitular Groups (%)*
	Ingushetian ASSR on December 5, 1936. Dissolved after the mass deportation of Chechens and Ingushetians on March 7, 1944. Restored as an ASSR on January 9, 1957. In 1990, Chechnya split off and declared independence. Ingushetia remained an autonomous republic within the RF.			
Kabardino-Balkaria	Founded as Kabardinian AO within the RSFSR on September 1, 1921. In 1922, expanded to the Kabardino-Balkarian AO. On December 5, 1936, raised to the rank of ASSR. After the mass deportation of the Balkars in 1944, transformed into the Kabardinian ASSR. Restored as the Kabardino-Balkarian ASSR in 1957. Since 1991, an autonomous republic within the RF.	753,531	Kabardins, 48 Balkars, 9	Russians, 32
Karachai-Cherkessia	Founded on January 12, 1922, as an AO of the Karachai and Cherkessians in the RSFSR. In April 1926, the Cherkessian part became a distinct national area (okrug). On April 30, 1928, incorporated into the AO of the Karachai, which was abolished after the mass deportation of the Karachai in 1944. On January 9, 1957, restored as the Karachai-Cherkessian AO within Stavropol' krai (region). In 1991, became an autonomous republic within the RF.	414,970	Karachai, 42 Cherkessians, 9	Russians, 42
North Ossetia	Founded on July 7, 1924, as an AO within the RSFSR. On December 5, 1936, raised in status to ASSR. After 1991, an autonomous republic within the RF.	632,428	Ossets, 53	Russians, 30 Ingush, 5

Source: Goskomstat SSSR (1991), *Natsional'nyi sostav naseleniya SSSR: Po dannym vsesoyuznoi perepisi naseleniya 1989* (Moscow: Finansy i Statistika).

Abbreviations: AO, Autonomous Oblast (autonomous region); ASSR, Autonomous Soviet Socialist Republic (autonomous republic); RF, Russian Federation; RSFSR, Russian Soviet Federated Socialist Republic; SSR, Soviet Socialist Republic (union republic).

TABLE 2.2

Ethnic Composition of SSRs, ASSRs, and AOs in the South Caucasus, 1989

Administrative Unit	*Status*	*Population*	*Proportion of Titular Nation (%)*	*Largest Nontitular Groups (%)*
Armenia	Founded on November 29, 1920, as an SSR. Between 1922 and 1936 part of the Transcaucasian Federal Democratic Republic. Became independent in August 1991.	3,305,000	Armenians, 93	Azerbaijani, 2.6 Russians, 1.6
Georgia	Founded on February 25, 1921, as an SSR. Between 1922 and 1936, part of the Transcaucasian Federal Democratic Republic. Declared its independence on April 9, 1991.	5,401,000	Georgians, 70	Azerbaijani, 5.7 Russians, 6.3 Armenians, 8.1
Abkhazia (within Georgia)	On March 4, 1921, founded as the Abkhazian SSR within the short-lived Transcaucasian Federal Democratic Republic. In 1925, combined with the Georgian SSR; in 1930, demoted to an ASSR within Georgia. Broke away from Georgia in August 1990. Status is still unresolved today.	525,000	Abkhaz, 17	Georgians, 46 Armenians, 14 Russians, 13
Ajaria[a] (within Georgia)	Founded on June 16, 1921, as an ASSR within the Georgian SSR. Today a part of Georgia.	392,000	Ajars, 63	Georgians, 23 Russians, 8 Armenians, 4
South Ossetia (within Georgia)	Founded on April 20, 1922, as an AO within the Georgian SSR. On September 30, 1991, declared its independence from Georgia. Its status remains unresolved.	99,000	Ossets, 66	Georgians, 29 Russians, 2
Azerbaijan	Founded on April 28, 1920, as an SSR. Between 1922 and 1936, part of the Transcaucasian Federal Democratic Republic. Declared its independence in September 1991.	7,021,000	Azerbaijani, 82	Russians, 5.6 Armenians, 5.6
Nagorny-Karabakh (within Azerbaijan)	Founded on July 7, 1923, as an AO in the Azerbaijan SSR. Declared its independence on September 2, 1991. Its status remains unresolved.	162,000	Armenians, 76	Azerbaijani, 22

TABLE 2.2 (*continued*)

Administrative Unit	*Status*	*Population*	*Proportion of Titular Nation (%)*	*Largest Nontitular Groups (%)*
Nakhichevan (within Azerbaijan)	Founded on February 9, 1924, as an ASSR; it was an exclave within the Armenian SSR, belonging to the Azerbaijan SSR. Today part of Azerbaijan.	295,091	Azerbaijani, 96	Russians, 1.3 Armenians, 0.6

Source: Goskomstat SSSR (1991), *Natsional'nyi sostav naseleniya SSSR: Po dannym vsesoyuznoi perepisi naseleniya 1989* (Moscow: Finansy i Statistika).

Abbreviations: AO, Autonomous Oblast (autonomous region); ASSR, Autonomous Soviet Socialist Republic (autonomous republic); SSR, Soviet Socialist Republic (union republic).

[a] There are no precise data for Ajaria. Ajars are distinct from Georgians mainly on the basis of religion. However, this was not usually, or was incorrectly, registered in Soviet statistics. The Georgian political scientist Gia Tarkhan-Mouravi puts the Ajar population at around 250,000 (conversation with the author, Tbilisi, 28 July 1998).

The system of administrative-territorial division had given the Soviet leadership an instrument for the control and stifling of national ambitions. However, the main historical significance of the system was unintended and lay elsewhere. Above all, this system contrived an institutionalized coupling between a given group and a given territory. This created a foundation for modern (territorial) nation-statehood in the Caucasus for the first time. In the pre-Soviet period, the "nation" was not at all institutionalized in the North Caucasus as a frame of reference for loyalty and source of identity, and it was only weakly institutionalized in the South Caucasus. Instead, collective action and identity were rooted in kinship, clan, and regional contexts, in religiously defined groups, or, in the South Caucasian cities, in class consciousness. The concepts of nation and nationality came to the Caucasus as a byproduct of its incorporation into the Soviet system.

It was the Soviet planners and cartographers who first institutionalized the nation and lent the concept a legal framework. Most of the larger ethnic groups in the Soviet Union were assigned a territory and equipped with institutions for cultural and social development: borders, national symbols, self-administration, a constitution, education and research institutes, and a mass media.[12] These institutions helped mold a national elite, which, in turn, could be incorporated into Soviet rule through the affording of material privileges or the opening up of opportunities for social mobility within central Soviet hierarchies. On the surface, the Soviet type sovereign nation-states that were created as building blocks of the Soviet Union looked "modern," but as with so many other Soviet modernization projects, they were, in fact, more a simulacrum of modernity. The principle of nationality had indeed been institutionalized: the nations were allocated territories with borders and acquired political and cultural institutions, the constitutional right to secession gave the impression of the right to self-determination of peoples, certain privileges were tied to the membership of a titular nation, and national membership was assigned and registered in identity papers. Nevertheless, these were quasi nation-states, and their parliaments had little influence, their borders little meaning, their symbols little allure; and their freedom to maneuver was tightly restricted by the central hierarchies of the Soviet Union. Most important, the right of the SSR to national sovereignty and independence, as enshrined in the Soviet constitution, was never meant to be more than a placebo.

With the creeping implosion of the Soviet center, however, the institutions where quasi-sovereignty resided took on power and significance. The process of post-Soviet nation and state building, as well as the resulting ethnopolitical conflicts, has been crucially shaped by the Soviet legacy, by those very institutions that were designed by the Soviet planner to reign in the "nation."

Toward the Post-Soviet Union

For the first time in the history of the Soviet Union, Gorbachev's policy of glasnost (open discussion) created a public sphere where political ambitions could be voiced. Among the first to occupy that public space were national movements in many of the union republics. A common feature of these mass movements on the periphery of the Soviet empire was that initially most of them presented themselves as pro-perestroika (restructuring) movements. By 1989, however, the national movements had turned to advocating more radical positions, increasingly exploiting the prospect of secession from the Soviet Union. Among the first to embark on the secessionist course were the popular fronts of the Baltic states, but the popular fronts of Armenia, Azerbaijan, and Georgia followed shortly thereafter, and with no less passion.

The political weight of popular movements was dramatically increased by the first partly free elections to the republican and local parliaments (soviets). Between February and June 1990, these elections were held throughout the Soviet Union, granting victories to the popular movements in many republics—for example, in Estonia, Latvia, Lithuania, Armenia, and Russia and, in October 1990, Georgia. The elections of 1990 injected democratic legitimacy into the local political process. Local leaders now had to change their point of political reference from Moscow to the republican level, and, most important, the Soviet rubber-stamp parliaments became a locus of real power.

The dismantling of the hierarchy of the Communist Party ran parallel to this electoral democratization. Gorbachev, in need of broad support for his reforms, shifted political decision-making away from the party to such newly founded political institutions as his presidency and the parliament of the Soviet Union. On March 6, 1990, Article 6 of the Soviet constitution, which guaranteed the primacy of the Communist Party, was amended, and a multiparty system was officially allowed. Gorbachev thus ended the principle of a chain of command that had tied the republics to the center. Predictably, the union republics and the autonomous republics grasped as much sovereignty as they could. By spring 1990, all the SSRs had passed declarations of sovereignty, and in the summer of 1990, most ASSRs followed suit. For most union republics, sovereignty in this context did not yet mean independence, but it did mean control over resources, property rights, taxation, and legislation. However, the Baltic states went further: Lithuania declared independence on March 11, 1990; Estonia and Latvia followed shortly thereafter that same year, on March 30 and May 4, respectively; and Armenia declared independence in August 1990.

From the summer of 1990 until its collapse, the Soviet Union was locked in a complex multilevel power struggle that was structured by the Soviet federal system. In Moscow, still the center of the Soviet Union, Gorbachev was maneuvering between the conservative Communist *nomenklatura* that wanted to preserve the old system and the democratic opposition that pressed for more radical reforms. In the republics, national democratic oppositions challenged the Communist *nomenklatura,* achieving more success where they were able to reinvigorate parliaments after the elections of March 1990. In several republics where the parliaments were still controlled by the old *nomenklatura*—for example, in Chechnya and in Azerbaijan—the national-democratic opposition became organized into extra-parliamentary mass movements, which dramatically increased the risk for a violent showdown between old and new elites.

By the end of 1990, political weight in the Soviet Union had clearly shifted away from the center to the republics and, within the republics, toward the national-democratic movements. In November 1990, in an attempt to hold the union together, Gorbachev presented a draft of a new union treaty that involved some decentralization of power to the republics but maintained a strong federal center in Moscow. In a referendum in March 1991, at least 70 percent of the electorate voted in favor of the renewed Soviet Union; however, the people of the Baltic states and Georgia did not take part in that referendum.

The strong vote for preserving the Soviet Union did not change the fact that the republics proactively took control over resources and property rights, thus engaging in a de facto dismantling of the Soviet system. The Russian Union Republic, under the leadership of Boris Yeltsin, was one of the leaders in this trend. The conservative forces became increasingly convinced that the new union treaty would seal the fate of the Soviet Union. On August 19, 1990, one day before the scheduled signing of the treaty, an emergency committee headed by Vice President Gennady Yanaev and including Chairman of the KGB Vladimir Kriuchkov, Prime Minister Valentin Pavlov, and Minister of Internal Affairs Boris Pugo staged a coup in Moscow. Although troops and tanks were sent in, the putschists acted indecisively, obviously surprised by the firm resistance of the Russian government under Yeltsin's leadership, and were not willing to use force. Within three days, the coup collapsed, and power shifted radically to Yeltsin and, more by default, to the other republican leaders. To all intents and purposes, the Soviet Union ceased to exist, and the unprepared republics were left to deal with the opportunities and risks that accompanied this unexpected independence. To be sure, not all societies managed the transition in a nonviolent way; internal wars flared up in Tajikistan, Moldova, and across the Caucasus.

Soviet ethnofederalism, which guaranteed the control of the center over the aspirations of the various ethnic groups for more than 50 years, proved to be an especially subversive institution by the dissolution of the Soviet Union. In particular, the equipping of the union republics with the prerequisites of statehood and the anchoring of their status as sovereign states in the Soviet constitution paved the way for the process of "sovereignization" that began in 1988. At the same time, the serial encapsulation of the federal subjects, the *matryoshka* or "Russian doll" federalism, provided considerable fuel for conflict. The autonomous republics and autonomous oblasts within the union republics viewed the latter's sovereignization and nationalization with concern, since they feared that the positive discrimination, which Soviet authorities had guaranteed the titular nations of the ASSRs, could be jeopardized. Vice versa, the union republics viewed with mistrust the tendency of "their" ASSRs to dispute subordination to them or even to make moves toward secession from the SSR. Thus, the weakening of the center led to a competition between union republics (SSRs) and autonomous republics and regions (ASSRs and AOs), which in Nagorny-Karabakh, South Ossetia, and Abkhazia ended in organized violence.

This competition was further exacerbated by the center through an alteration to the legislation on the right of secession for the union republics. In April 1990, the relevant law was complemented by an article ruling on the position of ASSRs and AOs in the event of the SSR seceding from the Soviet Union. The new law stated that, in this event, the affected ASSRs and AOs had the right, by means of referendum, to decide whether they would secede together with the SSR or remain in the Soviet Union.[13] Thus, for example, if Georgia decided to break away from the Soviet Union, the autonomous republics and autonomous oblasts within its territory would have the opportunity, after a referendum, to legally secede from Georgia and stay with the Soviet Union. This law was conceived primarily by the Soviet center as a brake on the independence movements in the SSRs: if a union republic wanted to split off from the Soviet Union, it would have to reckon with the secession of its "own" ASSRs and AOs. History rendered the law obsolete—the Soviet Union collapsed before it could be applied. However, between April 1990 and August 1991, the law provided considerable incentives for the ASSRs and AOs to intensify their separatist exertion from the SSRs, and this aggravated competition over sovereignty proved highly conflict-provoking.

Karabakh Armenians, Chechens, Abkhaz, and South Ossets often refer to this law in support of their claims to independence, but this is a doubtful legalistic argument. The amendments did not foresee the possibility of an ASSR or an AO becoming independent; the only option was for staying within the Soviet Union should the union republic, to which the ASSR or AO belonged, opt to secede. With the end of the Soviet Union as a state, the union republics had no choice but to secede, and the ASSR or AO could no longer opt to stay in the Soviet Union —an option that Nagorny-Karabakh, Abkhazia, and South Ossetia would indeed have wished to use. The law has lost all frame of reference. The right to independence—whatever experts on international law might say—is, in essence, a function of the real relations of power in the international system. This was quickly brought home to Karabakh Armenians, Chechens, and Ossets after 1991, when their quest for independence was met with no support by the international community.

After 1991, all union republics became independent. Those autonomous republics and oblasts which had also declared independence (Chechnya, Abkhazia, South Ossetia, Nagorny-Karabakh) were denied international recognition, however, unlike the union republics. Neither their "mother states" (Russia, Georgia, Azerbaijan) nor the international community recognized the independence of these territories. Four out of five wars in the Caucasus erupted over the status of former autonomous republics, the only exception being the civil war within Georgia, which is, however, closely linked to the secessionist wars of South Ossetia and Abkhazia.

Nations and State

Nationalism was declared dead twice in the course of the 20th century: once by "scientific Marxism," which predicted that the progress of the socialist societies would replace people's loyalty to national ideas with solidarity for the proletariat; and a second time by modernization theorists, who expected the fascination of individuals and social groups with national emotions and symbols to wane in a modern, globalizing, increasingly borderless world.[14]

The end of the Cold War brought nationalism back, both to the territories of the former Eastern Bloc and to public and academic discourses. The collapses of the Soviet Union and Yugoslavia, and the numerous armed conflicts and wars accompanying them, were interpreted as the "triumph of the nation," and predictions of nationalism becoming extinct in the name of radical enlightenment were revised.[15] Now, ethnic, national, and even cultural lines of conflict were proclaimed to be the dominant principle of order and disorder in a multipolar world.[16] The academic study of minorities and ethnic conflicts boomed, and events in the former Soviet Union, in former Yugoslavia, and in Rwanda seemed to trumpet the return of the ethnic.

The ethnic conflicts accompanying the collapse of the Eastern Bloc were interpreted as being caused by national processes that had been artificially kept in check by the socialist systems but which now broke loose with a vengeance. Such interpretations of events matched the primordial, substantial understanding of nation and ethnicity so dominant in Soviet practice and Soviet academic discourse. As described earlier in this chapter, the Soviet Union's ethnofederalist state structure, with its gradations of sovereignty for different ethnic groups according to their "level of development," was not simply a pragmatic means for installing Soviet power and overcoming national particularist interests. It was also an operationalization of Marxist-Leninist ideas about the stages of development through which peoples had to progress. The most developed groups, which had developed into real nations, thus had the right to their "own" union republic. Russians, Georgians, Armenians, and Azerbaijanis, together with 11 other national groups, were therefore assigned their own SSR. Other groups, such as the Chechens, the Ossets, and the Abkhaz, were only assigned autonomous provinces or regions.

Similarly, a substantial understanding of the "nation" also dominated academic thinking in the Soviet Union. Authors such as Nikolay Gumilev, who wrote extensively about the birth, triumph, and death of nations in the 1960s to 1980s, rose to spectacular prominence during the last days of the Soviet Union and in the early days of many nationalist movements.[17] The dominant understanding of the nation as an ethnocultural, substantial entity, capable or indeed forced to live, fight, and maybe die, lent the numerous nationalist movements that advocated the end of the Soviet Union a legitimacy which was difficult to contest. This was one of the many historical ironies that accompanied the demise of the Soviet Union.

In the 1960s to 1980s, two competing theories of ethnicity held sway in Soviet academic circles, but both had at their core an essential primordial understanding of ethnicity. Yulian Bromley (1921–1990), the director of the Institute of Ethnography of the Academy of Sciences of the USSR, formulated the official anthropological theory of the ethnos as a combination of such features as common territory, common language, common culture, and a distinctive ethnic consciousness that sets one ethnic group apart from others.[18] A maverick Soviet historian and geographer, Lev Gumilev, advanced an alternative understanding of ethnicity as a special biophysical force (*passionarnost,* in his terminology) compelling individuals and groups to unite in order to perform the creative work of transformation of natural environment. These groups tend to develop common ethnic consciousness, language, and culture.[19] Set against a panoramic world historical background, Gumilev's theory received much acclaim among historians, geographers, biologists, and the amateur public but was unanimously rejected by mainstream ethnographers. The outbursts of ethnic violence that accompanied the collapse of the Soviet Union put Bromley's rather bureaucratic theory to rest, while allowing Gumilev to gain more popularity among post-Soviet anthropologists. The primordial perspective on the nature of ethnic groups continues to be the bedrock of Russian anthropological thought.

Substantial conceptualizations of nation and ethnicity were also dominant in the discourse of mobilized national groups. Whoever had the chance to participate in the rallies of national movements in the late Soviet Union or has sat at the kitchen tables of the Soviet or post-Soviet periphery and listened to the passionate debates about the past, and especially about the future collective projects of Lithuanians, Georgians, or Chechens, will have inevitably encountered this. To attempt to deconstruct such substantial conceptualizations of the nation seemed hopeless: in the emotional and passionately conducted debates, the substantial qualities of one's own nation were regarded as a given self-understanding that could not be shaken. The nation was depicted in substantial ethnocultural terms, whereas the concept of a political nation, where ethnicity was not the main precondition, hardly resonated.

The massive mobilization force generated by nationalist identities in the Soviet Union in the late 1980s is indisputable, so it is tempting to take this as proof of a special quality intrinsic to national or ethnic bonding. Indeed, many commentators and many of the activists did so at that time. Nevertheless, no special bonding power of the national is required to explain mobilization in the name of a nation. It was the possibility, emerging in the course of the late 1980s, of realizing new collective political projects beyond the moribund Soviet system that lent the concept "nation" its potency, its mobilization effect, and its immunity to deconstruction. The concept of the nation as a substantial, real group was in great demand because the establishing and legitimization of new institutional rules and new polities relied on there being a "real" group as subject and beneficiary of these innovations.

In 1988 and 1989, hundreds of thousands demonstrated in Grozny, Tbilisi, Yerevan, Riga, Vilnius, and Tallinn, first in support of Gorbachev's perestroika, then against the Soviet Union, and finally for their independence—and all in the name of the nation. By 1993, the Soviet Union was gone, and wars had erupted in Chechnya, Georgia, and Nagorny-Karabakh. The Chechens challenged the Russian state and demanded independence. The Georgian state was challenged by the breakaway territories of South Ossetia and Abhazia. The Armenian exclave of Nagorny-Karabakh wanted to break away from Azerbaijan and join the newly independent Armenia.

It is tempting to assume a direct and causal link between national mobilization and the subsequent wars. However, as the case studies in this book show, there is no direct link between national mobilization and organized violence. National mobilization manifested itself in mass rallies, in the enthusiastic and often overly exaggerated public use of national symbols, in public discourse, and in the rewriting of national histories. Its central actors were the participants of mass rallies and those who, by virtue of their intellectual capacity or access to mass media, influenced and shaped the public discourse. In this climate of overheated national emotions, the risk of violence between members of ethnic groups did rise; for a long time, however, the level of spontaneous intergroup violence was extremely low, especially in those places where different ethnic groups had lived together for decades or centuries. These dense, interethnic relations withstood the national fever that gripped the capitals and the public discourse for an astonishingly long period, yet, in the end, neighbors did become enemies.

The rising interethnic tension between Russians and Chechens, Georgians and Abkhaz or Ossets, Armenians and Azerbaijanis, did not "automatically" translate into civil war. It took organization, resources, opportunity, and leadership by organizers of violence to turn interethnic tensions into sustained and organized violence. Once violence became organized, the mobilized masses rallying on public squares could no longer be viewed as the main actors; these were, instead, a few capable organizers with access to crucial resources, organizational skills, and military experience, who were willing to take the risk involved in waging war. The incentives and opportunities that shaped and constrained the actions of these organizers of violence were quite different from those of the hundreds of thousands who rallied on the main squares of the capitals, demanding national independence. Revolutions and wars are not the work *of* nations but are work in the *name of* nations. Nations and ethnic groups are not collective actors but symbols, and groups compete for control over them, while political entrepreneurs strive to institutionalize new rules of the game in their name. Taking what Roger Brubaker calls the "realism of the group" at face value detracts from identifying the real actors in the theater of violence—elites and counterelites, field commanders, paramilitary groups, militias, and entrepreneurs of violence.[20] Therefore, for all the flood of everyday language and interpretations, it is important to repeatedly deconstruct nations and ethnic groups as collective groups.

From a political science, and especially conflict research, perspective, the crucial question concerning the concept of the nation or the ethnic group is not to ask what a nation is but, rather, to investigate what the concept of nation does. Which groups can be best mobilized with the concept of the nation? What is the social and institutional context in which various groups fight over the control of the symbol "nation," and what is their program? And which institutional factors favor some and disadvantage others in their contest over the nation as a resource? Once these questions are posed, the focus of inquiry shifts away from the nation as a real, unitary group and focuses on interest groups competing over the nation as a resource, and on the institutional framework that structures the preferences and constraints of these groups. Whether, how, and by whom nation as resource can be employed depends on how the nation is institutionalized in political institutions, in laws, and in territorial state structures. Thus, it would be simplistic to claim that nations and nationalism caused the Caucasian turmoil at the end of the Soviet Union. Rather, it was the institutional legacy of the Soviet Union that shaped the ways in which the concepts of "nation" and "state" became contested.

The collapse of the Soviet Union urged all Caucasian polities to find a political answer to three crucial questions quickly, although these questions had taken centuries to be answered elsewhere. The first question regarded the final status of the polity: Would it be an independent, sovereign state or a province within a state? The second question was about ownership of the polity: Would it be the state of one specific national group or a state of all the people living on that territory? This question was no less explosive than the first, given the fact that none of the Caucasian polities was even close to being monoethnic. The third question related to the territorial extent of the polity: Would the borders drawn between the republics by Soviet leaders become the new internationally recognized borders, or would the borders be redrawn in order to better match the complex ethnic settlement patterns so typical of the Caucasus?

The political liberties that came with Gorbachev's policy of glasnost made it possible for these questions to be heatedly debated in public. The institutional legacy of the Soviet Union thus provided the structure of the fragmentation that arose around these questions. As the case studies show, the Caucasian societies favored different answers to these questions, which, in turn, led to different outcomes. Two observations, however, are notable. First, in contrast to events in the Balkans, the existing borders were not really contested anywhere. National aspiration centered on the international status of the territory, not on a change of borders. Second, there is the issue of how efficient the new states, independent of their final status, would be. How quickly would they develop state capacities? How solid would their new institutions be? How much protection would they be able to give minority groups? How capable would the new states be of regulating contenders for power and of controlling radicals within their own state? As the case studies show, the wars in Georgia, Azerbaijan, Armenia, and Chechnya were not related simply to the fierce contest over the status and the ownership of the new state but more to the fact that that the new states were unable to consolidate their power quickly and to accumulate state capacities.

3

Making Sense

Conflict Theory and the Caucasus

> The search for a single factor or a set of factors that explains everything is comparable to the search for the Holy Grail—noble but futile.[1]

In this book *conflict* is understood as a process in which two or more parties attempt to pursue their interests, which are perceived as mutually incompatible, by directly or indirectly seeking to reduce the other party's capacity to achieve its goals. Conflict is thus competition over resources and symbols, conducted in the framework of institutionalized procedures. Conflict is therefore the normal state of affairs in society. By contrast, *violent conflict* is understood as a process in which two or more parties attempt to pursue what they perceive as incompatible interests by trying to seize or destroy the property of the other party and/or to injure or eliminate the other party with the help of organized violence.[2] As a rule, violent conflicts are conducted outside all those institutions that a society provides and practices for dealing with conflict. From such a definition, the key question that conflict research needs to address is when and how conflict spins out of its institutional embeddedness and escalates into violence.

The emergence of violence is often perceived as a chaotic, irrational eruption. Wars "break out," violence "erupts," and social order "collapses." Such perceptions aptly capture the feelings of witnesses or victims of organized violence. However, again contrary to everyday perceptions, it is deeply misleading to depict violent conflicts as irrational, disordered, and chaotic processes. Undoubtedly, violent conflicts cause horrific devastation. Nevertheless, the normative rejection of destructive violence is no substitute for the analysis of the rational strategic calculations of those people organizing violence, investing in violence, and hence sustaining violence.

Social scientists cannot describe, let alone explain, events unless they are equipped with sufficient theory. Telling the stories of war and peace thus inevitably opens up the debate on the appropriate theoretical approaches that may be applied in order to collect, order, and interpret the "material" of which these stories are made. Behind these approaches are different and often competing epistemological positions that inform how knowledge of the observed social processes are gained and verified.

In this chapter, the specific analytical tools applied to the case studies in chapters 4 to 7 are discussed against the backdrop of recent conflict theories. The chapter starts with an overview of the findings in recent quantitative literature. This strand of research aims to identify those general factors that increase a society's propensity for violence in general, using a sample of most or all internal wars after 1945. Among the most prominent factors seen as increasing the risk for war are state weakness, low level of development, existence of resources for financing rebellion, complex patterns of ethnic geography, and terrain favoring rebellion. Next, these global propositions are complemented by a closer look at the microlevel of organized violence—by treating the organization of violence as a problem of collective action and identifying those factors and processes that are necessary for organizers of violence to overcome the many problems associated with collective, sustained violence. Finally, linking the two and expanding the explanatory power of both, an institutionalist approach to conflict research is introduced.

Risks for War: Global Propositions

Since the late 1990s, a number of quantitative comparative studies have sought to systematically identify those factors that make societies in general more prone to violence. In contrast to qualitative approaches, which are better suited to providing idiosyncratic, highly specific explanations for a small number of cases, these studies seek to uncover the generalizable factors that have an effect on the likelihood of war and which can be systematically traced across many cases. While sociological definitions of conflict and violence primarily focus on the processes that lead to the escalation of conflict, the quantitative strand of research literature focuses on structural factors that account for higher risks of conflict. Typically, such studies are based on a sample that encompasses all civil wars from 1945. The dependent variable is usually the occurrence or nonoccurrence of "internal conflict" (civil war, insurgency, internal war, or rebellion). These studies then test the effect of various independent variables such as "level of development" "regime type," "ethnic and religious fractionalization," and "mountainous terrain" on the dependent variable: that is, on the occurrence (or the length or the scale) of internal conflicts.

Since these approaches rely on statistical analysis for inferring causality, they require that their objects of interest—the war and the factors causing the war—are defined and "packaged" in such a way that it becomes amenable to statistical measurement and comparison.[3] Consequently, in terms of these studies, societies are at war or they are not, it is an ethnic war or it is not, the parties to the war are the government or they are not (in which case they are the rebels), the rebels are motivated by greed or they are not, and so on. This reductionism defies the tradition of sociological writing on conflict, with its emphasis on the dynamics of conflict; the shifting and blurring of boundaries; and the social construction of identities, motivations, and patterns of interaction as a result of conflict, not as its precondition, or independent variable. Furthermore, statistics may identify associations between a given factor and an outcome, but they usually do not illuminate the causal mechanism that explains this association. For example, one of the best established findings of quantitative conflict research is that a low GDP (gross domestic product) is associated with an increased risk of civil war, but which mechanisms actually cause this outcome are still hotly disputed. Despite these limitations, the general propositions that quantitative research have to offer provide a useful framework for comparison and are thus a rewarding starting point for this investigation.

The findings from recent quantitative literature point to six factors that increase a society's risk for internal war: a low level of economic development, a sudden loss of administrative capacities, opportunities for financing rebellions, recent previous wars, a complex ethnic geography, and terrain that favors rebellions. In the following sections, these findings are summarized, and their relevance and applicability in the context of the Caucasus are briefly discussed.[4]

Level of Economic Development

There is broad consensus that a society's level of economic development (usually measured by growth of per capita income, or by per capita income, or by average energy consumption) considerably influences the risk of internal conflict. Very poor societies are more prone than less poor societies to internal violence. Wealthy societies, by contrast, appear immune to organized violence. Collier et al. show that the level of per capita income, growth rate, and the structure of the economy—namely, dependence on primary commodity exports—have a significant effect on the risk of internal war. They estimate that doubling per capita income approximately halves the risk of rebellion.[5] Similarly, Fearon and Laitin show that, on average, reducing per capita income by $1,000 is associated with a 41 percent increase in the annual odds for the onset of civil war.[6] Hegre et al. found that in states moving from a very low to a marginally higher level of development, the risk of conflict also increases. If the level of development surpasses a certain threshold, roughly equivalent to the level of development found in Bhutan or Haiti in 1990, then the risk of conflict falls. Highly developed states are around eight times less at risk of conflict than are states with the highest risk level of development.[7] This might explain why, out of 127 internal wars since 1945, some 34 have taken place in sub-Saharan Africa and 33 in Asia, but only two occurred in the West.

Although there is much evidence that countries with low levels of economic development are at a typically higher risk of internal wars, it is not clear whether there is an actual causal link between a low level of economic development and civil wars; moreover, if there were such causality, the exact mechanism by which it works is not clear. Different studies have interpreted the correlation between a low level of economic development and a high propensity for civil wars in different ways. For example, Fearon and Laitin assume that the risk for war depends crucially on the government's capacity for effectively policing rural areas and combating insurgencies; hence, they interpret a low level of GDP as a proxy for the government's capacity to organize counterinsurgency.[8] Other authors see low levels of GDP as a sign of economic hardship, which lowers recruitment costs for rebels, or as an indicator that poverty may spark violence. Notably, these different interpretations, which are based on the same statistical findings, correspond to a quite different motivational structure for rebels. The first two interpretations see rebellion emerging when there is the opportunity to do so; the latter sees rebellion as being motivated by grievances. Both interpretations are consistent with statistical analysis of the data.

One of the benefits of such broad propositions is that it allows different regions to be put in global perspective. However, by global standards the Soviet and post-Soviet Caucasus probably does not qualify as a region marked by low levels of development. Even acknowledging the massive economic problems with which the Soviet Union was struggling in the last decade of its existence, the Caucasus of the 1980s must still be seen as a relatively well resourced region in comparison with other regions of the world. In 1990, the GDP in Georgia was approximately five times higher than the average of countries in the world's poorest quartile, even though the economy was stagnating during much of the decade and even shrinking toward the end (Table 3.1). In addition, the slow growth of the official economy in the early and mid 1980s was partly compensated for by the blossoming of the informal "shadow" economy. According to both anecdotal evidence and Soviet public perception, the shadow economy reached legendary levels in the Caucasus. The most conservative estimates assume that the size of the shadow economy was the equivalent of at least 30 percent of the official GDP in the last years of the Soviet Union (Table 3.2).

Real GDP is generally perceived as being the single most important indicator for level of development, but even if other measures of development are applied, it would be difficult to label the Soviet Caucasus as an underdeveloped region. While the benefits that the Soviet Union had to offer to its citizens considerably lagged behind what it had promised and could not compete with the West, its achievements were still impressive. Health care was widely available and free at the point of service; enrollment in secondary schooling was almost universal, because

TABLE 3.1
Development of GDP Per Capita, Constant 2000 $US

	1980	*1985*	*1990*	*1995*	*2000*	*2005*
Armenia	n.a.	n.a.	7,940	461	620	1,128
Azerbaijan	n.a.	n.a.	1,250	488	655	1,182
Georgia	1,670	1,986	1,493	458	648	971
Low and middle income (world)	864	899	961	1,035	1,190	1,435
Low income (world)	254	271	310	338	390	476

Source: *WDI Online: World Development Indicators*, online database (World Bank)
n.a., not available.

TABLE 3.2
Size of the Shadow Economy Relative to the GDP, Minimum Estimation (%)

	1990	*1990–1993 (average)*
Armenia	31	83
Azerbaijan	28	30
Georgia	33	86

Source: Yair Eilat and Clifford Zinnes (2002), "The Shadow Economy in Transition Countries: Friend or Foe? A Policy Perspective," *World Development* 30(7), pp. 1233–1254.

in the Soviet Union secondary school education was, with a few exceptions, free and mandatory; and a social safety net for pensioners was in place. While there was hidden unemployment, particularly in such economically backward regions as Dagestan, Nagorny-Karabakh, and South Ossetia, it was only with the violent escalation of conflict that unemployment really became a mass phenomenon. In sum, the Soviet Caucasus was by no means a region that suffered from a low level of development. Explanations that draw on atypical low absolute levels of development thus cannot easily be applied.

Likewise, Donald Horowitz's argument that economically backward, peripheral ethnic groups are more likely to rebel than groups that are relatively economically advanced cannot easily be applied.[9] Naturally, there were differences between the union republics in the level of economic development, with the Baltic republics being at the upper end and the Central Asian republics at the lower end. The differences between the Caucasian republics, however, were rather small. Moreover, the Soviet system put a high premium on equalization, and the Soviet redistribution system ensured that the differences in living standards across the population were remarkably small, especially in comparison with the dramatic gaps between social strata that have emerged all over the post-Soviet space.

To be sure, secessionist groups did refer to economic discrimination in order to legitimize their secessionist claims. For example, the Karabakh Armenians and the Abkhaz, in particular, complained that they were economically disadvantaged by the unloved republican centers. It is difficult to find substantial proof for these claims, however. Abkhazia was a rather affluent region within Georgia, mainly because of its privileged position as an all-Soviet *kurort* (tourist resort) and its flourishing export of tea and citrus fruits. Karabakh was certainly an economically backward region compared with urban centers such as Baku and Yerevan; according to economic indicators, however, it was more prosperous than most other regions in Azerbaijan. The perceived economic neglect was therefore more informed by what Karabakh could have been within Armenia compared with what it was within Azerbaijan.

Other indicators such as urbanization and education also show relatively little variance across groups within the Caucasus. But even if the North Caucasus, as a largely rural and little industrialized region, could have qualified as economically backward in relation to the central regions (mainly urban centers in Soviet Russia), this does not explain why only one group, the Chechens, embarked on organized violence, while other groups in the North Caucasus did not. Moreover, it also fails to explain why the Abkhaz, arguably a peripheral but a relatively prosperous (thanks to the thriving shadow economy) group in Georgia, opted for secession, whereas the poorer Ajars did not. Hence, neither an absolute low level of economic development nor a relatively low level of development (compared with other groups) is a factor that offers much explanatory power in the Caucasus. While expectations and fears over future economic development played a prominent role on the agenda of political actors and followers in the Caucasus, the economic situation, as it was, does not lend support to arguments that stress either economic discrimination or a general low level of development as explanations for internal wars.

Regime: Strength, Type, and Change

States are at risk when they are newly independent or when they have recently suffered political instability at the center. Fearon and Laitin estimated that the odds of a civil war starting are five times greater in the first two years of a state's independence than in other years. Political instability at the center also dramatically increases the risk of war. According to the same authors, a country that has suffered from political instability has a 67 percent greater chance of internal violence in the following three years than a country that did not suffer political instability.[10] Likewise, as noted above, there is a broad consensus that a low level of GDP per capita, which is interpreted as being an indicator of low administrative capacities, has a significant influence on the risk of violent conflict.

States that have undergone a rapid change from autocracy to democracy, or vice versa, are also at risk. According to Hegre et al., on average, regimes are 3.55 times more at risk of civil war on the day after a change of regime. This effect fades over time: one year after states have undergone a regime change, they face only a 1.89 times greater risk; after six years, they are no more likely to suffer violence than states that have not undergone regime change. Interestingly, the direction of regime change does not play a significant role—moves toward both autocracy and democracy are risky.[11] Contrary to commonly held assumptions, democratic states do not seem to be better protected than authoritarian states from the risks of internal wars. Collier and Hoeffler found no evidence that more democratic regimes were less vulnerable to organized violence than less democratic regimes, and they take this result as further evidence that the grievance script provides less explanatory power than the opportunity script. Fearon and Laitin reached similar conclusions, finding that the onset of civil war is no less frequent in democracies than in nondemocratic regimes, once they controlled for level of income.[12] However, they found clear evidence that regimes that are neither fully democratic nor fully authoritarian suffered from a markedly greater risk of internal conflict.[13] The same finding was reported by Hegre et al., who determined that authoritarian regimes and institutionally consolidated democracies are far less vulnerable to conflict than mixed systems or transitional regimes are. Very authoritarian and very democratic regimes display a similarly low conflict risk, while intermediate regimes are four times more susceptible to conflict. Semidemocratic and semiauthoritarian regimes combine a limited amount of public freedom with a limited amount of repression. This mixture can encourage conflict because the permitted public freedom makes the organization of resistance and the expression of protest against repressive politics possible.[14]

Instability and regime change certainly epitomize political developments in the Caucasus. All states in the region experienced political instability at the center, embarked on a rapid change from autocracy to democracy, and turned into weak transitional regimes en route. However, the Caucasian paths from political instability to violence show some peculiarities. The rapid devaluation of administrative capacities went hand in hand with national mobilization and a widening of the political space (liberalization). This conjunction of national mobilization, liberalization, and diminishing administrative capacities opened up various avenues that led to organized violence. As the Soviet state became weaker, it could no longer guarantee that competition between elites took place in line with institutionalized procedures, since it could no longer punish competitors who did not abide by the rules. Elite competition, as with most other aspects of politics, became "disembedded," as it was no longer played by the rules. In Chechnya, Azerbaijan, and, to some extent, Karabakh, nationalist counterelites, backed by mass support in the streets, captured the state by force. Likewise, state weakness also opened up windows of opportunity for realizing secessionist aspirations. Local elites in Abkhazia, Ossetia, Karabakh, and Chechnya wanted to seize the political opportunity that the weakening of the central state offered and opted for secession. The secessionist drive of these groups was without doubt further pushed by the lack of capacity and of political will of the newly ruling nationalist elites in Russia, Georgia, and Azerbaijan to offer credible security guarantees. Hence, it was not only the window of opportunity that triggered secessionist policies but also, especially in the case of Abkhazia and Karabakh, the lack of credible commitment of the new states to the protection of their national minorities. The structural weakness that prevents states from offering credible guarantees has been referred to as the commitment problem, and it certainly had an important role in the conflicts between Georgia and Abkhazia and between Azerbaijan and Karabakh.[15]

Financing the Rebellion

With the economic turn in conflict research, the financial viability of organized violence has come to the forefront, and researchers have sought to identify the important sources of income that finance rebellions. Potential sources are "lootable" natural resources such as oil, gems, and coca or opium poppy, as well as the taxing of illicit economic activities by rebels (for example, drug smuggling) and donations from a foreign patron or a wealthy diaspora. Both qualitative and quantitative studies suggest that the production of oil is associated with the onset of internal wars, particularly separatist conflicts.[16] With Collier and Hoeffler taking the lead, it is now broadly accepted that a high dependence on natural resources, primarily oil, makes a state more prone to internal violence.[17] However, while the link between oil and the risk of violent conflict is well established, the causal mechanisms are predictably opaque.[18] The existence of natural resources may provide an incentive for looting, it may motivate rebels to capture the state, or it may trigger secessionist movements that hope to gain control over the resources. A different line of thought, associated with the "resource curse," suggests that a wealth of natural resources often leads to distorted economic development, high levels of corruption, and poor governance, which may, in turn, fuel conflict more indirectly.[19] Also, natural resources may foster rentier states with weak ties to their societies and weak administrative capacities.[20] This may then lead to another factor that increases the risk of war—namely, the lack of state capacities.

Evidence from these case studies suggest that such lootable commodities, while not causing wars, help to prolong wars because rebels reinvest the profits from selling these commodities in the organization of violence. For example, in Afghanistan, the trade in gemstones and opium was an important source of income for the Northern Alliance of Ahmed Shah Massoud, but it cannot be claimed that trading in gemstones or drugs led to the onset of the war.

Finally, there is also evidence, both from case studies and from statistical analyses, that a large diaspora increases the risk of internal violence.[21] The donations and support from diaspora are often a crucial source of income for rebel movements. Well-known examples are the Tamil Tigers and the Kosovo Liberation Army, both rebel movements that were able to obtain, often by criminal means, material support for the cause from the diaspora.

In the Caucasus, only Azerbaijan and Chechnya possess natural resources of any significance—in both cases, oil. The diaspora argument, by contrast, is of wider applicability, if the definition of diaspora is relaxed. In the strict sense, only the Armenians possess a significant diaspora, and it was certainly crucial in helping to finance the war efforts. When the meaning of diaspora is broadened to include such diverse phenomena as the Chechen community living in Soviet urban centers (primarily Moscow and St. Petersburg) or ethnic kin groups living in neighboring states (such as the Ossets in South Ossetia who supported the struggle of the Ossets in North Ossetia, and the many volunteers from the North Caucasus who supported the Abkhazians' struggle against the Georgians), the support of the diaspora was in all cases of considerable relevance for the financing of war, *once it had broken out.* There is little evidence that the support of a diaspora was instrumental in explaining the outbreak of war.

Previous Wars

War breeds war. A factor that makes a society significantly more prone to organized violence is previous organized violence. Societies that have experienced conflict in the last five years are more prone to slip back into violence. Statistically, the risk of renewed war is twice as high as the risk of new war,[22] although this effect fades over time. After five years without war, the country has an "average" risk of war. This observation allows for different interpretations. Renewed conflict could point to hatred and motives for revenge, accumulated and strengthened during the first war as a core trigger. Alternatively, the previous conflict could have further weakened state capacities by damaging the economy and sapping political institutions. This, in turn, would make a renewed rebellion cheaper, since the government's counterinsurgent capacities would be reduced.

Another possible causal mechanism links renewed violence to the fact that in post-conflict societies, the organization of violence remains "cheap" because the logistics of war (weapons, command structures, networks, and maybe fear) are still widely available, and because widespread unemployment makes recruiting young males as fighters cheap.[23] In the Caucasus, two episodes of renewed war may serve as a test case for this proposition. First, there is the series of subsequent wars within Georgia; second, there are the two Chechen wars. In the case studies, the processes and mechanisms by which the previous war contributed to renewed wars are traced in detail.

Ethnicity: Diversity and Inequality

Perhaps the most original contribution of large-*n,* quantitative cross-country studies, running counter to widely held popular beliefs, is that ethnically or religiously diverse societies do not have a higher risk of violent conflicts than do more ethnically homogeneous societies.[24] Collier and Hoeffler as well as Hegre et al. demonstrated that ethnically fractionalized societies are more secure than more homogenous societies. They hypothesized that in diverse societies, consisting of numerous ethnic groups, it is more difficult for organizers of violence to recruit along ethnic lines, simply because the pool for recruits is smaller.[25] They also found, however, that this only occurs when the largest ethnic group is less than 45 percent of the total population. When the largest group makes up 45 percent or more, the risk of violence significantly increases. The authors argue that this is because groups that form a relative or absolute majority are tempted to use their numerical dominance to discriminate against smaller groups, which, in turn, stirs discontent. "Ethnic dominance" is therefore seen as a major factor in increasing the risk of war.

Ethnicity per se is thus not a causal factor. However, once a society has become unstable, ethnicity takes a prominent role in shaping the dynamics of violence. In 51 percent of all internal wars since World War II, at least one party to the conflict recruited mainly along ethnic lines; in 18 percent of all wars, recruiting was also done at least partly along ethnic lines. Only roughly one-third (31 percent) of all wars cannot be labeled ethnic wars.[26] Furthermore, once tensions escalate into war, there is evidence to suggest that ethnic wars tend to be longer than wars not fought along ethnic lines.[27]

Last, economic and cultural discrimination against ethnic groups has been seen as the root cause of many conflicts.[28] Ted Gurr and his research group (in the Minorities at Risk Project) indicated that economic discrimination against minorities constitutes a major risk factor.[29] A number of cases, such as Peru, Colombia, Kosovo, and Macedonia, strongly support this assertion.[30] Quantitative research has also tried to test the "worldwide" validity of the discrimination argument. Neither Collier and Hoeffler nor Fearon and Laitin found a significant correlation between inequality within countries (measured by the Gini coefficient) and the risk of war. However, neither study was equipped to measure income inequality *between* ethnic groups because the inequality within the population of a given country is what was measured. These measurements are therefore blind to possible inequalities between different ethnic groups.[31] Consequently, the argument that inequalities between groups may breed violence cannot be discarded, although this does not imply that ethnicity itself is a cause of conflict. Instead, it implies that commonly held grievances within an ethnic group can motivate conflict. It also implies that ethnicity can facilitate mobilization and recruitment in the course of conflicts, and that an ethnic conflict is likely to breed more mutual negative stereotypes, which makes a resolution more difficult to reach.

In the Caucasus, four cases of war occurred in an ethnodemographic situation that would qualify as ethnic dominance. In Chechnya (73 percent), Karabakh (76 percent), South Ossetia (66 percent), and Abkhazia

(46 percent), the largest ethnic group clearly outnumbered other groups. In all cases, it was the titular group (Chechens in Chechnya, Karabakh Armenians in Karabakh, Ossets in South Ossetia, and Abkhaz in Abkhazia) that wanted to secede, thus initiating a downward spiral that led to violence. Interestingly, however, in was not necessarily the titular group that was the numerically dominant group. In Abkhazia, the titular group formed a clear minority with only 17 percent of the overall population. Any explanation of conflict processes in the Caucasus that draws on "ethnic dominance," therefore, has to explain how, in at least one case, the initiative for secession came from a minority group. Ethnic dominance as an explanation is also weakened by the converse cases. Ingushetia (70 percent), Kabardino Balkaria (48 percent), North Ossetia (53 percent), and Ajaria (63 percent) would also qualify as areas of the Caucasus with ethnic dominance, but all have avoided violent conflict. Hence, while ethnic dominance may increase the risk of conflict, it does not always lead to conflict. Therefore the mechanisms that helped defuse tensions related to ethnic dominance are of key interest.

Since ethnic dominance points to an ethnodemographic situation which, in turn, is formed by existing borders and by the ascription of membership to a specific ethnic group, any explanation that is based on ethnic dominance must refer to how "ethnicity" was institutionalized in the Soviet Union. Soviet ethnofederalism provided certain ethnically defined groups with particular territories and vested these territories (the union republics, the autonomous republics, and the autonomous oblasts) with political institutions. These political institutions proved to be a powerful organizational resource that made mobilization easier along *predetermined ethnic lines*. The political institutions of the Soviet Union thus created a path dependency for splits along ethnic lines, which may or may not have occurred without this institutional framework. This then points to the fact that ethnicity per se is never an explanation for conflict; rather, the way ethnicity is institutionalized and how this institutionalization becomes contested in periods of rapid social change explains conflict. Seen in this way, it becomes clear that ethnicity is not an a priori given but a social construct that emerges through history, and that "ethnicity" is contingent on both the discourse of a group about its own identity and on the political institutions in which certain aspects of this ethnicity are enshrined. Both are subject to change over time. By contrast, quantitative research, with its high premium on simple categories, tends to take ethnicity as a given attribute to a group and is therefore guilty of implicitly perpetuating a primordial position.

In a brilliant and polemical article against the use of oversimplified typologies, Valery Tishkov warns that "the basic methodological weakness of such theories of conflict analysis lies in their vision of groups as collective bodies with needs and universal motivation—not as situations, feelings, or acts of speech."[32] Adopting such a perspective allows us to reconcile the fact that many internal wars (all but one in the Caucasus, and almost two-thirds of all internal wars since 1945) have a clear ethnic dimension, while at the same time ethnicity per se does not seem to be a cause of conflict: most multiethnic societies are at peace, most ethnic minorities do not rebel, and ethnically diverse societies are no less stable than homogeneous societies. However, ethnic boundaries, while not a *cause* of conflict per se, become reinforced or even reinvented *during* conflict. The salience of ethnicity can therefore be the result of the "ethnicization" of conflict. Cultural difference becomes important in the course of conflicts, for it is the material from which the barriers between groups are built. Cultural difference is the quarry, the stone from which serves to build walls between groups. These stones, however, are continually being moved, and cultural difference is a product of this continual work at building barriers; it is, so to speak, a permanent building site.

Furthermore, cultural difference is relational—the perception of the one group depends on how the "other" group is perceived and is constructed accordingly, and this perception changes precisely under the impact of conflict and violence. The perception of cultural difference is more a consequence than a cause of conflict. If groups clash, they deepen existing cultural differences or even invent new ones. This engenders a narrowing of cultural possibilities. Conflict brings about the destruction of multiple possibilities of identification: the number of available fits is reduced, the flexibility of the remainder diminishes, and the perception of the other is strengthened. Once such a process starts, it matters little whether the differences perceived by the participants are deeply rooted in cultural everyday life or are superficial and newly invented. Group conflicts can equally well be organized on the narcissism of small differences as on a border between civilizations. The conflicts in the Caucasus provide evidence for how ethnicity was reconfigured and perceptions and relations between groups became subject to change, once groups engaged in conflictive competition.

Finally, ethnicity, which is, after all, embodied in cultural norms of how things are done, may be a proxy for available social capital. Ethnic ties can be used to grease the social relations that are essential for collective action and, consequently, for organized violence. Ethnic social capital, while by no means being the only or the most important social capital, makes recruitment and financing easier and helps in finding sponsors abroad. After all, diaspora support, which has been identified as a major source of funding for organized violence, works precisely through ethnically defined social capital.

Terrain

The statistical data indicate that mountainous terrain increases the risk of conflict and wars tend to be longer when they are fought in mountainous countries. This finding obviously resonates well with the suggestive image of the noble but fierce mountain peoples, a cliché that, sadly, still inspires writers to write books like *Caucasus: Mountain Men and Holy Wars*.[33] The interpretation of this finding is less romantic, however. It is assumed that mountainous terrain affords the rebels a military advantage by providing shelter and hideouts and that mountains increase the government's costs of controlling the territory. Both may increase the opportunity for organizing violence. The connection between terrain and the risk for internal violence has not attracted much attention, perhaps because it is hard to imagine a viable policy prescription against the negative effects of mountains, at least outside the Soviet Union under Stalin. In 1944 Stalin deported many of the indigenous mountain peoples, and the Soviet Union invested considerable resources in resettling mountain dwellers in the plains.

In the Caucasus, "mountainous terrain" as a factor offers a treacherous parsimony. The fact that all violent conflicts in the Caucasus took place in mountainous regions seems to confirm that a high risk of conflict is associated with terrain that favors rebellion. However, there are good reasons for not putting too much trust in the simplicity of this argument. First, there is little to be gained from this observation since the Caucasus is a very mountainous region, but, as stated earlier, not all potential hotbeds have escalated to violent conflicts. So, while the mountainous terrain cannot be excluded as a factor in increasing the propensity for conflict in some cases, it is not a universal explanation. Second, a closer look at the actual fighting indicates that the strong correlation between physical geography indicators and conflict must be interpreted with caution. The character of the terrain obviously did not matter much at the start of the struggle for power, as the conflicts were centered around the capitals and not in the mountains.

In the case of the Georgian wars, terrain only became important when the western province of Mingrelia became the key theater of violence. Terrain was also not particularly relevant in the South Ossetian war, which was fought primarily around the capital, Tskhinvali. In fact, high mountains were more of a problem for the rebels since the vital connection with North Ossetia was blocked during winter. Even the war in Abkhazia was not influenced that much by the mountains and forests since it was fought primarily in the narrow corridor along the coast, with very little guerrilla activity. Likewise, in Karabakh, terrain initially favored not the rebels but the Azerbaijanis who had occupied strategic positions in the mountains overlooking Karabakh's capital of Stepanakert. The war in Chechnya followed a similar pattern. Initially, the conflict centered on the capital Grozny and a few other urban centers in the plains of Northern Chechnya. The mountains in the South of Chechnya served as a safe haven for regrouping and logistical support. Terrain grew more important when the Russian army started to control the plains and the rebels were pushed to their strongholds in the mountains. Hence, while it is plausible that terrain has affected the duration and, above all, the tactics of the rebels, there are no simple linkages between terrain and the onset of war.

From Risk to War: Organization of Violence

Having risk factors does not automatically lead to organized violence. This is because organizers of violence, notwithstanding their motivations and objectives, face massive difficulties. First, they must recruit members to join an organization, the activities of which impose great risks and considerable personal costs on members. Second, they must sustain this organization by providing internal cohesion, organizational structure, and discipline. Third, they must finance the expensive logistics of organized violence: vehicles and fuel for transportation must be provided; weapons, ammunition, food, and medical supplies must be purchased; rewards for the fighters and especially for the leaders must be distributed; and perhaps some material support for the families of killed and injured fighters may be granted.

In facing recruitment, leaders of organized violence have to overcome what Mancur Olson has famously called the "free rider problem."[34] Since many of the collective benefits of a "rebellion" victory will be realized independent of individual participation within the rebel movements, and because the high costs and risks involved in participation provide very good reason not to join the movement, organizers of violence usually find it difficult to recruit individuals to their organizations.

In theory, there are a few ways to overcome this collective action problem. Motivation for the "right cause" alone, while it certainly plays an important role, is usually not enough to recruit members to rebel movements, and it is certainly never enough to sustain the movement.[35] To overcome collective action problems, organizers of violence have to make use of the material and social endowments that they have at their disposal.[36] In other words, they have to materially reward participants (or at least promise future rewards), and they have to mobilize participants by making use of the bonds of shared norms.

Material endowment can come from different sources. Organizers of violence may generate profits from the extraction of natural resources such as oil or diamonds;[37] from donations from the diaspora;[38] from taxing the population; from control over segments of the legal, illicit, or illegal economy; or from sponsors abroad. The amount and the type of material endowment to which organizers of violence have access depend partly on the natural resources of the country and partly on its economic structure and on its neighbors. None of this can be easily changed.

Social endowment refers to the social ties of trust, to general or specific reciprocity, and to the mechanisms of social control that exist within certain segments of society and that make the coordination of collective action easier. A famous concept that subsumes these social qualities is "social capital," which, since Robert Putnam's study, is most often positively associated with being a precondition for democracy.[39] However, social capital can go both ways, and networks, reciprocity, shared norms, and trust are also valuable ingredients for the organization of violence.[40] Under certain circumstances, social capital can be activated and used for organizing social action.[41] To be sure, there is nothing inherent in the concept of social capital that predetermines that this collective action should be directed toward community development rather than organizing raids on the neighboring village.[42] Social capital is therefore a concept that captures social ties within a society suited for overcoming collective action problems, but it does not state how and to what ends these ties are used.

Thus, the feasibility of organizing violence depends on both a specific mix of material rewards and the invocation of social capital, and both are highly contingent on the given social, political, and natural conditions. In theory, material and social endowments could be used in a compensatory manner—that is, a lack of material resources could be compensated for by tapping deeper into existing social capital, and large assets in social capital could compensate for lacking material resources. While it is possible for organizers of violence to acquire new sources of material resources, however, existing social capital is limited, and it is very difficult to build new social capital in a short period of time. Therefore, in practice, social and material endowments are not quite compensatory; whereas organizers of violence may succeed in opening up new sources of revenues, they must rely on what social capital is already there. The significant factor is thus how successful organizers of violence are in making use of existing social capital, and under what circumstances society is willing to put its social capital at the service of the organizers of violence.

Social capital may reside in ethnic, religious, or communal ties, or it may have been accumulated through repeated interaction in socioprofessional or cultural networks. Once more, counter to conventional wisdom, ethnicity does not necessarily imply a "higher" or "specific" amount of social capital available within a group. As shown in the following chapters, the social capital on which the various organizers of violence in the Caucasus relied varied from case to case, but all of the social ties that were used were of a much more specific fabric than just "ethnicity." This again highlights the fact that ethnic groups are not collective actors. What brings agency to ethnic groups are small but dense networks that stem from communal ties, kinship, and socioprofessional interaction.

Recruitment is only the beginning of organized violence. Organizers of violence also have to think about the sustainability of their organization. Sustained organized violence requires internal cohesion, the ability to recruit new members, and the capacity to finance the logistics of organized violence. The difficulties involved are similar to, but nevertheless distinct from, those associated with the recruitment stage. Any rebel movement that wants to sustain its existence needs at least some success on the battlefield, otherwise it will soon lose its credibility. To a large degree, military success depends on internal cohesion and discipline. Thus, organizers of violence need to move beyond recruitment and need to build up internal sanction capacities. If they do not succeed, the movement will not be able to operate successfully on the battlefield, and it will probably fragment into smaller, barely coordinated units without a unified command structure. Such a dispersed structure may be quite adequate and successful for waging guerrilla warfare, especially when mainly terrorist tactics are applied, but it is not adequate for winning on the battlefield against an army. As the experiences in Georgia and especially Chechnya dramatically proved, highly fragmented "rebel" organizations also hinder the emergence of efficient state institutions, which, in turn, lead to new waves of organized violence.

Sustaining violence depends on a constant supply of revenue. Many theories of rebellions assume that the success of rebel movements depends on the distribution of rewards only after victory—for example, after the state has been captured or the province has become de facto independent. Such models look at the rewards for the fighters (which, if the fighters are highly motivated and confident, could indeed be postponed until after victory), but they overlook the fact that organized violence requires a constant investment in the logistics of war. Consequently, there is a need to generate profits not only *after* the war but *during* the course of violence. This necessity affects the dynamics of violence. Most notably, it facilitates the emergence of a situation that can be called a "market of violence."[43] Because sustaining violence is expensive, organizers of violence engage in economic activities that characteristically combine legal business, organized crime, and warfare. Organizers of violence then transform into entrepreneurs of violence.[44]

Entrepreneurs of violence create an economy that tends to be integrated into transnational networks of trade and investment, and they engage in the trafficking of drugs and weapons, in kidnapping and extortion, and in taxing the shadow economy. Profits are reinvested or kept in offshore banks. Gradually, short-term economic interests replace long-term political ones, and entrepreneurs of violence may become interested in avoiding significant battles and sustaining profit instead. Such a situation can be understood as a market of violence: as an economic area dominated by civil wars, warlords, or robbery, in which a self-perpetuating system emerges linking nonviolent commodity markets with the violent acquisition of goods.[45]

Once a market of violence is established, there is a strong rationale for the warlords to stabilize the status quo. If government officials receive a share of the revenues from the market of violence, or are themselves acting as warlords, they have an interest in prolonging the violence at low levels. In such cases, sustaining low-level violence with reduced risks becomes a rational objective of both the "rebels" and the "state." This understanding contradicts the view of prolonged war as a communication problem or as the result of anarchy. This market is characterized by the lack of large battles because neither side is ready to commit substantial resources to winning the war. All violent conflicts in the Caucasus developed for a certain period into markets of violence in which combat operations were combined with profitable economic activities. In Georgia, markets of violence did not last long in comparison with such classic cases as Afghanistan, Lebanon, Sierra Leone, and the Democratic Republic of Congo. Chechnya, in contrast, has been completely torn apart by rival entrepreneurs of violence. The establishment of statehood in Chechnya went awry because the successful field commanders were more interested in perpetuation of the market of violence than in restoration of the state. In the permanent struggle for power between the "rump state" and the violent entrepreneurs, the remaining state institutions were dismantled, institutions capable of containing conflicts were devalued, and the rump state was deprived of the resources required to crack down on the private organization of violence. As a consequence, Chechnya sank into anomie and internal conflict, which, among other factors, provoked the second Russian invasion in 1999.

The shift from a mainly politically motivated war to a partly or overwhelmingly economically motivated war has important consequences. Entrepreneurs of violence have a vested interest in prolonging the functioning of their "markets." They may thus obstruct or undermine any political settlements, even if the terms seem to take into account the stated objectives of the movement. In other words, political solutions, which may work for the settlement of politically motivated conflicts, do not work once the conflict has developed into a market of violence.

Unsurprisingly, this shift from a politically motivated war to an economically motivated market of violence is not reflected in the official statements and discourses of the organizers of violence. Circumspection is therefore required regarding the motives they profess. The definitiveness of these discourses, mostly based on wrongs suffered and the quest for justice, as well as exaggerated friend-foe distinctions, may be deceptive. The differentiation between the normative framing of the conflict and the rules guiding the incentives of relevant actors is essential. This is not to say that the normative framing of a conflict by the parties and other interested observers is just a fancy story of good and evil told by profit-maximizing warmongers. Making sense of violence (perpetrated or endured) is a crucial function of normative frameworking and has strong implications for the chances of post-violence rapprochement and healing. Of even more immediate practical influence for the organization and channeling of violence is the mobilizing power of the normative story. In terms of mobilizing young people to fight, kill, and die it may come second only to the organization of fear.

Finally, the organization of violence depends on leadership. Notwithstanding the suggestive power of rational choice theories, which are inclined to explain the organization of violence as a process that is very much guided by the invisible hand of universal cost-benefit calculations, leadership is crucial. However, telling the stories of the leaders of organized violence in the Caucasus enters normatively slippery terrain. What they all have in common is a skill for organization, a certain amount of social and material capital that they were willing to invest in organized violence, and a charismatic enough personality that appealed to followers. But whereas some became presidents (such as Robert Kocharian in Armenia), others ended up as the most wanted terrorists in Russia (such as the Chechen warlord Shamil Basayev) or were killed in Russian covert actions (such as the first president of Chechnya, Dzokhar Dudayev). Musa Shanibov, a military leader in the war in Abkhazia, retired to his previous life as a university professor in his hometown of Naltchik in Kabardino-Balkaria.

Arguably, the fact that some organizers of violence became politicians, whereas others were killed and still others became terrorists depends not only on the personality, the political convictions, and the actions of these leaders but also on their success on the battlefield; on the political economy of international relations, on which the fate of the struggles for independence depends; and on dominant public opinion (which, for that matter, most often follows the political economy of international relations, albeit often with a certain time lag).

Assigning normative labels to the leaders of organized violence is not the primary objective of this book. Of more relevance is following their various career paths and highlighting similarities and differences in the way they put their organizational skills and their social and material endowments in the service of organizing violence. Organizers of violence acquired specific know-how in very different environments. Organizational skills, for example, were acquired in the Soviet army, in the police force, or in the criminal underworld. Social capital stemmed from their well-known and respected families or from their prestige as nationally famous athletes, especially wrestlers. Some had none of this but nevertheless became effective commanders, such as Samvel Babayan, a car washer who became Karabakh's most efficient and ruthless military leader and later defense minister of the unrecognized enclave. It is telling that the sources of their material resources were less diverse than the sources of their social capital. All of the successful organizers of violence were either already quite active in the shadow economy of the late Soviet Union or they quickly learned how to tap into it. Finally and perhaps most important, at a certain stage in their career, all organizers of violence were invited by politicians to participate in the state. These attempts to co-opt commanders into state structures backfired in many cases and ended with the collapse of any remaining state structures.

Tracking the specific trajectories of organizers of violence—from their origins in Soviet-style networks of social interaction; through their time as independent field commanders and violent entrepreneurs; to defense ministers, presidents, or terrorists—helps to unpick the stories of war and peace in the Caucasus.

Expanding the Theory: Institutions and Conflict Analysis

The conjunction of a specific ethnic demography institutionalized by the Soviet Union and the weakness of the central state account for an atypically high risk of conflict in the Caucasus. These risks were then amplified by what could be called pathological social constellations such as atypically high opportunities for either capturing or secession from the state, a massive commitment problem on the side of the new states, and a climate that was highly favorable to ethnic entrepreneurship. This added up to a breeding ground for the organization of violence, and, in four polities, groups capable of waging war emerged. However, some polities could opt out of organizing violence, whereas others, despite sharing most characteristics with those that spiraled into war, could not. For example, South Ossetia, Abkhazia, Karabakh, and Chechyna waged war, whereas Ajaria, Dagestan, Ingushetia, Kabardino-Balkaria, and Karachai-Cherkessia avoided violence. Of particular interest here are the circumstances and conjunctures that helped some polities to successfully overcome the fatal problems associated with state weakness, while other polities proved unable to rebuild a functioning statehood from the rubble of collapsed Soviet institutions.

Similarly, ethnic entrepreneurship in the Caucasus was potent enough to capture the state, but in Chechnya, Georgia, and Azerbaijan, it was not potent enough to sustain it. Some leaders who came to power on the tide of nationalism have been unable to retain power. Abulfaz Elchibey in Azerbaijan, Zviad Gamsakhurdia in Georgia, and Dzokhar Dudayev in Chechnya all lost presidency and power, and then the state, relatively rapidly. All three left behind failed states wracked with escalated ethnic conflicts, and the reconstruction of these states has still not been fully achieved. There were some factors that enabled the careers of ethnic entrepreneurs to develop but hindered successful state building precisely in those polities in which ethnic entrepreneurs were initially most successful.

In addition, the general propositions of conflict research fail to illuminate how the various armed movements in the Caucasus solved the problems associated with recruiting and financing once tensions had been transformed into organized violence. Consequently, the following areas also need to be explored: how followers were recruited, and how recruits were turned into fighters; how fighters were armed and paid, and from where the weapons and finances came; what the specific mix of material resources and social capital that organizers of violence successfully exploited was, in order to build up a military organization; and, generally, how the logistics of war were addressed, and what specific factors proved beneficial to or hindered this endeavor.

The analysis of these issues is by necessity context-specific since the trajectories, if not the structural preconditions, of an individual conflict unavoidably depend on social, cultural, and political factors and constellations that are in all likelihood highly idiosyncratic. The theoretical lenses of this study therefore need to be expanded in a way that allows the idiosyncrasies of a specific conflict process (its trajectory) to be captured, while at the same time not losing sight of the structural factors that accounted for the risk propensity of a given society and the pathological social constellations that made the organization of violence more likely. Hence, the story of "actors who seek to fulfil their dreams, make alliances, learn from one another and make mistakes"[46] needs to be included, and, since social action is always to a large extent path dependent, those factors that structure the actions and interactions of relevant actors need to be described carefully. In short, the integration of an action-theoretic paradigm into a structuralist paradigm is needed. Bridging the actor-structure divide requires a focus on the interactive strategies of actors operating within institutional settings that, at the same time, enable and constrain these strategies. Such an approach has become known as actor-centered institutionalism[47] and is closely associated with the new institutionalism in social science.[48]

In analyzing the trajectories of conflict processes, institutions—which are, in the broadest sense, simply "the rules of the game"—become the most relevant unit of analysis. They are crucial for an understanding of actors and their strategic interactions because actors depend on socially constructed rules to direct their action. Institutions constitute actors, actor constellations, and the mode of interaction within this constellation. Moreover, they define who is able to participate in a particular political arena, they determine what actors think is both possible and desirable, and they shape the strategies that actors choose in pursuing their preferences. Institutions are rule-bound and repetitive patterns of human interaction. They are "the humanely devised constraints that shape human interaction. In consequence they structure incentives in human exchange, whether political, social, or economic."[49]

Focusing on the institutional framework of a society therefore allows an understanding of how the expectations, fears, and preferences of actors are shaped, and how these preferences then translate into the strategies that actors pursue—the strategic choices that trigger counter-strategies by other actors and culminate in an interaction which then may or may not lead to violence. Besides incorporating an actor-centered perspective into the analysis, an institutional approach also brings the great benefit that it is not blind to locality or to history. The institutional framework of a given polity will inevitably have a distinct local flavor, as institutions emerge and get rooted during a long historical process, shaped by cultural, geographical, and political idiosyncrasies. This is even true for the Soviet Union, the seemingly isomorphist institutions of which were locally grounded and blended with local informal rules of the game.[50] Focusing on the specific institutional framework of a society thus grasps the specific local conditions that have shaped preferences and strategies, and it is precisely this highly differentiated local institutional framework that accounts for variance in the trajectories of conflicts. In that sense, the institutional framework of a specific polity can be understood as the crucial intervening variable that explains variance in outcomes across cases that seem to have many, if not most, structural similarities.

Neo-institutionalist approaches, in a multitude of nuances, figure prominently across all disciplines of the social sciences and cover a fascinatingly wide array of issues. For example, scholars have used institutionalism to explain economic performance, variance in welfare policies across European states, large-scale historical change, the behavior of bureaucracies, and the success of rural development projects. Political scientists in comparative politics analyze political institutions to explain domestic politics, and researchers in international relations investigate the effects of institutions (regimes) on international cooperation. However, institutionalist approaches do not figure prominently in the field of conflict research.[51] There appears to be no work in the field explicitly centering on an institutionalist approach, despite the enormous heuristic and explanatory power that institutionalist approaches offer to the study of conflict processes.[52]

Similar to what has been said earlier on social capital, there is a certain ambivalent quality to institutions: institutions do not only defuse conflict, they can also breed conflict. Indeed, both outcomes—organized violence and the avoidance of it—are equally the result of a society's institutional framework.

Institutions can defuse conflict, thus providing societal stability, via two main mechanisms: institutions can provide procedures to accommodate the diverging interests of competing social groups, thus reducing the motivation to organize violence, and they can provide coercive capacities (monitoring and sanctioning capacities), thus reducing the likelihood that actors actually pursue rule-breaking strategies. Hence, the feasibility of organizing violence is reduced. Both the accommodating function and the coercive function of institutions helps to "embed" conflict. Conflicts are then dealt with (processed) according to known rules and procedures, and any defiant behavior from actors is negatively sanctioned. This reduces the likelihood of conflict spinning out of control and turning into organized violence. However, this embedding of conflict processing should not be confused with a conflict-free society. Conflicts may still exist, but they are routinely dealt with in a procedural way, and actors usually adhere, either because the threat of negative sanctions for defiance are credible or because the benefits of nonviolent conflict processing exceed the potential benefits of unilateral, non-rule-abiding behavior, or both.

The accommodating capacity of institutions makes it unlikely that actors actually want to organize violence, and the coercive capacities of institutions make it difficult (expensive) for actors to do so. The accommodating capacities are often attributed to democratic institutions. Democratic procedures ensure that different groups in a society have a voice in shaping the politics of the polity they share. Political institutions designed to protect minority groups help to accommodate tensions between different groups, and complex power-sharing arrangements can balance the various interests of different groups.[53] None of the accommodating functions—representation, minority rights, and power sharing—need to be provided by formal political institutions, enshrined in the constitution or the legislation of a country. These functions can equally well be provided through informal, unwritten institutions. Informal mediation, informal mechanisms of power sharing, or even informal, yet routinely practiced buying off or cooptation of political contenders by the dominant elite may all add to the stability of a society. For example, within the Soviet Union, informal power sharing between ethnic groups within an autonomous region or territory was routinely practiced. An informal system of quotas that assigned a more than proportional share of key posts within the republic to members of the titular nation was in place in all ethically mixed regions where the titular nation was a minority.[54] In multiethnic regions, such as Kabardino-Balkaria and Dagestan, the ethnic composition of the elite was carefully balanced in order to avoid one group achieving a dominant position.[55]

The coercive capacities of institutions—that is, the ability to monitor and sanction norm-defying behavior—is usually attributed to the power of state institutions: specifically, to the state's administrative capacities and its legitimate monopoly of violence. It is thus the law-enforcement bodies of a state that actually ensure that the rules of the game are adhered to. By this logic, a sudden weakening of administrative capacities is seen as dramatically increasing the risk of organized violence. As with the accommodating functions of institutions, the coercive function need not be exercised by formal institutions. Arguably, many regimes derive their stability not from strong state institutions but, rather, from informal yet highly institutionalized patron-client relations.[56] Such informal patron-client networks may substitute for state institutions, but, more often, they merge with state bureaucracies to form hybrid arrangements, which are nevertheless stable and quite effective in providing regime stability, as the longevity and persistence of many patrimonial regimes aptly demonstrates.

Institutions do not always defuse conflict; indeed, under certain circumstances, they may breed conflict. By a twist of fate, they may turn into a subversive power that actually undermines the stability they have helped to preserve in the past. Institutions do not change easily. Even though the rules of the game are usually stable, and actors rely on these rules in their expectations and strategies, this does not mean that all or even most actors are content with this institutional equilibrium. Certainly, at least a significant coalition is, but for those who are not content with the current situation, the risks and costs associated with changing the rules may simply be too high. They may fear the uncertainty that will come once the actual set of rules becomes defunct, or they may be locked in a power asymmetry, which makes them unlikely to succeed in changing the rules against the will of the dominant elites. Nevertheless, institutional change happens; indeed, it is one of the constants of society.

Institutional change may happen incrementally, as a result of shifting coalitions and the changing bargaining power of actors, or it may be triggered by external shocks to the institutional framework.[57] Rapid and exogenously induced institutional change is by default conflict prone. A weakened institutional framework may prompt the disembedding of conflict—conflicts are no longer "processed" according to shared norms or procedures, because one or both parties to the conflict seek to achieve their objectives by force. A weakened institutional framework also leads to increased competition, because actors see an opportunity to redesign the institutions in their favor. In such a situation, the competition between actors turns into a "winner-takes-all" game, and the increased stakes lead to increased risk taking, which, in turn, increases the risk of violent escalation. Moreover, a change of the institutional framework will also lead to a change of the distributional consequences of institutions: As a result of changes in the institutional framework, some social actors will get more, while others will lose out, and this will affect the power balance. Since actors base the decision of whether to pursue a risk-avoiding or risk-seeking strategy on their perceptions of their relative strength vis-à-vis other actors, a sudden change in the distributional function of institutions may dramatically increase the propensity for actors to engage in high-risk strategies, thus increasing the propensity of conflict and violence.

An institutional approach is a heuristic device that allows the identification of relevant critical junctures in the trajectories of conflicts, and as such it requires an inductive research strategy. The reason for this inductive strategy is straightforward and dictated not by methodological reasoning but by the sheer complexity of social life. The universe of specific arrangements of institutions is infinite, and societies across space and time have produced highly diverse institutional arrangements. But whereas the universe of institutional solutions may by infinite, the functions that an institutional framework fulfills or fails to fulfill *with regard to conflict processing* (respectively, conflict escalating) are not; the institutional framework in general shapes incentives and constraints of social actors. More specifically, the distributional function of institutions determines who gets what; hence, the relative power of actors within a society is a function of the distributive consequences of the institutional framework. Whether an actor will pursue a defensive, risk-avoiding or aggressive, risk-seeking strategy therefore depends on its relative power vis-à-vis other actors and thus, ultimately, on the institutional framework.

Summing up, the *distributional consequences* of institutions and *their capacity to embed conflict by accommodation or coercion* are highly important for the analysis of conflict trajectories. It is the specific institutional framework of a society that accounts for, among other things, how ethnicity is institutionalized, what social capital is available to groups, how leaders mobilize and control followers or fail to do so, and how states become consolidated. Hence, it is by focusing on the specific institutional framework of a society (and its changes) that the global propositions of conflict theory and the microlevel foundations of organized violence can be woven together into a coherent narrative.

4

Wars over Chechnya

Background

In 1991, Chechnya unilaterally declared its independence from Russia. Since then, Russia has waged two wars, 1994–1996 and 1999 to the present day, in an attempt to secure control over the secessionist republic. The wars in Chechnya have been by far the bloodiest of all the conflicts in the post-Soviet Caucasus. Indeed, when compared with all civil wars that took place after World War II, only four wars claimed more lives relative to the prewar population. These were the wars in Afghanistan, Laos, Vietnam, and Liberia. The Russian military campaign has killed approximately 50,000 civilians (60 out of a prewar population of 1,000) in what it has framed as an attempt "to restore the constitutional order." In the West, the public perception associates the ongoing conflict in Chechnya today mainly with protracted guerrilla warfare and sporadic terrorist attacks on Russian targets, with links to Islamic fundamentalism. Such a perception is deeply flawed, however, and is based only on a small and by no means representative segment of the gruesome realties of the conflict, which, in 1991, began as a political struggle for an independent, secular Chechen nation-state. Back then, the Chechen national aspirations were very much the same as those of Latvians, Estonians, Lithuanians, Armenians, and Georgians.

Chechnya is situated in the northeast region of the Caucasus. To the east, north, and west, the republic borders with the Russian regions of Dagestan, Stavropol' krai, Ingushetia, and North Ossetia; to the south, it borders with Georgia. Its territory encompasses 15,678 km. About one-third of the territory is in the plains north of the Terek River, which crosses Chechnya west to east. The southern part of Chechnya, covering another one-third of the total territory, is mountainous—the highest mountains are over 4,000 m high—and poorly accessible. The capital, Grozny, was founded in 1812 as a military outpost of Russian colonial-

ism in the North Caucasus and aptly named "the threatening." It and the other larger settlements—Gudermes, Shali, and Urus-Martan—all lie in the middle part of Chechnya, between the mountains in the south and the Terek Plains in the north. Most of the intensive fighting took place here; rebels used the mountains in the south as their safe retreat and as a lifeline for military supplies. A large part of the military supplies were brought over mountain paths from Georgia, Dagestan, and Ingushetia.

The available demographic data for prewar Chechnya are not very precise. The reason for this is that, until 1991, Chechnya, together with the much smaller Ingushetia, constituted the Chechen-Ingushetian ASSR. All data from the Soviet Census of 1989 thus relate to the Chechen-Ingushetian ASSR (these data are provided in table 2.1). Extrapolating from the data in the Soviet Census, it can be estimated that, in 1991, the population of Chechnya proper was around 836,000, of which about 700,000 were ethnic Chechens and the rest were predominantly ethnic Russians living in Grozny. Since 1991, almost all the Russians have left Chechnya.

Chechnya was always one of the poorest regions of the Soviet Union and was massively supported by the center in Moscow through subsidiary funding, or transfer payments. In 1991, unemployment reached 30 percent.[1] Since the 1970s, up to 25,000 people temporarily left the republic each year to work as seasonal laborers.[2] Agricultural land is scarce. Chechnya has little industry apart from the oil industry, which developed in Grozny due to the considerable oil reserves of the republic. Most positions in the oil industry, especially qualified and managerial posts, were filled by Russians. Before World War II, the Chechen oil fields were the most productive in the Soviet Union after those in Azerbaijan. By the beginning of the 1980s, however, the reserves had clearly shrunk. In the 1980s, 7.5 million tons of oil were extracted per year, making up 1.5 percent of the annual oil production of the Soviet Union. By 1993, annual production had fallen to 2.6 million tons, and the reserves shrank to a modest 30 million tons. The large oil refinery in Grozny, at which both locally extracted oil and oil from Azerbaijan and Siberia were processed, produced around 17 million tons of oil products in 1991. Two years later, the amount had fallen to 1.2 million tons.[3] Hence, neither Chechen oil reserves nor oil processing had a strategic significance for Russia in the 1990s. After 1991, however, the huge profits from refining locally extracted oil, and the illegal export of oil from Siberia and Azerbaijan via Grozny, did play an important role in the internal struggle for power in Chechnya. After 1990, Chechen dependence on oil revenue grew rapidly. Already by 1991, one-third of the Chechen budget was covered by revenue from oil production and export.[4]

Chechnya became part of the Romanov Empire only after putting up an epic resistance against Russian colonizers that lasted for almost half a century. In the Chechen nationalist narrative, the Russian conquest of the North Caucasus and the colonial wars against the Chechen tribes are the first of many instances of a genocidal policy of the Russian state against the Chechen nation.[5] The gruesome policies that Russian colonialists applied in their attempt to overcome Chechen resistance—punitive raids, scorched earth policies, forced migration and exile, and the massacres of entire villages—are seen as being repeated by the Russian military today. After the collapse of the Tsarist Empire, Chechnya became part of the short-lived North Caucasian Republic, only to be reincorporated into the new Bolshevik state in 1922. As happened in other parts of the Soviet Union, the Soviet conquest brought mass terror, mass arrests, and deportation to the Gulag (forced labor camps), religious persecution, and the Sovietization of most aspects of cultural life, including the shift from Arabic to Cyrillic letters. In 1934, the territory of Chechnya was combined with the neighboring Ingushetian AO to form the Chechen-Ingushsetian ASSR within the Russian Soviet Federated Socialist Republic (RSFSR). But only ten years later, on February 23, 1944, Chechens and Ingush from all over the USSR were rounded up and deported to Central Asia. The newly formed ASSR was dissolved, and for the next ten years, even the names "Chechnya" and "Chechens" disappeared from public view. In total, 387,229 Chechens and 91,250 Ingush were deported.[6]

Mass treason and collaboration with the German Wehrmacht were given as the official reasons for the deportation of an entire people. Although the German Wehrmacht barely reached the North Caucasus, its approach in 1942 stirred renewed resistance among Chechens against the Soviet power. According to the NKVD, the People's Commissariat of Internal Affairs (the predecessor of the KGB, the Committee for State Security), up to 6,000 fighters were active in Chechnya, waiting for an occasion to join forces with the German army against Soviet power. In contrast, during World War II, some 29,000 Chechens, among them many volunteers, had fought with the Soviet army against Nazi Germany, but this did not spare them from mass deportation to the steppes of Kazakhstan. It has been estimated that around 18 percent of the deported died due to forced labor and harsh natural conditions.[7]

The Chechen deportation lasted until 1956, when the Communist Party under Nikita Krushchev's leadership condemned the deportations, restored the Chechen-Ingushetian ASSR, and allowed the Chechens and the Ingush to return. Around 200,000 survivors returned. Many found their homes occupied by new settlers. The continuing mistrust of the Russian state toward the Chechens found its manifestation, among other things, in the fact that, contrary to common practice, the first secretary of the republic's Communist Party was always a Russian. All leading Chechen politicians of the 1980s and 1990s were born in exile in Kazakhstan.

Despite the particularly ferocious attempts at Sovietization, Chechen society, perhaps more than other Caucasian societies, has proved itself to be particularly resistant. In key areas, such as law and justice, loyalty and solidarity, and religion and identity, traditional forms of local organization were preserved. Older Chechens relate that, after the Stalin era, no Chechen was ever brought before a Soviet court of law charged with a serious crime. Instead, law was administered according to the traditional legal canon, the *adat,* and enforced by the clans.[8] Such tales may be exaggerated, but they highlight the extent to which traditional ideas about law, as well as traditional procedures for its enforcement, were preserved during Soviet times. Islam, the source of much of customary law called *adat,* also resisted Soviet atheist campaigns. Adherence to Islam remained an important part of Chechen cultural identity, even if the open practicing of religion was not possible in the Soviet Union.

The considerable resistance of Chechen society toward Soviet institutions and Soviet culture brought about the parallel existence of two normative systems. This strange juxtaposition of contrasting, often mutually exclusive, norms and procedures, present in all Soviet societies, was particularly prominent in Chechnya.[9] The fact that, to a large extent, the Chechens were sidelined in terms of opportunities in the Soviet Union, made the system even more entrenched. In the Soviet Union, it was difficult to have a career as a Chechen. Even within their "own" republic, key political and economic positions were by and large beyond the reach of Chechens. This was in contrast to other ethnic republics, in which representatives of the titular nation had good career chances up to a certain point. For this reason, the emergence of a Chechen-Soviet elite took place very slowly. Thus, after 1991, a class of decision-makers, who were able to stabilize the political situation and ensure a relatively conflict-free transition in many Union republics and autonomous territories, was lacking in Chechnya.

The existence of a parallel system of norms proved to be historically powerful. It explains, alongside other factors, the speed with which Soviet institutions were dismantled after 1991. The high social self-organization of the Chechens turned out to be a double-edged sword, however: on the one hand, it doubtless contributed to the efficient organization of resistance against Russia; on the other, precisely this capacity for self-organization was to become a great obstacle to the establishment of state structures. Another important feature of Chechen society that has not only survived Soviet modernization but was presumably strengthened as a result of Soviet discrimination against Chechens was an unqualified loyalty to the extended family, thus implying high resistance to the Soviet state's demands for obedience. However, this provided a competitive advantage in many areas of Soviet life. In a system in which scarce goods could only be acquired by means of strongly institutionalized networks, family solidarity and communities of protection and revenge based on clan and family membership constitute an advantage. Not without reason were Chechens among the most successful groups in the Soviet Union in the field of organized crime.

Traditional Chechen society is clan-based, and many observers see *teip* (clan), an exogamous, patrilineal formation whose members claim descent from common male ancestors 12 generations removed, as the central organizing principle of Chechen society.[10] Soviet and Chechen ethnographers have established elaborated lists of *teip*s, counting around 135, which are subsumed to nine *tukkum*s (clan associations, without an official head). Much has been said by observers about the clannishness of Chechen society, and both the Chechens' stunning success in putting up guerrilla resistance against the Russian army and their equally grand failure in establishing viable state structures in the interwar period (1996–1999) have been attributed to a fragmented, yet highly mobilized clan society.[11] Recent empirical work, however, suggests that the importance of the clan as a social unit, capable of collective action and thus playing a political role, has been massively overstated, both by romanticizing Chechen nationalists and by orientalizing Russian and Western observers in search of a hidden transcript for chaotic North Caucasian politics.

Sociologist Georgi Derluguian sees the functions of the clan primarily as a repository of collective reputation that can be used as social capital in interaction beyond the face-to-face society of the village or neighbor, as a network of trust that can be invoked for very practical purposes such as securing a job or finding a business partner. Elena Sokirianskaya, who recently conducted fieldwork in Chechnya, reaches similar conclusions. She finds that *teip* exists as a part of national identity and has a symbolic value; however, she does not find support for the assumption that *teip,* as a collective actor, has a role in shaping political interaction.[12] These findings of Derluguian and Sokirianskaya are thus much in line with what recent empirical research has to say about "clans" in Central Asia. Whereas their symbolic value as markers of identity may be high, they are, just like "nations" and "ethnic groups," not collective actors, and their influence on creation of the post-Soviet Central Asian states has been much exaggerated.

The role of the extended family is of unquestionably crucial importance in Chechnya, however, both traditionally and as a present-day survival strategy, forced on Chechen society by more than a decade of war, lawlessness, and dramatic economic deprivation. Sokirianskaya points out that in colloquial usage, Chechens and Ingush often use the word *teip* (clan), when they actually refer to an extended family member (usually the man's parents, their siblings with spouses and children, cousins and second cousins with spouses and children).[13] With the economic crisis that plagues wartorn Chechnya, the importance of extended family networks for solidarity and mutual support grows, together with family nepotism. In addition, when the security situation is very bad, and the few available job opportunities are within criminal business or the security agencies, the recruitment tends to be more and more via relatives and family. Social and political mobility becomes group based and family oriented—a development that, arguably, tells us more about a society's crisis and survival mode than about its traditional "clannishness."[14]

The Chechen Revolution

In November 1990, an All-National Congress of the Chechen People was convened in Grozny. There, 1,000 delegates, each representing 1,000 Chechens living in the Soviet Union, met to debate the cultural and national concerns of the Chechen people, its future, and its past. This was an unprecedented event, made possible by the spirit of glasnost and perestroika that had led to national mobilization throughout most capitals and most borderlands of the Soviet empire. Among the congress' many guests of honor was one Dzokhar Dudayev, at the time commander of a division of strategic bombers stationed in Estonia. Dudayev was the first Chechen to reach the rank of a general in Soviet history. The high-ranking guest lent a shine to the proceedings—a career in the Soviet army in Chechnya. Dudayev was basically a foreigner to his own land. He was born in Kazakhstan, like almost all of his generation, and made his career in Russia. He was married to a Russian woman and spoke better Russian than Chechen. Nevertheless, and to the surprise of many, the congress voted the high-ranking foreigner in as chairman of the executive committee of the All-National Congress of the Chechen People. Whether is was because Dudayev, as an outsider, was not caught up in the rivalries between local factions or whether his high military rank inspired the delegates, the first national leader of the Chechens in post-Soviet times turned out to be a Soviet Air Force general. Dudayev wholeheartedly embraced his new political career, but it proved to be a short one, with a disastrous end for himself and with most dire consequences for his people. Dzokhar Dudayev died in April 1996, when a Russian rocket homed in on him via his satellite phone.

As was the case with all the other national movements that formed in the Soviet Union, the Chechen national congress understood itself to be the only legitimate representation of its people. The legislative body (Supreme Soviet) of the Autonomous Republic of Chechnya-Ingushetia, however, even though it had been freely elected in 1990 for the first time in Soviet history, was considered by most Chechens to still be an instrument of Soviet rule. Under Dudayev's leadership, the national congress soon began to put pressure on the Supreme Soviet, to force it to adhere to the more radical politics of the congress. The short test of strength ended with a triumph for Dudayev and the congress. On November 27, 1990, the Supreme Soviet passed a resolution declaring Chechnya-Ingushetia a "sovereign republic."[15] Chechnya-Ingushetia became thereby the 11th ASSR to have passed a declaration of sovereignty. Although the declaration avoided the word "independence," it was more radical in tone than many of the other declarations of sovereignty passed at that time by all subjects of the Russian Federation. There was no reference to the Soviet Union or to the Russian Federation. Instead, in Article 1, the Chechen-Ingushetian Republic was declared to be a "sovereign state, founded as a result of the self-determination of the Chechen and Ingush peoples." At the same time, the declaration avoided an ethnonationalist, exclusive stance: in Article 3, it was written that "the bearer of sovereignty and the source of state power in the Chechen-Ingush republic [is] its multinational population" —a clear indication that the Supreme Soviet sought to avoid possible friction between Chechens, Ingush, and Russians.

With this success, Dudayev left Chechnya and returned to his division in Tallinn, to a heated political atmosphere every bit as nationalist-separatist as in Chechnya. In the Baltic states, the independence movement was even more strongly articulated and radical than in the rest of the Soviet Union. In March 1990, Lithuania had declared its independence from the Soviet Union. In May 1990, Latvia followed suit. Possibly, the euphoria of a national breakthrough in the Baltic had an influence on the mood of the general population and precipitated further events. In any case, in June 1991, Dudayev returned to Grozny and convened the second Congress of the Chechen People. With this development, a political process was initiated, which Dudayev and the Chechen media would soon baptize the "Chechen revolution." The first step was for the congress to rename itself into the "National Congress of the Chechen People." Immediately after this, the new National Congress proclaimed the foundation of a Chechen state outside the Soviet Union and outside the Russian Federation and simultaneously declared that, pending parliamentary and presidential elections, all power would reside in the executive committee of the National Congress.

The Chechen revolution gained momentum as a result of political events in Moscow during the August Putsch of 1991. When Russian President Boris Yeltsin confronted the Soviet putschists in Moscow, Dudayev organized a counterdemonstration against the putschists in Grozny. The protest against the putsch turned quickly into a militant demonstration against the Soviet system, against Communism, and for Chechen independence. On August 21, 1991, it became clear that the coup in Moscow had failed and that the Soviet Union had de facto, if not de jure, ceased to exist. In the course of the following days, Soviet power was radically dismantled in Chechnya. Soviet government buildings were occupied by demonstrators, starting with the telegraph office, in a deliberate reference to Soviet revolutionary mythology. Reinforcements for the barricades in Grozny flowed in from all regions of Chechnya. Barricades were erected, prisons were opened, and green flags—symbols of Islam—replaced Soviet red flags.

In early September, Dudayev, with a handful of armed retainers, enforced the "self-dissolution" of the now completely powerless Supreme Soviet. Power in Chechnya had now in actual fact shifted to the executive committee of the National Congress. The Chechen revolution dismantled all Soviet political institutions more quickly and more thoroughly than did all other national independence movements of the Soviet Union, in part because the institutions of Soviet power had only superficially penetrated Chechen society. Subsequently, however, it was this institutional tabula rasa that rendered the consolidation of the new state impossible.

The comparison with the Baltic experience is telling: here the new national elite had taken control of the existing political institutions and turned them into instruments for the achievement of independence. The "revolution" ran its course essentially "legalistically," within the relevant political institutions. The Supreme Soviet established itself as a locus of legitimate power—as was the case in the other Soviet republics—which, following the first free elections, were dominated by members of the Popular Fronts. The extra-parliamentary representative institutions of the national-democratic movements, the so-called People's Congresses, continued to exist in parallel. This political configuration made it possible for national elites to play a good-cop, bad-cop game with Moscow. The Supreme Soviet took a moderate national stance, while the Popular Congress assumed a more radical position. Together, they steered a course aiming for national independence without bloodshed. In Chechnya, by contrast, the Supreme Soviet, even after the elections of 1990, did not become a locus of real power. Dudayev's National Congress, an ad hoc gathering with little procedural legitimacy, but which had a charismatic and determined leader with high popularity among Chechens, had little difficulty in outmaneuvering the Supreme Soviet.

A further difference between Chechnya and the Baltic is worth noting. There was no broad class of Soviet Chechens who benefited from the Soviet Union. This is partly connected with the fact that Chechens suffered more severe discrimination than most other Soviet nationalities. They were underrepresented both in the Soviet elite and in the administrative elite of Chechnya itself. Consequently, there was no broad local elite wanting to preserve certain elements of the old system in the post-Soviet epoch. This was another reason that Dudayev's revolution was more radical than other revolutions in the collapsing Soviet Union.

In all probability, Soviet state power disposed of the means to counteract the Chechen revolution. An army base was located outside Grozny, and the police and KGB disposed of considerable resources. It was not the means that were lacking, but the political will to use them. The central hierarchy, which could have mobilized the organs of state power, collapsed. With the defeat of the putschists in Moscow, the Soviet Union ceased to exist, and the president of the collapsing empire, Gorbachev, could not and did not want to use security forces. The new Russia under President Yeltsin initially even supported General Dudayev, who immediately sided with Yeltsin during the August coup, and was counted as being a natural ally in the struggle against the old Soviet *nomenklatura* and the putchists.

The "self-dissolution" of the All-Soviet Supreme Soviet and the dismantling of the Soviet structures on all administrative levels took place very much with Yeltsin's support. Only when Dudayev openly declared independence to be his highest goal, and set a date for presidential elections in Chechnya, did Moscow react. On November 8, 1991, President Yeltsin declared a state of emergency in Chechnya, which, however, was then lifted by the Russian Duma on November 11. On the same day, Russian airborne troops tried unsuccessfully to set foot in Grozny airport, which was blocked by Chechen fighters. The contingent returned to the barracks, and Dudayev held the election and was elected president with 90 percent of the vote. His first decree proclaimed the independence of Chechnya. His newly elected parliament granted him all powers necessary to defend the sovereignty and independence of Chechnya.

In Moscow, for the next two years, a power struggle raged between Yeltsin and the Duma, which held the political attention and the resources of the new political elite. Between December 1991 and the autumn of 1994, Moscow left Chechnya alone. This period will go down in Chechen history as a time of lost opportunities: in these three years, Dudaev did not manage to secure a basis for economic reforms or for a functioning statehood. Instead, he got caught up in a struggle for power between rival elites, which was often conducted with weapons. The first coup attempt against Dudayev took place in March 1992, under the leadership of the head of the Terek district administration, Umar Avturkhanov, who apparently was motivated by a quest for a share in oil revenue.[16] To get a grip on the increasing internal opposition and avoid a looming removal from office, in April 1994, Dudayev dissolved the parliament and installed a presidential regime. This step did not halt the increasing anarchy.

In the summer of 1994, Moscow regained interest in events in the breakaway republic and began to support the opposition against Dudayev with weapons and money. In August 1994, the new Provisional Council under the leadership of Umar Avturkhanov declared that it had taken power in Chechnya. In November 1994, several hundred armed supporters of Avturkhanov, supported by Russian soldiers, attempted to take Grozny. Dudayev's armed fighters repelled the attack and took several dozen Russians prisoner. One month later, Russia shifted from a policy of covert intervention to open military intervention.

Some specific factors help explain the Chechen revolution. First, unlike the Baltic states and Armenia, Chechnya lacked the segment of moderate, Soviet-educated nationalists who would have been able to incorporate nationalist aspiration into the political institutions of the Soviet system. As a result, the nationalists formed ad hoc political bodies with little procedural legitimacy, whereas the Supreme Soviet and a large part of the economic elites sided with Moscow and were perceived as antinational. As the rifts between the two camps grew, politics in Chechnya became more and more extra-constitutional. Second, nationalists had in General Dudayev a determined leader and an able organizer, who would use "brawn" to pursue his agenda. Third, the national leadership could make use of a powerful nationalist narrative that emphasized the eternal struggle between the Russian state and the Chechens, including the victimization of the freedom-loving Chechens. Dudayev, himself a product of the Soviet system and very much a member of the Soviet *nomenklatura,* capitalized on this discourse to mobilize support. Fourth, the demographic dominance of Chechens (73 percent) over Russians (26 percent) explains the rapid success of the Chechen national revolution: the numerically superior Chechens, united in their rejection of the Soviet system, encountered almost no resistance on the part of the unorganized Russian minority. However, the price for the swift success of the Chechen revolution was growing fragmentation within the leadership and the inability to consolidate statehood. Eventually these factors led to violent conflict with Russia.

The First War, 1994–1996

In December 1994, more than three years after the Chechen declaration of independence, the Russian army entered Chechnya with 40,000 soldiers. The question naturally arises of what prompted the Russian polity to change its policy of grudging toleration so abruptly and to send a huge, but unprepared, poorly trained, and unmotivated army to Chechnya. The answer is found primarily in Russian domestic politics, especially in the electoral campaign of a president struggling for his political survival, as well as in the debate between "Kremlin hawks" and "Kremlin liberals" competing for the favor of the president and thus for power.[17]

In the autumn of 2004, a year before the Duma elections and 20 months before the presidential elections, Yeltsin's popularity had reached an all-time low in all opinion polls. Yeltsin and his inner circle hoped to gain political dividends from a short and successful military campaign in Chechnya. The plan was to stage Yeltsin as preserver of Russian unity and guarantor of law and order, and for this to be rewarded by the electorate. Yeltsin was persuaded of the necessity of such a "small, victorious war"[18] by a coalition of hawks in his immediate proximity, who hoped thus to further minimize the influence of liberals in the presidential cabinet.[19]

Externally, the Kremlin legitimated the war with reference to the necessity of restoring constitutional order in Chechnya. In actual fact, ever since its declaration of independence in 1991, Chechnya existed in violation of the Russian Constitution, which does not permit the secession of subjects. In addition, in the three years of its de facto independence, Chechnya had turned into a market of violence in which organized crime flourished. Both issues constituted major problems for the young Russian state, but there was no hint of a threat to national security to prompt such a massive military action.[20] Although Russian officials repeatedly alleged that there was a risk that the country would break up, in December 1994, the spreading of separatism from Chechnya to other republics (the so-called Caucasian domino effect) was very unlikely. The political elites of the respective national republics in the northern Caucasus were almost solely recruited from the junior ranks of the old *nomenklatura,* who viewed their future as lying *nolens volens* within the framework of the Russian Federation. The horrendous economic price, in the form of mass unemployment and an almost compete halt in production, which the Chechens paid for their go-it-alone strategy, convinced the leaderships elsewhere in the federation of the rationality of loyalty to Moscow.

The presence of Chechen oil reserves also fails to explain the Russian invasion. Oil production in Chechnya was far too small (less than 1 percent of the entire Russian oil production in 1996) for the reserves to be viewed as strategically important. Finally, it has been argued that Chechnya, as an oil-transit country between the oil fields of the Caspian basin and the Russian export terminal of Novorossiisk, is of great significance for Russia. However, this argument does not hold, either, as Chechnya is easy to replace as a transit country. A pipeline circumventing the republic was already being planned by 1996 and was operational soon thereafter.[21]

The war proved to be anything but small and victorious. It soon became clear that this was to be a protracted, bloody, and unpopular war in which small, mobile, and highly motivated Chechen units inflicted humiliating losses on the rapidly demoralized troops and exposed time and again the weakness of the Russian army in the eyes of the public.

Shortly before the war, the Russian minister of defense, Pavel Grachev, boasted that only one regiment of paratroopers and two hours were needed to take the capital of Grozny. As it turned out, nearly three weeks of intense urban combat was required before the Russian army finally captured what was left of the center of Grozny. As many as 25,000 civilians died in a weeklong air raid and artillery fire in the sealed-off city, and large parts of the city were flattened. The Russian army lost 4,000 soldiers.

During the campaign, the Russian army and security forces from the Ministry of the Interior committed numerous and, in part, systematic war crimes against civilians. Notorious were the "filtration camps"—large detention camps in which security forces held large numbers of Chechen males between 16 and 60, in order to "filter" rebel fighter from innocent civilians. There is well-documented evidence that severe torture was systematically used in these camps,[22] and it was common practice to extort ransom payments from the relatives of detainees; often, relatives also had to pay for the dead bodies of their sons and fathers. Atrocities against the civilian population happened on a routine basis. The case of the village of Samashki, where Russian army units killed about 100 civilians, gained a sad notoriety.[23]

In June 1995, an audacious raid on the small southern Russian town of Budennovsk, led by the most famous and arguably most effective Chechen field commander, Shamil Basayev, propelled the Chechen war again into the headlights of Russian and Western media interest. On June 14, 1995, Basayev and a few hundred armed men attacked and captured a police station and the town hall and then seized the hospital, taking around 1,500 hostages. After several days, Russian Special Forces tried twice to storm the hospital compound. They encountered fierce resistance, and many hostages were killed in the crossfire. Basayev demanded that, in exchange for the hostages, the Russian government halt military actions in Chechnya and begin a series of negotiations. On June 19, most of the hostages were released, and Basayev's group left Budennovsk and returned to Chechnya. In total, 105 civilians and 25 police and army personnel were killed in the siege.

Soon after, in August 1996, in what is one of the most humiliating defeats of a modern army, a few thousand Chechen fighters recaptured the city of Grozny in a surprise attack, surrounded or routed its entire garrison of around 10,000 Russian troops (mainly from the Ministry of the Interior) and blockaded the Russian army unit at their nearby base.

Clearly, the "small, victorious war," which was supposed to have made Yeltsin into the preserver of the unity of the fatherland and the guarantor of law and order, had become an enormous political albatross. In order not to endanger Yeltsin's reelection, the Russian leadership finally began to search for a political exit from the military cul-de-sac. On August 25, 1996, the Russian plenipotentiary General Aleksandr Lebed and the Chechen head of staff Aslan Maskhadov signed the Accord of Khasavyurt in the presence of Tim Guldimann, the head of the OSCE (Organization for Security and Co-operation in Europe) mission in Grozny. This declared that both parties aimed to find a solution to the conflict by the year 2001. The all-important question of the republic's status was thus deferred. The Russian troops pulled out, and Chechnya was in the hands of a coalition of field commanders.

Undoubtedly the most famous among them was Shamil Basayev. Basayev's "career" is in many ways highly symptomatic of the darker side of the post-Soviet transition and reflects Chechnya's misfortunes. Shamil Basayev was born in 1965 in a village near Vedeno, in southeastern Chechnya. He was named after Imam Shamil, the legendary leader of anti-Russian resistance in the 19th century. After graduating from school and serving the mandatory two years in the Soviet army (where he was a firefighter), he worked for a few years on a collective farm in southern Russia. In 1987—the year perestroika began—Basayev moved to Moscow (the big city of opportunities) and enrolled in the Moscow Engineering Institute of Land Management. Later, his roommates claimed that he successfully used his friendship with foreign students to start a computer-import business, a virtual goldmine in the late 1980s. With the collapse of the Soviet Union and the confrontation between Dudaev's Chechnya and Yeltsin's Russia, Basayev's career took a new turn. When Russia, in reaction to Chechnya's unilateral call for independence, declared a state of emergency and issued an ultimatum, he hijacked an Aeroflot YU-154 plane, en route from Mineralnye Vody in Russia to Ankara in Turkey on November 9, 1991, and threatened to blow up the plane unless the state of emergency was lifted. The hijacking was resolved peacefully in Turkey, with the plane and passengers being allowed to return safely and the hijackers being given safe passage back to Chechnya.

In 1992, Basayev recruited a few hundred volunteers from various regions of the North Caucasus to form the so-called Abkhaz battalion. He took it to Abkhazia to fight on the side of Abkhaz separatists (where he was helped by Russian army units) against the Georgian government. It was in Abkhazia that he gained experience as a field commander, and his reputation as an exceptional military leader (and as a gifted entrepreneur of violence, who knew how to profit from war) began to grow. Basayev's Abkhaz battalion later became the most formidable unit in the Chechen war.

Little is known about his activities immediately after his return from Abkhazia. Some sources claim that he fought on the side of the Azeris against Karabakh Armenians, albeit with less success than in Abkhazia. In 1992 or 1993, he seems to have spent some time in Pakistan and maybe in Afghanistan making contacts with Islamic fundamentalist organizations. There he also met a few of his fellow countrymen and was impressed by how well they had mastered Arabic. As Basayev later told a journalist, he was quite sure at that time that, upon their return to Chechnya, these young men would achieve great authority among their people, because they were so well educated in Islam and in the Arabic language.[24] He soon returned to Chechnya and became a patriot-businessman, building up wealth within the shadow economy. When the war started in December 1993, Basayev and his Abkhaz battalion were in the forefront of Chechen resistance. In addition to his raid on Budennovsk, he played a major part in the recapturing of Grozny in August 1996. By 1996, he was promoted to commander of the Chechen Armed Forces. After the retreat of the Russian army in the summer of 1996, he stepped down from his military position in December 1996 to run for president but lost to Aslan Maskhadov, who had been commander in chief of the Chechen resistance during the war. In an attempt to co-opt Chechnya's most famous warlord (and potential renegade), the new president appointed him prime minister.

Between the Wars: Chechnya 1996–1999

After Russian troops had pulled out, the victorious Chechens announced that parliamentary and presidential elections would take place on January 27, 1997.

Since 1989, free elections have been recognized around the world as a ritual, marking a new beginning and the consolidation of a new political order. It was hoped that elections in Chechnya would also serve these functions. The attempt went awry. In spite of the free and fair elections, which were greeted with enthusiasm by the Chechens, between 1996 and 1999 Chechnya became an example of a lawless, crime-exporting, failed state: armed crime increased dramatically, as did the organized kidnapping business.[25] By the end of 1999, several hundred people, mostly Chechens and Dagestanis, were victims of kidnapping. State authority no longer functioned—it was eaten up by the unending rivalry between warlords. Instead of moving from Soviet order to a consolidated, democratic polity, Chechnya was characterized by the almost complete dismantling of all Soviet state institutions, the proliferation of alternative but ineffective institutions, the loss of control over the means of violence, failure to incorporate armed groups in the state, and the radicalization of Islamic discourse.

The leader of the revolution and the first president, Dzokhar Dudayev, did not have much time to build new political institutions, nor was he apparently very enthusiastic about doing this. Already in 1994, in order to counter increasing internal opposition, Dudayev dismissed the parliament, which he himself had called into being. He encountered no resistance. Dudayev was then killed in action toward the end of the first Chechen war, in April 1996.

The end of the first war in 1996 provided a new chance to strengthen Chechnya's institutions. In January 1997, parliamentary and presidential elections took place. The OSCE afforded organizational and financial help and dispatched election observers. The military commander of the Chechen rebels, Aslan Maskhadov, won with 59.3 percent of the votes in the first round of voting, clearly ahead of the most popular of the field commanders, Shamil Basayev (23.5 percent).

Aslan Aliyevich Maskhadov was born in 1951 in exile in Kazakhstan. In 1957, his family was allowed to return to Chechnya. Like his predecessor Dudayev, Maskhadov was in the military. He graduated from the Tbilisi Artillery School in 1972, served from 1990 as a local commander of Soviet rocket forces and artillery in Vilnius, capital of the Lithuanian SSR, and retired from the Russian army in 1992 with the rank of colonel. He was a brilliant officer, a secular-minded person, and, despite the fierce military resistance he led against the Russian army, a moderate politician willing to negotiate with Russia.

In spring 1997, it appeared that Chechnya and its new president had a fair chance. The agreement between Russia and Chechnya foresaw to delay the thorny question of Chechnya's final status; Russia, still very much plagued by internal political struggle seemed to be willing to refrain from using force, and the international community represented by the OSCE had just made it clear that it supported Chechnya's consolidation. But Maskhadov quickly found himself enmeshed in a struggle against internal opposition, which made it hard to centralize power, much less to shift it from one-man rule to institutional governance. New state institutions proved incapable of asserting themselves over the field commanders, who sought to defend their independence from the state. Moreover, resistance against central rule was increasingly framed as a struggle against un-Islamic institutions and practices.

In December 1998, Zelimkhan Yandarbiyev, who had assumed the role of acting president for a few months after Dudayev's death, set up an Islamic body, the Supreme Sharia Court, in an attempt to wrestle away legislative powers from the parliament, thereby ensuring that all laws were consistent with Islam.[26] At the same time, Vice President Vakha Arsanov, being a bitter opponent of the president, pushed for the formation of a State Shura,[27] as a council of influential and respected religious and political leaders who would have the right to issue instructions to the president and the parliament. Vakha Arsanov was then a leading member of the opposition to President Maskhadov, which consisted mostly of field commanders, and the rationale was simple and transparent: the Shura would serve the loose coalition of field commanders, jealously guarding their own power, as an instrument for the final disempowerment of Maskhadov.[28] Arsanov expressed this actual content as follows: "The Shura is not an opposition, but the legitimate authority of the Sharia, and the current president and the vice president, i.e. me, must delegate their power to the Shura. This will, *inshalla,* soon happen."[29]

The hard-pressed president attempted to counter these attacks by preempting the opposition. On February 3, 1999, he signed a decree introducing, with immediate effect, the Sharia in Chechnya. He stripped the parliament of legislative responsibility, sacked the vice president, and declared his intention to establish a purely consultative Shura.[30] The opposition immediately announced that they would boycott the presidential Shura and persisted with the establishment of their own Shura. On February 9, the oppositional Shura convened and announced that it was immediately taking over the business of government. Among the 34 members of the oppositional Shura were sacked Vice President Vakha Arsanov, former President Zelimkhan Yandarbiyev, former Foreign Minister and Islamic zealot Movladi Udugov, and the two influential field commanders, Salman Raduyev and Shamil Basayev.[31]

In this way, the dismantling of the state was brought to a successful conclusion: in early 1999, in Chechnya, there was a president without power, a parliament without responsibility, a president's Shura and an oppositional Shura consisting mostly of field commanders. There was no longer a constitutional court, but then there was no constitution as such, as the president himself had suspended the constitution in preparation for a new one based on the Sharia, which still had to be written.

Much of the process of dismantling state institutions had been carried out with reference to Islamic principles. Yet, the trajectory of Chechnya's dissolution cannot be reduced to the antisecular forces of radical Islam. Part of the Islamic discourse should be understood as a smokescreen, behind which entrepreneurs of violence, warlords, and criminals pursued their tactical objective: to curb central authority, so that it was incapable of interference with their economic activities. Alternatively, the unmaking of the Soviet system, and the war that democratic, secular, and pro-Western Russia had unleashed against its own citizens, had set in motion a far-reaching sociocultural change within Chechen society and the wider North Caucasus. One result was an ambiguous, powerful, and extraordinarily complex process, driven by many factors, which can be captured only tentatively by the term "Islamization." One factor behind this was the return to ethnocultural traditions that the collapse of the Soviet Union made possible. More important, perhaps, were attempts to find new common values under the strain of war with Russia. The activity of Islamic missionaries, which flocked to Muslim regions of the former Soviet Union in the mid 1990s, and the chance to access their generous funding furthered the process of Islamization. During the Soviet era, Chechnya was a secular society, not only in the public realm but also in the daily life of the population, although religion remained an important frame of reference for the self-identification of Chechens. In the wake of the collapse of the Soviet Union, Islam entered public life. In 1998, there were over 400 mosques in Chechnya, and from 1998 on, almost the entire population has designated itself as practicing Muslims.[32]

The war against Russia accelerated the process of Islamization. The Chechen struggle for independence at the end of the 20th century exploited the organizational potential of Islam, as a century earlier Imam Shamil had done against Tsarist Russia. Shamil also conceived of his war as an Islamic war, making it possible to replace clan loyalties with a religious-political program possessing a great capacity for mobilization, over and above that of the clans. It was this program that first gave the Caucasian mountain dwellers a common identity, which stood above clan structures and ethnolinguistic group allegiance, and lent the war against Russian theological sanctification. In this way, Islam advanced to a concept functioning effectively to achieve outward resilience and inward unity. In the North Caucasus, Islam replaced the nation, which had only limited potential for mobilization. Islamization, however, proved to be a double-edged sword. As an instrument for mobilization, and for finding sponsors in the Islamic world, Islamization succeeded. At the same time, however, it contributed decisively to the further fragmentation of society: the importation of alternative norms led to normative competition splitting society, often along generational lines. Established conflict-regulation procedures were devalued. The few remaining state structures were dismantled in the name of Islam, leading the Chechens further and further along the road to anomie.

In the Caucasus, the most radical form of Islamization was represented by the Wahhabites, a term used in the Caucasus and Central Asia as a synonym for "Islamic fundamentalists." The term goes back to Muhammed ibn-Abdul Wahhab, a scholar and cleric, who preached in the 18th century in northeast Arabia. Ibn-Abdul Wahab conceived of himself as a reformer who wanted to purge Islam of everything that did not come directly from the Koran. Wahhabism therefore rejects as un-Islamic the local type of Islam that existed in the Caucasus, which combined elements of Sufism with customary law (*adat*). Since the traditional regulatory frameworks of Chechen society—especially the centrality of clergy and the elders—are questioned, Wahhabism contains considerable social explosiveness.

Before 1993, there were virtually no Wahhabists in the North Caucasus. As a result of the war and the influence of Arabic missionaries, their number has grown considerably. In particular, young men seem to find Wahhabism attractive. Wahhabism propagates high social solidarity and mutual material support, along with the chance to jump the traditional barrier of seniority and achieve prestige and riches while still young.[33] The field commander Shamil Basayev, in his mid-30s, answered the question as to why Chechnya is receptive to Wahhabism in the following way: "The usual generational question—a conflict between fathers and sons. The older generation is completely delegitimized, while the younger, searching for a better fate, turns to Islam."[34]

In another interview, he recalled how he met with adherents of

Wahhabism in Chechnya. At the time, he was deputy prime minister. He recalls that, visiting a Wahhabi camp, how surprised and stunned he was to find that nobody seemed to react to his arrival and his saying "salam." Everybody just continued with what they were doing. Struck by such an evident break with traditional Caucasian politeness, he asked why "they behaved so strangely toward a visitor, a guest, why nobody got up to meet me, nobody displayed joy, expressions of warmth. They answered: Sit down and do your own work. They explained that for them, there was no such a thing as an elder in age or elder in rank. This estranged me from them."[35]

As becomes clear from Basayev's reaction, Wahhabism in Chechnya is met with considerable suspicion because of its threat to the established social order. This can be exemplified by a cursory look at the evolution—or, rather, the devolution—of the justice system in Chechnya. According to the March 1992 constitution, Chechnya was a constitutional state. The new Chechen penal code, introduced after the recapture of Grozny, was based on the Sharia, however, and introduced Sharia courts. The practice of these Sharia courts was met with skepticism and resistance in Chechen society. The procedures were considered to be subjective, and often very young and poorly trained judges commanded little credibility and respect.[36] Moreover, the Sharia justice was compatible with neither the secular Soviet law nor the Chechen customary law (*adat*), the two institutionalized legal concepts in Chechen society. In particular, the fact that young men became judges went against the traditional Chechen notion of gerontocracy.

Factually, therefore, in many regions, the Soviet penal code remained in force. This legal pluralism was recognized by the authorities in Grozny and openly addressed. The Chechen interior minister, visibly doing his best to make a virtue out of a necessity, explained that each offender could choose the legal system under which he wished to be judged.[37] In the meantime, however, the existing legal pluralism, along with the appointment of young men as judges, not traditionally admitted to this role, proved to be extremely destabilizing. It hollowed out the entire legal system and contributed to the erosion of social norms in relation to law and justice.

The threat of the complete dismantling of the remaining political institutions was only one challenge that the new president had to tackle. Another, more tangible, was the open resistance of many field commanders to central authority. In 1996, the state in Chechnya was de facto not much more than a coalition of field commanders, who had extremely effectively organized anti-Russian resistance. In the postwar period, however, the coalition proved short-lived and unstable. Armed conflicts between groups were common, but, as it turned out, Maskhadov's attempts to incorporate armed groups into the state apparatus, and thus subordinate them to a common commander and democratic, legitimate control, failed. Nominally, various branches of the government and bureaucracy controlled armed troops: the president controlled the National Guard and an antiterror unit; the Ministry for State Security controlled the Sharia Guard and the so-called Islamic Regiment; the national security service controlled the border troops. In actual fact, all these armed units remained the personal troops of their respective field commanders, and all attempts to integrate them into state structures failed.

President Maskhadov made an initial attempt to incorporate the armed groups in July 1997. He decreed the formation of a professional army, the National Guard, under a unitary command structure. This move quickly failed in the face of opposition from the field commanders, who did not want to surrender control of their battalions. After it became clear that it was impossible to establish central control over the armed groups, Maskhadov reacted by trying to co-opt influential field commanders into the state. The commander of the Islamic Regiment, Arbi Baraev, was appointed deputy commander of the National Guard, and his troops were incorporated into the structure of the Ministry of State Security. Another field commander, Shamil Basayev, was appointed prime minister in January and given the task by the president of either integrating the illegal armed groups or dissolving them.[38] Basayev was then one of the most powerful field commanders, at the head of around 1,000 disciplined fighters. But Maskhadov's strategy of co-opting the field commanders into the state, and thus gaining control of the armed forces, went awry. On July 13, 1998, armed clashes took place between the National Guard of the president and Baraev's Islamic Regiment. Nominally, at this time, the Islamic Regiment was part of the National Guard and the rebel Baraev was their deputy commander.[39]

After these clashes, Maskhadov dissolved by decree all armed groups. In addition, he demanded that all foreigners who formed illegal armed groups and spread religious ideologies were to be expelled from the country. This decree was directed at Islamic fighters from the Arab world, many with experience in Afghanistan, who had established training camps in Chechnya. The best known of the foreign field commanders was a Saudi who went by the name of Amir Khattab. He commanded a unit of several hundred men and proved to be an effective fighter during the first Chechen war. Some of his military actions were filmed and distributed on Islamic websites. This may have contributed to his alleged success among militant Islamic fundamentalists as a prominent fundraiser for the Chechen war.

The consequence of Maskhadov's decree was that almost all field commanders moved into open opposition to the president and attempted to remove him, with the accusation that he was pro-Russian and anti-Islamic. Simultaneously, they argued that secular state institutions, meaning the office of president, the parliament, and the Constitutional Court, were un-Islamic institutions, too. In the fall of 1998, Maskhadov's authority was destroyed, and it was obvious that his power was restricted to Grozny. Maskhadov's attempts to integrate the armed groups into the state failed.

The Second War, 1999–Present

In the summer of 1999, the second war over Chechnya began. It was triggered by the invasion of Dagestan by militant Islamic rebels from Chechnya, as well as by a series of bomb attacks in Moscow, for which the Russians held the Chechens responsible.

In August 1999, several hundred Chechen Islamist rebels, under the leadership of field commanders Shamil Basayev and Amir Khattab, invaded the neighboring republic of Dagestan with the declared aim of "liberating" it and uniting it with Chechnya into an Islamist republic. The Chechen Islamists encountered bitter resistance from the local population of Dagestan, who were soon supported by Russian security forces. Not without difficulty, the Russian army drove the Islamists back into Chechnya. This Russian army campaign found massive resonance with the Dagestani and Russian populations.

Shortly after the rebel incursion into Dagestan, bombs exploded in Moscow on September 6 and 13, 1999, completely destroying two apartment blocks; 228 people died. On September 16, another 16 died in a bomb explosion in Volgodonsk, a city in the Rostov region. Politicians, Russian security services, and the public immediately blamed the Chechens for the attacks, who, however, denied any responsibility. Up to the present day, Russia has shown no proof of Chechen involvement in the attacks. But reeling from these terrible attacks, and from the raids of Islamist fighters in Dagestan, the readiness for a second war against Chechnya soared in the population. The Russian relief campaign in Dagestan grew quickly into a large-scale war against Chechnya, and it became very clear that the Russian army had waited for a pretext to get even on the battlefield.

The Russian army attacked positions inside Chechnya with heavy artillery and from the air, finally entering Chechnya in October 1999 with an overwhelming force of 100,000 men. This initially very successful and extremely popular war benefited first and foremost the then prime minister and presidential hopeful, Vladimir Putin. Yeltsin had only appointed the head of the secret service, Putin, prime minister in August 1999 and, at the same time, had made very clear that he wished to see the new premier as his successor as the Russian president. Putin was almost unknown when he became prime minister, and the approval of the population was initially around 2 percent. After four weeks in office, Putin's popularity had surpassed the 60 percent mark: trenchant words and a ruthless, and telegenically presented, prosecution of the war in Chechnya had made the new man into a bearer of hope. One of the first things he did was to promise a harsh crackdown on Chechen terrorists: "We'll get them anywhere. If we find terrorists in the shithouse, then we'll blast them in the shithouse. That's all there is to it."[40] As the war started, Putin's rating soared over the rubble of Grozny. Six months later, he won the presidential elections in the first round.[41]

The second Chechen war differed from the first in many respects. This time, the Russian army adopted a different tactic. Rather than sending poorly trained and vulnerable light motorized units into urban warfare, they relied on heavy artillery and aviation, including high-altitude bombing, before the infantry took the devastated cities and villages. The loss of human life and the destruction of infrastructure were enormous, but by March 2000, the Russian army captured all larger settlements, including the capital, Grozny, and largely drove Chechen rebels out of the flat north of the country. Nevertheless, the rebels remained capable of guerrilla warfare, typically targeting Russian and pro-Russian officials, security forces, and military and police convoys and vehicles.

Another difference from the first war was that this time Russian policy makers understood that the outcome depended not only on success in the battlefield but also on success in the information war. In the first war, the Russians almost completely ignored the informational side of the war. In an instinctive move to keep journalists out, which is characteristic of all armies but especially of the Russian army, they treated journalists as unwelcome visitors, but not much effort was invested in preventing them from reporting from Chechnya. Journalists, both Russian and foreign, slipped into Chechnya, and as a result of harassment by state authorities, they often went there with the help of locals and reported from the Chechen perspective. Very often, media reports and broadcasting reflected exclusively Chechen positions, and the public, especially in the West, deciphered the Chechen war primarily as a national resistance against the Russian state which exercised a measure of force that was clearly beyond their tolerance.

By August 1999, Russian leaders had learned the lesson. During the second Chechen war, journalists were "guests" of the Russian army, they were witnessing "police operations," and the perspective of Chechen victims was virtually absent from Russian TV screens. Instead, images of tortured and executed Russian prisoners of Chechen criminal gangs were widely shown, and such videos were presented to European politicians. In January 2000, President Putin appointed Sergey Yastrzhembskiy "assistant to the President of Russia in the coordination of analytical-information work of federal organs of executive power, participating in the counterterrorist operation on the territory of the North Caucasus region, and in conjunction with the mass media." This murky, Soviet-style title meant, in effect, that Putin had just created a state bureaucracy that was actually something like a ministry of propaganda. The message that Yastrzhembskiy hammered home via the Russian mass media time and again was that Russia was conducting surgical counterterrorist strikes against Chechen bandits and terrorists, many of which were financed by Islamic sponsors.

At home, this version gained popular support with a population that was still in shock from the horrible apartment bombings in Moscow in summer 1999, and that was yearning for stability and order (*poryadok*). Initially, it did less well in the West, especially because Russia excluded Western journalists, as well as relief and human rights organizations, from Chechnya and reduced the role of the OSCE to a minimum, thus making it clear that it saw Chechnya as an exclusively domestic problem and did not want any interference. Rifts between the West and Russia over Chechnya deepened as, in a strange moment of international politics, Chechnya became intertwined with NATO's war against Serbia over Kosovo. In March 1999, NATO started an operation to force Serbia to stop its attacks on Kosovo. NATO acted in the spirit of United Nations principles but without a Security Council resolution. Russia, which had actually vetoed such a resolution, saw NATO's air strikes as an arrogant demonstration of power, as a violation of international norms and regulations, and, ultimately, as a threat to the very cornerstone of international law—the ban on intervening in the domestic affairs of a sovereign state.

NATO air strikes ended in June 1999. A month later, the second Chechen war began. When the West expressed criticism and protest over gross violations of human rights by the Russian army, Russians widely defied these criticisms as hypocrisy. Had not the "West," by bombing Serbia, violated international norms? Frictions over Chechnya, and over Kosovo, led to a sharp deterioration in European-Russian relations, culminating in the Parliamentary Assembly of the Council of Europe's (PACE) decision to temporarily suspend Russia's voting right.

In Europe's eyes, the war in Chechnya was a national struggle for independence, and Chechen fighters were usually referred to as "rebels." It took another watershed event in international politics to change that. After the attacks of September 11, 2001, on the World Trade Center by the Islamic terrorist network Al-Qaeda, Russian public relations worked hard to communicate to the world that Russia's war in Chechnya was, in fact, just another (and indeed older) front in the global war on terror. One rather bizarre aspect of the ratcheting-up of the informational warfare was that soon after 9/11, "news" regarding the connection between Chechnya and Al-Qaeda and the Taliban began to flood relevant websites and Internet discussion forums. While some were formally correct but of little relevance—for example, the fact that the Taliban had recognized Chechnya's independence—other "news" was of a more inventive nature. For example, shortly after 9/11 it was reported that Russian secret services had found flight simulator software and maps of European cities in Chechnya; and when Enduring Freedom launched its offensive against the Afghan town of Mazar-i-Shariff, rumors spread out that the town was defended by 2,000 hardened Chechen fighters who had come to help the Taliban in their last stand.

But however exaggerated and often clumsy the Russian public relations offensive was, the European perspective on the Chechen war began to change, as did the nature of the Chechen war. Chechen fighters, no longer able to put up military resistance, relied more and more on terror and increasingly referred to global jihad. Islamic websites prominently featured the Chechen war as an important front in the jihad against the secular West, and the statements of Chechen field commanders published on these websites bore more and more resemblance to the discourse of Islamic fundamentalism. These changes in style and attitude should be treated with caution and not accepted too quickly as a proof of the "jihadization" of Chechen resistance, or even of Chechen society. The new Islamic symbolism of resistance may also reflect a new fundraising strategy of the Chechen rebels and an attempt by the global jihad industry to hijack the Chechen national struggle for its own propaganda efforts. However, it was very clear that, in 2000, Chechen resistance no longer spoke the language of its first leaders—namely of Soviet-trained, secular, professional army officers such as Dudayev and Maskhadov.

On June 6, 2000, Chechnya experienced its first suicide bombing when a young woman, Khava Baraeva, drove a truck loaded with explosives through a Russian security forces checkpoint. Since then, suicide bomb attacks, sometimes executed by women or girls, have become a part of the war against Russia.

On October 23, 2002, a commando unit of 42 Chechen gunmen took more than 900 people hostage at a Moscow theater, demanding an immediate end to the Russian presence in Chechnya. The hostage crisis ended tragically on October 26, when Russian troops stormed the building. The 130 hostages died from the incapacitating effects of knockout gas that the Russian Special Forces had pumped into the building before their raid. All the terrorists were killed, some of them executed while unconscious from the effect of the knockout gas.

On September 1, 2004, some 30 gunmen took control of a secondary school in the small town of Beslan, in North Ossetia, and seized over 1,000 hostages, most of whom were children. Following a tense two-day standoff, Russian Special Forces raided the building. The fighting lasted more than two hours. In the end, 331 civilians, mostly children, as well as 31 hostage-takers and 11 Russian Special Forces soldiers, were killed in the fighting.

Shamil Basayev, former prime minister of Chechnya, a national hero, and a once-ardent admirer of Ernesto "Che" Guevara, took responsibility for both of these ruthless terrorist acts by issuing a statement on an Islamic website. Basayev had escaped the second siege of Grozny but had lost a foot as he crossed a minefield. Despite the fact that Russia put a bounty of US $10 million on his head, he was still at large, hiding in the mountainous south of Chechnya and occasionally granting interviews to journalists. On July 10, 2006, Shamil Basayev was killed in the village of Ekazhevo, in Ingushetia. According to Chechen sources, Basayev was riding in one of the cars escorting a truck filled with explosives in preparation for an attack when the truck exploded, killing Basayev. Russian officials claim that this explosion was the result of a planned special operation.

"Normalization" and "Chechenization": The New Faces of the Chechen War

By spring 2001, large-scale military operations came to end, and the Chechen war entered yet another phase. Russia found itself challenged with countering the threats of ongoing guerrilla warfare that increasingly resorted to terror attacks on civilians, while at the same time managing a hugely expensive postconflict reconstruction and finding a political settlement that could act as a base for a real peace-building process. Judging from the formal steps adopted, Russia was playing by the book. An overwhelming military force had tipped the balance of power radically in favor of Russia and successfully insulated the remaining rebel units from overt mass support, pushing them into the mountainous south. Russia then began to transfer political power to loyal local elites and tried to secure legitimacy by holding a referendum (on March 23, 2003) on a new Chechen constitution (which naturally foresaw Chechnya as a part of the Russian Federation). On October 5, 2003, presidential elections were held, and in November 2005, a parliament was elected.

However, social realities in Chechnya belie this process of "normalization." The constitutional referendum and the presidential and the parliamentary elections were, according to the univocal statement of observers, neither free nor fair but clearly managed by the Kremlin. Far from shifting power to democratically legitimized representatives of Chechen society, the Russian strategy toward Chechnya actually empowered a small and ruthless clique of local strongmen, which came to exercise a regime of terror. This placed the burden of war once again on Chechen society, but it was not a way to peace.

By 2006, Chechnya was a poor, fragmented, deeply traumatized society, over which a ruthless and exploitative local clique governed with the blessing and support of Russia. The new strongman of Chechnya was the 30-year-old Ramzan Kadyrov, who was appointed prime minister in March 2006. Ramzan Kadyrov is the son of Akhmad Kadyrov, who was elected president of Chechnya in 2003. Eight months later, Akhmad Kadyrov was assassinated by a bomb blast in a Grozny stadium during a World War II victory parade, and his son Ramzan took over. Both Akhmad and Ramzan had fought against Russia in the first Chechen war but had then switched sides. The Kadyrov family relies on a large militia of ethnic Chechens, the so-called Security Service of Akhmad Kadyrov, commonly known as the *kadyrovtsy,* commanded by Ramzan. The core of the *kadyrovtsy* consists of relatives and covillagers of the Kadyrov family, but its ranks are filled with many former rebel fighters who switched sides and are now engaged in raids against their former brothers in arms. The militia is estimated to number around 4,000 men, which makes it by far the largest armed formation in Chechnya, apart from the Russian army. After 2002, this militia was legalized by Russia as a part of the Ministry of Internal Affairs of the Chechen Republic. *Kadyrovtsy,* acting as a proxy for Russian power, are now doing most of the fighting against the remaining rebels. Human rights organizations have repeatedly reported that *kadyrovtsy* are responsible for serious and routine human rights abuses committed in Chechnya on behalf of the state.[42]

Russia's president, Vladimir Putin, apparently greatly appreciates the services of Ramzan Kadyrov, and he decorated him with the highest honor of the Russian Federation, the Order of Hero of Russia. Immediately after the assassination of Akhmad Kadyrov, President Putin received Ramzan in the Kremlin and assured him of Russia's support. The imagery of this meeting, which was broadcast on Russian television, could have been taken from an American movie: a don promoting a young offspring to the rank of captain, giving him a free hand in his chiefdom in exchange for unconditional loyalty. The fact that Ramzan owns several black Hummers and uses a gym (named after himself) as his unofficial headquarters further contributes to the movie imagery.

In a report coauthored by the International Helsinki Federation for Human Rights (IHF), the International Federation for Human Rights (FIDH), the Norwegian Helsinki Committee, and Center "Demos" and

Human Rights Center "Memorial," the situation in Chechnya at the end of 2005 was described as follows:

> There are two Chechnyas today. In the first one the life of a human being means nothing. The smallest suspicion, however groundless, is sufficient for someone to be seized by armed men in camouflage, to be subjected to torture and murdered. In this Chechnya, armed clashes and artillery bombing of settlements continue. In the villages and towns the rebel networks attack groups of Russian federal servicemen and policemen. Blood continues to be spilt and there is no hope for peace in the near future. In the other Chechnya, life has normalized. Houses and bridges are being built, fields cultivated, and representatives of federal and security services with active support of the population successfully combat the remaining contracted foreign fighters and local bandits. It does not matter much that this Chechnya, constructed by the Kremlin propagandists, exists only in the virtual space. The important thing is: many people in and outside Russia believe (or pretend to believe) in this Chechnya. At the core of this virtual construction is the plan for "political settlement" implemented by Kremlin. This process is based on rejecting the possibility of negotiations with the warring side, the creation of republican institutions and transferring certain types of authority and functions to them, including that of identifying and eliminating the Chechen fighters. These structures have been given a mandate for uncontrolled violence and, according to human rights groups, in 2004–2005 they were responsible for the majority of crimes committed against civilians in Chechnya.[43]

Human Costs of the Chechen Wars

Figures of casualties in civil war are notoriously unreliable. According to official Russian figures, the first war (1994–1996) took the lives of 4,000 Russian soldiers. This figure seems much too low, however. Russian statistics on the first war usually did not include casualties among Interior Ministry troops and the police. More realistic estimates put the figure at around 7,500. With regard to civilian casualties of the first war, many observers estimate that around 40,000 civilians were killed, but figures range from 20,000 to 100,000. The number of Chechen fighters killed is even harder to estimate; most accounts, however, indicate a figure of around 4,000.

Establishing the numbers of casualties for the second war is possibly even more difficult than for the first war, since Russian censorship and the information blockade now work very efficiently. According to official figures from the Russian Ministry of Defense, the casualty toll of all the power-wielding agencies with troops deployed in the period from September 1999 to December 2002, when the large-scale military campaign came to an end, was 4,572 servicemen killed and 15,549

TABLE 4.1
Number of Casualties of the Chechen Wars

	Russian Soldiers	*Chechen Fighters*	*Civilians*
First War, 1994–1996	7,500[a]	4,000[b]	40,000[c]
Second War, 1999–2002	4,500	3,000[d]	13,000[e]

[a] This number is my own estimate, based on figures from Russian sources, nongovernment officials, and Western reporting.

[b] According to Chechen figures, the Chechen losses were between 2,000 and 3,000 fighters (Gall and De Waal, 1997, p. 360). Dunlop, 2000, puts the number at 4,000. There are no official Russian figures.

[c] Chechen sources put the number at 100,000; this number was also mentioned by General Lebed before his peace-seeking mission. The Moscow human rights organization, Memorial, whose activists documented casualties throughout the war, put the number at 50,000, half of whom died during the Russian storm of Grozny (December 1994–March 1995). Dunlop, 2000, estimates that there were 35,000 civilian casualties. Besides the storming of Grozny, the storming of other cities and villages in Chechnya led to high civilian casualties. The numerous, mostly pointless violent "mopping up" operations of the Russian army cost further lives. Finally, up to 8,000 "disappeared" in the so-called filtration camps, which the Interior Ministry established, supposedly to sift out fighters from civilians. These numerous and massive infringements of human rights have been documented in detail (Human Rights Watch, 1995; Human Rights Watch, 1996; Kovalyev et al., 1995a; Orlov, Cherkasov, and Sirotkin, 1995; Orlov and Cherkassov, 1998; International Helsinki Federation for Human Rights, 1996).

[d] Russian figures for rebel losses are contradictory and inconsistent. In March 2001, the General Staff stated that in the course of the "antiterrorist operation," over 10,000 rebels had been eliminated between October 1999 and March 2001. At the onset of the war, the same General Staff had put the number of rebels, in various, mutually contradictory statements, at between 5,000 and 20,000. On the basis of reports of the military agency AVN, as well as reports from the nonstate, pro-Chechen website kavkaz.org, it can be concluded that the weekly losses of the rebels since the transition to guerrilla warfare are slightly less than those of the Russian army. Chechen Head of Staff Maskhadov put his own losses in May 2001, directly following the heaviest losses of the war, at 1,500 ("Russian Crackdown in Chechnya Killed 40,000 Civilians"). This number seems to be realistic.

[e] There are no Russian figures for civilian casualties. In May 2000, Chechen sources already spoke of over 40,000 victims. This figure, equaling the total casualties of the first war, is probably exaggerated. In the first war, most of the civilian casualties died in the storm of Grozny. In the second war, however, the cities had largely already emptied. Many of the civilian population sought refuge in the mountains or tried to get over to Georgia through mountain passes. A documentation of this mass flight is provided by a report of a team from Médecins Sans Frontières, 1999, based on interviews with refugees. The majority of the displaced civilian population fled to safety in neighboring Ingushetia. During the battle for Grozny, the city was inhabited by an estimated 40,000 people. If the civilian casualties were as high as during the first storm of Grozny in January 1995, then the number of civilian casualties by February 2000 must be put at 8,000. The bombardment and the storming of further settlements up to March 2000 took further lives, as did the numerous mopping-up actions of the Russian security forces. Estimating very conservatively, the second war had taken the lives of around 13,000 civilians by August 2001.

TABLE 4.2
Total Number of Internally and Externally Displaced People at a Given Time, 1999–2001

Year	*To Ingushetia*	*To Georgia, Azerbaijan, and South Russia*[a]
September 1999	50,000[b]	6,000
October 1999	100,000[c]	10,000
November 1999	225,000[d]	14,000
June 2000	170,000[e]	
March 2001	150,000[f]	6,000
August 2001	150,000[g]	

[a] My calculations, based on the figures of the Azerbaijan Interior Ministry and Russian and Georgian newspaper reports. Blank spaces indicate data not available

[b] "Russian Federation/Northern Caucasus: Tens of Thousands of Newly Displaced," *ICRC News 39*, 30 September 1999. (available online at http://www.reliefweb.int).

[c] "Caucasian Early Warning Network: Region Ingushetia (Internally Displaced)," Caucasus region policy brief, October 1999 (available online at http://www.reliefweb.int/w/rwb.nsf).

[d] "UNHCR Briefing Notes: Timor, Chechnya," UN High Commissioner for Refugees (UNHCR), 30 November 1999 (available online at http://www.reliefweb.int/w/rwb.nsf).

[e] "UNHCR North Caucasus," UN High Commissioner for Refugees (UNHCR), 30 June 2000 (available online at http://www.reliefweb.int/w/rwb.nsf).

[f] "UNHCR Briefing Notes: Sierra Leone/Guinea, Chechnya/Ingushetia, Afghan Refugee Children," UN High Commissioner for Refugees (UNHCR), 16 March 2001 (available online at http://www.reliefweb.int/w/rwb.nsf).

[g] "Emergency Action of the Red Cross and Red Crescent Movement for the North Caucasus and the South of Russia, July 2001," ICRC, 23 August 2001 (available online at http://www.reliefweb.int/w/rwb.nsf).

wounded—a total of 20,121 servicemen—enough to man two motorized rifle divisions.[44] Since then, rebels continue to inflict losses on Russian and increasingly on pro-Russian Chechen forces and police, but reliable data on the death toll of this low-intensity partisan war are not available. (Table 4.1 presents the figures.)

The first war triggered extensive, if short-lived, refugee movements. In 1995, around 250,000 Chechens were internally displaced.[45] The majority of the refugees found shelter with relatives and friends in the mountains, in the north of the country, and especially in neighboring Ingushetia. The destruction of settlements was limited, since the Russian army seldom employed artillery and aviation for extended periods of time during the first war; Grozny, the center of which was literally razed to the ground by Russian artillery, was the exception.

The numbers of internally displaced people in the second war are well documented in the reports of the UNHCR (United Nations High Commissioner for Refugees), ICRC (International Committee of the Red Cross), and other international organizations (Table 4.2). In total, the refugee numbers were greater than in the first war. In particular, however, in contrast to the first war, the majority of the refugees did not return quickly. Due to the heavy, often week-long bombardment with artillery and aircraft, the infrastructure suffered far more damage than in the first war. In addition, the fear of repression, arbitrary arrests, and "disappearances" in one of the notorious filtration centers was great and justified.

Organization of Violence: Funding, Recruitment, Arming

The Chechen rebels have put up formidable resistance against an army that outnumbered them by at least ten to one, not to speak of the far superior weaponry that Russians had at their disposal. Obviously, Chechen rebels were able to overcome the organizational and logistical difficulties of rebellions, the core of which are financing and recruiting. The following paragraphs highlight the mechanisms by which this was achieved.

Sources of funding for the Chechen rebels changed over time, as did the underlying dynamics of violence. Generally speaking, however, there were five sources: profits from the shadow economy, profits from oil extraction and oil reexport, ransom payments for hostages, donations by the diaspora, and donations by foreign Islamic sponsors.

The initial accumulation of money for the wars to come took place within the shadow economy of the dying Soviet system. The funding of the Chechen rebellion is inseparably connected with the short-lived regime of Dzokhar Dudayev, the so-called Chechen revolution, and the unprecedented economic opportunities that the gold-rush days of a collapsing empire offered to some. In the very early days of post-Soviet Russia, it was said that control over just 1 km of the Russian border was enough to become a millionaire. Between 1991 and 1993, Dudayev's regime controlled more than 300 km of the Russian border. Between 1991 and 1993, Chechnya was transformed into an enormously profitable, illegal, but tolerated free-trade zone, which made millions for its owners. When Chechnya declared and de facto got independence in 1991, it suddenly had an international airport free of controls, as well as open borders to Georgia and Russia at its disposal. At the same time, Chechnya remained in the ruble zone and received payments from the Russian federal budget, especially for wages and pensions. This position at the intersection of the still state-regulated Russian market and the world market, alongside the almost complete absence of state controls, made Chechnya a miracle of the shadow economy and an El Dorado for organized economic crime.

Consumption goods, especially entertainment electronics and textiles, were imported duty free in Grozny and resold for a large profit in Russia, while weaponry from Russia was exported to the world market. Soviet arsenals and the weaponry of the West Group of the Soviet armed forces (then withdrawing from Central Europe) ensured that there was a plentiful supply.[46] In 1993, it was possible to acquire automatic weapons at the central market in Grozny without any problems. Grozny also became a financial center for illegal earnings. The godfathers of the Chechen mafia, especially influential in Moscow, laundered their money in Chechnya, including the millions they made by forging the notes of exchange of the Central Bank. In one of the most infamous cases, a group "earned" at one fell swoop a sum in rubles then equivalent to US $700 million.[47]

Another source of income for Dudayev's regime, which, arguably, created even higher profits, was oil. In 1993, some 2.6 million tons of oil were extracted in Chechnya, with a value of US $250 million at the world market price of that year. Between 1991 and 1993, around one-third of Chechnya's budget was financed by proceeds from the oil business.[48] Locally extracted oil brought nice profits, but the revenues from the reexport of cheap Russian oil were incomparably higher.[49] In spite of the economic blockade imposed by Russia after 1991, oil continued to flow into Chechnya from Siberia to be processed in the refineries in Grozny. Large amounts of this oil were then exported. Officially, between 1991 and 1994, some 23 million tons of oil were exported via Grozny.[50] However the actual export was likely to be much higher, since Russia's oil barons used Grozny as an outlet to illegally pump cheap Russian oil onto the world market for hard currency revenues. Naturally, a large part of the illegal proceeds flowed to Russia, but a substantial part remained in Chechnya. Conservative estimates put the share of revenues remaining in Chechnya at US $900 million.[51] As the first war began, oil deliveries to Chechnya finally came to an end, but locally extracted oil was still available. Dudayev was initially quite successful at establishing central control over the distribution of profits from the oil sector that gave him leverage over ambitious field commanders and explained the relative unity of Chechen resistance during the first war.[52] During the war, however, Dudayev lost his grip on oil profits, and his successor, Aslan Maskhadov, was never able to recentralize control over the distribution of oil profits.

In 1998, at least 400,000 tons of oil, of 843,000 tons produced, was extracted illegally, outside the control of the Chechen state.[53] The tapping of the pipeline and the illegal extraction of oil by organized criminal groups, but also by private households, became endemic. These small household refineries became the most important and almost only source of income for innumerable Chechen families. The whole of the North Caucasus was supplied by their oil products, first and foremost poor-quality gasoline. The extent of this "private" extraction is exemplified by fact that, in the course of a three-day operation in November 1998, Chechen security forces closed down 112 such household refineries. Nevertheless, it proved to be impossible for the state to centralize oil revenues, and Maskhadov was thus robbed of the possibility of stabilizing his regime by means of a patron-client network redistributing oil revenues. In a desperate move, he decreed in June 1999 that the Interior Ministry, the Ministry of State Security, the National Security Service, and the National Guard could keep all the illegally extracted oil that they confiscated.[54] This obvious attempt to cut off possible rivals from oil revenues, while at the same trying to keep his ministries in line (which were like an umbrella organization for private militias anyway), did not work but led to further fragmentation of the state institution.

After the second Russian invasion of 1999, the new pro-Russian administration in Chechnya again made efforts to recentralize oil revenues. In early 2001, the company Grozneftgaz was created to run the oil and gas reserves. At that time, 51 percent of the capital belonged to the Russian state, and 49 percent was given to the pro-Russian Chechen administration that increasingly acted as Russia's proxy. Backed by an overwhelming Russian military force, this effort was met with more success.

Toward the end of the first war, outright criminal activities started to complement profits made in the shadow economy and the oil sector. The most notorious was the ransom business. A few cases involved foreigners, such as the kidnapping of Vincent Cochetel, head of the UN Mission in Ossetia (1998); of the Italians Pocaterra, Lombardi, and Valenti (September 1996); of the Italian press photographer Mauro Galligani (1997); and of the three employees of Russian television channel NTV (1997). They were all freed following the payment of a considerable ransom, but four employees of a British telecommunications company were killed in December 1998. These cases are only the tip of an iceberg, however. In fact, from 1996 on, hundreds of people in Chechnya and the bordering republics, especially Dagestan, became victims of kidnapping. People-trading had developed into a branch of the economy in a full-blown market of violence.

During the first war, Russian and Chechen forces had already traded in living and dead bodies. The Russian army sold the Chechens the corpses of their fallen and demanded ransoms for the freeing of prisoners, who quite often were not prisoners of war but civilian men over 15 years of age who were arbitrarily being held captive. Chechens, for their part, sought to exchange Russian prisoners for their relatives. Families who needed to buy the release of family members but lacked Russian hostages could "acquire" these from other Chechens. The director Sergei Bodrov portrayed this macabre trading in people in his film *The Prisoner of the Caucasus* (Russia 1996).

The end of the war by no means put an end to the people trade. Its structure, however, changed. The kidnapping business now became systematic and purely economically motivated. The number of kidnappings shot up after 1994. Forthwith, around a third of all kidnappings in Russia took place in the North Caucasus.[55] According to figures provided by the Russian Ministry of the Interior, between 1992 and 2000 there were 1,815 cases of kidnapping in the North Caucasus, with a peak in 1996 (427 cases) and 1997 (361 cases).[56]

There is no evidence that the Chechen field commanders were exclusively and systematically orchestrating the kidnapping business. Instead, the kidnappings were organized by well-run criminal groups that had connections beyond Chechnya, but these groups could not operate in Chechen territory without the protection and permission of the local strongmen. Field commanders, if not directly involved in kidnappings, would presumably have at least received a share of the profits. There are no data on the proceeds from the kidnapping business, and estimates are very difficult. But there is some anecdotal evidence. According to Russian sources, US $10,000 for a kidnapped Russian soldier and $20,000 for an officer was the usual price.[57] Ransoms for rich civilian hostages may have been many times higher. For the freeing of the NTV journalists or of western victims of kidnapping, several hundred thousand dollars were supposedly paid.[58]

Another source of income was racketeering. According to a report by the Main Directorate for the Struggle against Economic Crime, around

4,000 enterprises in Russia were in the grip of "ethnic mafias." A substantial number of these enterprises were under the control of Chechens, who donated some of their profits to the rebels.[59] Financial support also flowed from the Chechen diaspora in Russia, in the former Soviet Union, and from the diaspora in Turkey, Jordan, and Saudi Arabia, which date back to the emigrations of the 19th century. The Chechen diaspora supported the struggle for independence with voluntary donations; to some extent, however, a "war tax" was also collected, comparable with the war taxes collected from the Albanian, Kurdish, and Tamil diasporas in their corresponding wars.

Finally, considerable "donations" from Islamic sources started to flow after the first war. The Russian domestic secret service, the FSB, reported large financial flows to Chechnya from the Arab Emirates, from Egypt, from Libya, from Kuwait, from Qatar, from Afghanistan, and from Saudi Arabia, chiefly via Turkey and Azerbaijan. Money needed on the spot would then be brought to Chechnya from the latter countries by courier. In addition, from 1998 on, the Russian secret service has repeatedly claimed to have intelligence of funds flowing to Chechnya from circles close to Al-Qaeda. These assertions are hard to verify, and the FSB is certainly a source that needs to be treated with extreme caution. However, it is more than likely that the Chechen rebels were able to attract a considerable share of the global funding for jihad.

The availability of funding is one—and perhaps the most important—factor that explains the successful recruiting of fighters. Other factors are linked to social and cultural conditions. Chechens are traditionally a martial society, for whom fighting is associated with winning honor and prestige. Handling weapons is regarded as an essential component of manhood and is therefore widely practiced. Just as deeply anchored in the population is the desire for independence from the Soviet Union and Russia. These two circumstances do not provide a sufficient explanation for the organization of violence in Chechnya, but they do account for the relatively large recruitment pool and for recruitment being relatively cheap. Initially, the pool of men in Chechnya who were willing and able to fight probably totaled around 20,000. This made for speedy and flexible recruiting. Thus, the repeated claims of the military leader of the rebels, Aslan Maskhadov, that he could easily increase the number of his troops tenfold, if necessary, were perhaps slightly exaggerated but basically correct.

During the first war, and in the beginning of the second war, four groups of fighters could be distinguished. First, there were well-equipped, disciplined, and experienced units, commanded by well-known field commanders, which as a rule had access to substantial funding and operated quite independently. These units were the backbone of the Chechen rebels, and some of them turned into standing militias that efficiently opposed the central state.[60] The first such armed group in Chechnya was organized by a former police officer and successful illegal market entrepreneur, Bislan Gantemirov. His Party of the Islamic Way was, in reality, a paramilitary organization. It became the core of the National Guard, which provided armed support to the Chechen revolution of August and September 1991. Gantemirov's men also forced the self-dissolution of the Supreme Soviet in 1991.

The second group was made up of occasional fighters, who either joined a unit for a limited period of time or themselves created a small company to fight against the Russian army relatively independently. It was the numerous fighters from this group who made the first Chechen war a truly popular movement with mass support in the general population. An article that appeared in *Izvestia* in January 1995 describes the fighter from this group thus:

> He is twenty-five, wears a black leather jacket and blue jeans, and carries a Kalashnikov automatic. In peacetime, he flies regularly to Iraq and buys clothes, shoes, kitchen appliances, TV stands and other things. Thus, his main "military profession" is as a middle-level wholesale trader bringing in middle-level revenues. Dudaev, as a president of an independent Chechnya, is completely irrelevant to him. What are not irrelevant are his business, his wife and children, and his house, which he is ready to defend by force of arms.[61]

The third group of fighters consisted of the numerous self-defense militias, which formed in almost every village, to protect the inhabitants against attacks from the Russian army and, at times, also from the rebel units.

The fourth group (which was perhaps never larger than a few hundred fighters) included the so-called foreign mujaheddins. In particular, the Saudi field commander Khattab, who had already fought in Afghanistan, attracted public attention. Khattab arrived in Chechnya in February 1995 and immediately attained fame by distributing a video of an ambush sprung by him and costing 100 Russian soldiers their lives. In the interwar period, Khattab ran a training camp in Chechnya. He was regarded as useful for tapping the funds of the international jihad industry for the Chechens. After 1999, the stream of mujaheddins increased from, especially, Afghanistan, Saudi Arabia, Yemen, Egypt, and Turkey. According to unverifiable Russian sources, foreign mujaheddins were supported by Osama bin Laden and trained in camps in Afghanistan.[62] The main websites of the international jihad industry seem to back this up.[63]

The bulk of the fighting was done by the first two groups, and the part-time fighters served as a pool that commanders could tap into whenever a large-scale operation, which demanded more men, was planned. Units were most often based on extended families and neighborhood ties (which often overlap). It was common practice that most families had at least one male among the fighters. Peer pressure and ideas of honor may have contributed to this, but having relatives among the fighters also served as a security guarantee.

Estimating the number of fighters in the first Chechen war is difficult (Table 4.3). Aslan Maskhadov, the chief of staff of the Chechens, put the strength of the Chechen forces in Grozny at the start of the war at around 1,000. Only the 500-strong National Guard—whose core was the Abkhaz battalion, veterans of the war in Abkhazia, and the 200 men of the President's Guard—had been trained and equipped.[64] The rebel numbers, however, must have rapidly swollen, since volunteers flocked to Grozny from every village to support the resistance against the Russian army. The Russian secret service put the number of fighters

TABLE 4.3
Estimation of Chechen Rebel Strength

Year	*Number of Fighters*
1994	1,000
1995	7,000
1999	9,000
2000	7,000
2001	4,000
2002	3,000

Source: These are my own estimates, based on Russian figures, interviews in Chechnya, and Western media reports. Nikolai Patrushev, director of the domestic secret service, the FSB, put the number of rebels in February 2001 at 5,000 (*Jamestown Monitor* 7(23), February 2001). The commander of the Interior Ministry Troops, General Vyacheslav Tikhomirov, put their number at between 3,000 and 5,000 (*BBC Monitoring Service,* United Kingdom; March 22, 2001, Story Filed: Thursday, March 22, 2001 6:02 AM EST). The Chechens put their strength in March 2001 at between 6,000 and 7,000 (Shamil Basayev, interview in English by Azzam Publications, "Jihad in Chechnya," available online at http://www.qoqaz.co.za/ [accessed August 12, 2001]).

shortly after the beginning of the war at between 5,000 and 7,000.[65] At the end of the first war, there were around 7,000 experienced and equipped fighters in Chechnya. This number then rose quickly in the face of the second Russian invasion. Volunteers with combat experience from the first war joined the troops of field commanders; in the winter, enlistment as a fighter often constituted the only way to earn a living. After the second fall of Grozny in 1999, many units dissolved, but a few thousand fighters withdrew into the mountains.

After funding and recruitment, a third barrier that a rebel movement has to overcome is weapons procurement. In the context of the collapsing Soviet Union, this was by far the easiest task. No armed groups on the territory of the Soviet Union encountered problems in arming themselves in the early 1990s. The weaponry of the Chechen rebels came almost exclusively from the arsenals of the Soviet army. In June 1992, Russia withdrew all military forces from Chechnya. Almost all the weapons and all the equipment were left behind. In this way, the following weapons came into Chechen hands: 42 tanks (T-62M and T-72); 66 armored vehicles (BMP-1, BMP-2, BTP-70, and BRDM-2); 30 122-mm howitzers (D-30); 58 120-mm mortars (PM-38); 18 GRAD multiple launch rocket systems (B-21); 523 rocket-propelled grenade launchers (RPG-7); 18,832 AK-74 rifles and 9,307 AK-47 ("Kalashnikovs"); and 533 sniper's rifles and 1,160 machine guns.[66] Furthermore, there are clear indications that a large part of the weaponry of the withdrawing West Group of the Soviet forces was sold on the world market via the "free trade zone" of Chechnya.[67] Some of these weapons would have stayed in Chechnya. More weaponry was acquired from former Soviet armament factories in Estonia and Moldova.[68]

Chechen rebels had no air force and almost no artillery. In the main, the rebels used light, mobile weapons of Soviet make, suitable for guerrilla warfare: automatic guns (AK-47 and AK-74) and machine guns (PK); light mortars; and the RPG-7, a shoulder-fired weapon used against tanks, bunkers, and light vehicles.

The rebels seemed to have had few problems in keeping supply lines open. The routes over the border to Georgia and, via Dagestan, to Azerbaijan, are passable, and thus the post-Soviet arms markets in both of these countries could be accessed. Large amounts of supplies come additionally from the Russian army, either from the Russian garrisons in Georgia and Armenia or directly from the Russian army in Chechnya. Corruption among troops and officers is so great that weapons are regularly and systematically sold to the enemy. In the summer of 2001, the price of a Kalashnikov from the Russian army was around $100. In 1991, such a weapon had cost six times more on the market in Grozny.[69] The presence of the Russian army in Chechnya has thus lowered the price of weapons for the Chechens.

Chechen Lessons

At first glance, the case of Chechnya offers much support for the classical script of a nationalist, secessionist war, including all the well-known elements of bitter historical memories, a tradition of violent conflict, and a policy of discrimination.

In the Chechen national discourse, the topos of the eternal war against Russia played an important role, as did the bitter memory of the deportation by Stalin. Both doubtless proved themselves to be key resources for the national mobilization, initially for Dudayev's revolution, and later, as Russia did indeed bring war to the country, for the mobilization of the guerrillas.

The Soviet policy of discrimination continued after Chechens returned from exile in Kazakhstan. Generally speaking, Soviet authorities did not trust Chechens. The ethnic quota—an all-important instrument of Soviet ethnic policy—was mostly adhered to, meaning that positions within the *nomenklatura* within the Chechen-Ingushetian ASSR were distributed in a ratio of 5:4:1 (five Chechens, four Russians, one Ingush). This quota, though, did not adequately reflect demographic distribution. Moreover, the key positions in education and in the important oil sector were mostly given to Russians. In addition, the first party secretary, by far the most important position and usually held by a member of the titular nation, was always a Russian.[70]

Since most influential white-collar positions within the Soviet system were occupied by Russians, there was, unlike most other ethnic Republics within the Soviet Union, no Chechen Soviet middle class, which could have taken the role of a moderate, secular-minded nationalist elite willing to compromise with its counterparts in Russia. Instead, most of the supporters of Dudayev's Chechen revolution and most fighters came from the rural population. Around 70 percent of Chechens lived in rural areas, but the large urban population (in 1990 Grozny had around 400,000 inhabitants, roughly one-third of the population) was mostly

Russian. It was also among the rural population that the labor surplus was the greatest. Tens of thousands of Chechens left the republic every year as seasonal labor migrants. This labor surplus among the male rural population may also help explain the large pool from which rebels could recruit. The last element in this script was the collapse of the Soviet system in August 1991, which finally opened up a window of opportunity for the realization of the Chechen national aspiration.

However, in light of the chain of events described in this chapter, the nationalist-secessionist script seems to be if not wrong then insufficiently convincing. The Chechen wars did not happen as an unavoidable tectonic movement but unfolded from specific and often highly idiosyncratic conjunctures of factors and events, which are often only remotely linked to the elements of the classical script. In other words, the unfolding of what was, in retrospect, the classical script depended on factors and conjunctures that are not part of that script.

The leitmotif of the Chechen road to war was the dismantling of state institutions and the repeated failure to consolidate state institutions and statehood.

In contrast to the majority of the successful new national elites in the post-Soviet space, the first leader of the Chechen nationalist movement, Dzokhar Dudayev did not even attempt to harness the organizational potential of the existing Soviet institutions for his purposes. In the Baltic states and in the states of the South Caucasus, the Supreme Soviets were "nationalized," thereby winning new legitimacy, and the Ministry of the Interior and its security forces were put into the services of the new national regimes. By contrast, Dudayev created a parallel structure, the National Congress. He thereby denied himself the organizational and material resources of the old system, instead relying on his charisma and popularity, a fervent nationalist ideology, and armed support from rural followers. Such a regime proved to be weakly embedded and highly vulnerable to internal fragmentation. Moreover, Dudayev's regime was financially dependent on revenues generated by shadow economy entrepreneurs who were exploiting the illegal free-trade zone of Chechnya. This coalition of nationalist ideology and shadow economy entrepreneurship—the patriot-businessmen-axis—had no interest in establishing a functioning statehood, since this would have seriously threatened the shadow economy and organized crime. In other words, the most important sponsors of the regime had a rational interest in preventing the establishment of an internally effective state with an enforcement capability. Rising criminality and growing internal opposition, together with his very autocratic attitudes, weakened Dudayev's position both within Chechnya and as a partner in negotiations with Moscow, a development he tried to counter by stirring more national fervor. The situation rapidly deteriorated, and Russia could no longer ignore the problem. The fact that the Russian policy could find no better way to deal with the situation than launching an ill-planned, disastrous, full-scale war must be attributed to the Russian domestic political struggles described above.[71]

The first war ended with the completely unexpected retreat of the Russian army. But the sociopolitical terrain, on which the victorious Chechens could have erected their polity, had become even more difficult. The war—as most wars do—had brought to power a few successful entrepreneurs of violence who had well-equipped, well-trained, and well-funded militias. These new strongmen were more interested in the perpetuation of an economy of war than in the reconstruction of statehood, which would have implied transferring power and economic claims to an elected president and new state institutions. Aslan Maskhadov, the military genius who had led the guerrilla war, became, with the blessing of OSCE observers, Chechnya's newly elected president, but he failed to subdue or co-opt field commanders. He also did not succeed in concentrating in his hands the distribution of the material resources, especially revenues from the shadow economy and oil profits. Thus, he never had the means to build up a patron-client network, and he could not bring into play the single most successful means of securing regime stability in the post-Soviet states. In a permanent struggle for power between the rump state and entrepreneurs of violence, remaining state institutions were gradually dismantled. Under the pretext that the parliament, the Constitutional Court, and the office of president were un-Islamic institutions, field commanders sought to abolish the remaining organizational potential of the state. When, in 1998, Maskhadov desperately attempted to preempt this by disempowering the parliament and transferring power by decree to an ad hoc Islamic council (Shura) under his leadership, the dismantling of the state was formally concluded.

From then, still more fragmentary powers came into play, and they reduced the societal capacity for peace even more. The second Russian invasion caused tremendous material destruction, forced hundreds of thousands to flee, and added thousands to the already horribly high death toll of the first war. The Chechen rebels have increasingly accessed the funds of the international jihad industry and thus have availed themselves of a source of finance that is particularly difficult to block. They have also changed their tactics and resorted to outright terror attacks, so that now the process of "jihadization" is under way. It is therefore of little consequence that the majority of the Chechen population does not support fundamentalism or terrorism but is, after more than a decade of war, simply yearning for basic physical and economic security.

For thousands of young men with guns, however, the economy of war has become the only field of gainful activity, and the forces of this market, for them, may be stronger than any of the normative foundations on which a Chechen polity could be built. Moreover, in what is perhaps the greatest tragedy of Chechnya, it is hard to think of a normative framework that seems acceptable for most and strong enough to withstand the powers of fragmentation unleashed in Chechnya. Both the traditional rules of *adat* and the newly imported norms of Islamic fundamentalism have proved unstable foundations. It is also probable that the norms of secular, democratic statehood have been discredited for a long time to come by a secular, modern, democratic state (Russia) waging a barbaric war, and by its murky attempts at simulating democratic normalization after the war. In Chechnya, it seems, the societal capacity for peace has been destroyed. In this regard, Chechnya is above all else a lesson in the devastating spiraling dynamic of violence.

Chechnya also holds a few lessons for international research into the risks that precipitate war. As described here, the original accumulation of capital for war took place in the veritable boom that the Soviet shadow economy experienced at the end of the Soviet Union. The shadow economy was also the main source of funding for other incidents of war in the Caucasus. Yet, the exploitation of the opportunities in the shadow economy does not necessarily lead to war; in the case of Chechnya, those who benefited the most combined high enthusiasm for a national *cause* (however vaguely defined) with much less enthusiasm for a national *state,* thereby aggravating state weakness and internal fragmentation. Other sources of funding had a role, too. Profits from reexported Russian and locally extracted oil fueled rebellion. The lack of central control over the distribution of these profits further added to fragmentation. But there is little evidence that the oil deposits caused the original organization of violence; oil profits played a minor role as a causal factor in Dudayev's moves toward independence. In the course of the sovereignization of the subjects of the Russian Federation after 1990, local elites encountered few problems in appropriating a fair share of profits from their mineral resources. The expensive and risky establishment of an independent state was by no means necessary. Neither do Chechnya's oil deposits serve as a motive for the Russian intervention. In 1993, only 2.6 million tons were pumped—less than 1 percent of the total output for Russia—and this is far too little to hold any strategic importance.

The single most powerful explanation for the second war in Chechnya is the previous war. In this respect, the argument that wars breed new wars is clearly supported. As Collier and Hoeffler predicted, it was not a desire for vengeance that triggered the war; rather, it was the incursion of two renegade commanders into the neighboring republic of Dagestan. What motivated this raid is far from clear. What made it possible was the existence of two idle, but well-armed and well-trained, militias in search of a mission.

The effect of ethnic dominance is difficult to gauge. The fact that Chechens were the largest ethnic group and that Russians were poorly organized and not mobilized certainly contributed to the speed of the Chechen revolution, which met no resistance at all. However, there was no interethnic conflict between Chechens and Russians in Chechnya. Russians opted for exit—many had left Chechnya even before the war started—and today, there are hardly any Russians living in Chechnya.

Finally, the mountainous terrain has had some effect on the duration of the war, as rebels have been able to retreat into the mountains and war supplies have been trafficked along mountain paths. However, the most decisive fighting has taken place in the urban environment, and the political conditions that paved the way to violence were first laid down in Grozny. Therefore, there is no evidence that terrain has causally contributed to the unleashing of the war in Chechnya.

5 Wars in Georgia

Background

In the bygone Soviet space, Georgia was without doubt the land of plenty and wonder. Located just south on the impressive mountain chains of the high Caucasus, every year hundreds of thousands of Soviet tourists visited its resorts on the Black Sea, relaxed on its beaches, and enjoyed excellent cuisine, fine wine, fresh fruits, hospitality, and the omnipresent public display of *grandezza* and style, which is so cultivated by Georgians. In the collective imagination of the Soviet public, Chechnya stands for the exotic, yet dangerous and wild Caucasus, and Georgia is its no less exotic but tamed and hospitable counterpart. Georgians were quite comfortable with the way their country and their culture were perceived in the Soviet Union, and they contributed to their national clichés, which, after all, served the tourism industry and brought cash into the country. Despite the fact that Georgia later produced an oppositional national elite whose radicalism and uncompromising stand toward the Soviet Union proved to be exceptional even by the standards of the late Soviet Empire, many Georgians are well aware of the fact that Georgia's special position within the Soviet Union was not entirely to its disadvantage. It is not uncommon for Georgians jokingly to toast to "the colony we have lost—to the Soviet Union," a reference to the opportunities that the exploitation of the Soviet shadow economy offered (a field which the Georgians, according to abundant anecdotic evidence, had perfected). When, in the early 1990s, a series of internal wars devastated the country, undoing all remnants of functional statehood, this came as no less unexpected and shocking for the Georgian population than it would for the populations of Germany or Norway today.

Between 1989 and 1993, there were three related wars in Georgia. The first, over the breakaway region of South Ossetia, began in Novem-

ber 1989, escalated in January 1991, and then flared up again in June 1992. The second war was fought between rival Georgian groups bidding for political power; it began in December 1991 and ended in November 1993 and was triggered by the violent overthrow of President Zviad Gamsakhurdia by a coalition of opposition politicians and warlords. The third war was over the breakaway Autonomous Republic of Abkhazia; it began in August 1992 and ended in September 1993 with the defeat of Georgian troops. The conflicts over South Ossetia and Abkhazia remain formally unresolved to the present day. In both cases, the secessionist entities have asserted themselves militarily but have failed to gain international recognition.

The wars have cost up to 13,000 lives and have produced the second largest ethnic cleansing in the former Soviet Union, when Abkhazian forces "cleansed" 200,000 mostly ethnic Georgians from the breakaway republic. But even in catastrophe and war, Georgia at least partly held up to its theatrical, dramatic style where tragedy and comedy are closely intertwined. It seems unusual for a sculptor and a playwright to become the leaders of the two largest paramilitary forces, while the president is the translator of Baudelaire into Georgian and the son of Georgia's best-known modern novelist. All three leaders were drawn from Tbilisi's close-knit intellectual elite. Perhaps, therefore, it is also not surprising that it is quite hard to find a Georgian who had participated in any of the militias and who had a rank lower than colonel. It seems that these armies, commanded by artists and intellectuals of a sort, consisted only of officers. And finally, it may also be characteristic of Georgia that the leaders of the eventually defeated paramilitaries were pardoned by President Shevardnadze and allowed to return to a life as privateers; Shevardnadze, in turn, after having lost power in the so-called Rose Revolution, retired unharmed. In Georgia, it seems, the gestures of pardon are respected more than the thrust for vengeance. This, at least, sets the wars in Georgia apart from other wars in the Caucasus region.

Georgia (69,700 km^2) lies in the South Caucasus and has an extraordinarily varied ecology, with alpine, subtropical, and semiarid climatic zones. To the west, the country is bordered by the Black Sea; the northern border is formed by the Caucasus mountain chain. Here, Georgia borders on the Russian North Caucasian republics of Karachai-Cherkessia, Kabardino-Balkaria, Ossetia, Ingushetia, Chechnya, and Dagestan. In the southeast, Georgia has borders with Azerbaijan; in the south with Armenia and Turkey. Around 65 percent of Georgian territory is over 800 m above sea level; 30 percent lies over 1,500 m and is mountainous. The territory of contemporary Georgia was incorporated into the Russian Empire at the beginning of the 19th century. After 1917, Georgia became an independent republic for a short time before being forcefully incorporated into the new Bolshevist state in 1921. In 1936, Georgia received the status of an SSR within the framework of the Soviet Union.

Georgia has a multinational population; in 1989 it had 5.4 million inhabitants, 70 percent of whom were Georgians. Armenians (8 percent), Russians (6.3 percent), Azeris (5.7 percent), Ossets (3 percent), and Abkhaz (1.8 percent) were the larger minority groups. There were three autonomous, ethnically defined regions within Georgia. The Autonomous Region of South Ossetia in the north, and the Autonomous Republics of Abkhazia and Ajaria in the west, at the Black Sea coast. The Abkhaz comprised only 17.8 percent of the total population of 525,000 in their ASSR. The Georgians, with 45.7 percent of the population, constituted the largest group.

In South Ossetia, in contrast, the titular nation constituted 66 percent of the total population of around 100,000. With 29 percent of the population, Georgians made up the largest minority. A further 100,000 Ossets lived outside the AO in the rest of Georgia, and 335,000 Ossets lived in North Ossetia, which now belongs to the Russian Federation, and which is linked with South Ossetia by a tunnel through the

Caucasus Massif. In Ajaria, the third autonomous region in Georgia, about 63 percent of the population were Ajars.[1]

Georgia possesses no mineral resources. The products of Georgian agriculture, especially wine and other alcoholic beverages, but also citrus fruits, grown mostly in Abkhazia, and tea, brought large profits on the Soviet market (especially in the shadow economy). Living standards during the Soviet period in Georgia were noticeably higher than in other Soviet republics, with the exception of the Baltic states, even if this is not reflected in the official Soviet statistics.[2] The 1980s in Georgia was a period of especially rapid growth in the shadow economy, and at the end of the decade (i.e., at the end of the Soviet Union), significantly more was produced in the shadow economy than in the official economy. Even if reliable data are lacking, it can be cautiously estimated that there had been no negative growth in per capita income in Georgia before the escalation of the first of the three conflicts, the war against South Ossetia in November 1989. After 1989, the consequences of the collapse of the Soviet Union were exacerbated by the effects of the internal wars in Georgia, and the Georgian economy started to shrink dramatically: in 1990 by 11.1 percent, in 1991 by 20.6 percent, in 1992 by 43.4 percent, and in 1994 by 40.0 percent.[3] The civil war for power in Tbilisi and the war against Abkhazia took place, therefore, in a period when the official economy barely existed any more.

Georgia's Way to War

During the early years of perestroika, Georgia was a relatively peaceful republic, ruled by an ethnically homogenous Georgian *nomenklatura* that was organized into closely knit patronage networks and skilled in exploiting the lucrative opportunities offered by the Georgian shadow economy. A Georgian nationalist discourse opposing Soviet assimilationist policies had been present sporadically since the 1970s, but a real opposition movement had not existed. It was not until the beginning of 1988 that an oppositional nationalist discourse similar to that which existed in the Baltic states and Armenia—a discourse representing religious, cultural, and political concerns—established itself in Georgia.[4]

Among the first oppositional groupings was the Ilya Chavchavadze Society, founded by the dissidents Giorgi Chanturia, Irakli Tsereteli, and Tamar Chkeidze. The Ilya Chavchavadze Society was a broad platform for dissidents and parts of the liberal intelligentsia. At the same time, foreign-language specialist Zviad Gamsakhurdia and musicologist Merab Kostava, both dissidents who had spent some time in Soviet prisons and thus had considerable prestige within the emerging national movement, created the Helsinki Union. At that time, both groupings were mainly concerned with issues of Georgian national culture. In 1988, radical leaders broke away from these groupings to form new, more politicized and more nationalist movements: Gamsakhurdia and Kostava formed the Society of St. Ilya the Righteous, Tsereteli founded the National Independence Party, and Girogi Chanturia built up his National Democratic Party. The latter was the first group with an explicitly separatist program. Already in its early stages, what was to become the leitmotif of the Georgian national movement became visible: small groupings with only rudimentary internal organizational capacities, formed around charismatic leaders and personal ties rather than a program, with a tendency toward fragmentation and radicalization.

The nationalist tide soon grew stronger and developed variations on a general theme, such as Georgian victimization, distortion of Georgia's national history, prohibition of a national memory, and imposition of Russian-Soviet foreign rule. Even the pro-Communist Rustaveli Society appropriated the main elements of the nationalist discourse (short of the demand for independence).[5] Beginning in 1989, the radical Georgian nationalists dominated the public sphere. The more radical groupings around Chanturia, Kostava, Tsereteli, and Gamakhurdia were pivotal in organizing mass demonstrations in Tbilisi. Already in November 1988, the national opposition mobilized up to 200,000 demonstrators in order to protest a proposed constitutional change that would have given the new USSR Congress of People's Deputies the right to impose union law over republican law. By the end of 1988, the national mobilization had clearly developed into a real political power, posing a serious threat to Communist rule.

National mobilization in Georgia proper was mirrored (and in large part dependent on) national mobilization in Georgia's autonomous republics. The first wave of national mobilization hit Abkhazia. Abkhazia was an autonomous republic within Georgia with 525,000 inhabitants, of whom 45.7 percent were Georgians, 14.3 percent Russians, and 14.6 percent Armenians. The Abkhaz made up 17.8 percent of the population.[6] The Abkhazian-Adygean language group belongs to the North Caucasian linguistic family, akin to the Chechen-Dagestanian group and not related to the Kartvelian family of languages of which Georgian is a member. There are both Orthodox and Muslim believers among the Abkhazian population. The relationship between Georgians and Abkhaz was not free of tension during the Soviet period. The severe policies of repression under Stalin, Abkhaz' fear of Georgian demographic and political dominance, and the competition for resources between Tbilisi and Sukhumi (mainly over money transfers from Moscow, but also over cadre positions in Abkhazia and control of lucrative segments of the shadow economy) had caused political friction. As long as Soviet rule was firmly established in the region, however, this friction had not led to violent conflict between the local Abkhaz and Georgian populations.

In 1957, 1967, and 1977, Abkhazian cultural movements and parts of the intelligentsia (and some high-ranking Communist Party functionaries in 1977) requested that Moscow integrate Abkhazia into the territory of the Russian Soviet Federated Socialist Republic (RSFSR). The Soviet leadership turned down the Abkhazian request each time but compensated them by putting together a package of concessions and increased regional investment. These compensatory measures led to the Abkhaz' gaining disproportionate access to resources and to key political positions. This was particularly true at the end of the 1980s when Tbilisi was losing its grip over local Abkhazian affairs. In 1990, some 67 percent of the ministers in the Abkhaz government were Abkhaz.[7] As economic control went hand in hand with administrative power in the Soviet system, Abkhaz controlled most of the local economy.

When the national tide grew stronger among Georgians and Abkhaz, each group started to promote its discourses about past injustices. The Abkhaz complained about the shifting of demographic proportions in their republic. Primarily due to the immigration (including a government-led resettlement) of Megrelian (western Georgian) peasants to Abkhazia during the Soviet period, the proportion of Georgians in the autonomous republic had risen from 28 percent in 1914 to 45.5 percent in 1989, thus heightening competition over scarce land.[8] Abkhaz also complained that per capita investment in Abkhazia was only 40 percent of the level of investment in the rest of Georgia. This was factually correct but incorrectly interpreted as ethnic discrimination since Georgians were the largest ethnic group in Abkhazia and would thus be the main victims of a discriminatory policy. Furthermore, Abkhazia, as the "Soviet Riviera," was without a doubt one of the wealthiest regions of the

Soviet Union and enjoyed a far higher standard of living than the rest of Georgia.

The Georgian population in Abkhazia, meanwhile, complained about the disproportionate allocation of key positions in Abkhazia. In particular, control over the distribution of land was important, since produce from the Abkhazian agricultural sector, including tea, tobacco, wine, and citrus fruits, brought huge profits on the Soviet market. The Georgians in Tbilisi accused the Abkhaz of having special connections to patrons in Moscow and regarded the Abkhazian national movement as an existential threat to the ultimate objective of Georgian independence from the Soviet Union.

In June 1988, some 58 Abkhaz Communists sent a letter to the Nineteenth Party Conference in Moscow demanding the uncoupling of Abkhazia from the Georgian SSR. This demand awakened Georgian fears of a repetition of the scenario in Karabakh , when an autonomous entity in one former Soviet republic sought to be integrated into another. A mass demonstration in Abkhazia took place in March 1989 near Sukhumi at Lykhny, a place that is significant in Abkhazian history and mythology due to its holy tree and the fact that it was the historical residence of Abkhazian rulers. Some 20,000 people, including Abkhaz members of the Communist elite, signed the Declaration of Lykhny, calling for the promotion of Abkhazia to the status of a union republic, which implied secession from Georgia. The declaration was published in Abkhazian newspapers on March 24, 1989. In July 1989, the first cases of intercommunal violence occurred. Sixteen people died and hundreds were injured.[9] The clash was provoked by an attempt to divide the University of Sukhumi into two parts, one of which was to become a branch of Tbilisi State University.

The Georgian national movement reacted to Abkhaz mobilization and especially to their demand to join the Soviet Union as a union republic with a new call of its own. Throughout the country, mass demonstrations took place, combining anti-Communist and anti-Abkhazian slogans. The anti-Abkhazian mood strengthened, especially among the Georgian community in Abkhazia. In March 1989, the news of a mass demonstration of Abkhaz—at which, again, the secession of Abkhazia from Georgia had been demanded—led to one of the largest protests in Tbilisi's history. The Georgian Communist Party leadership, fearing a loss of control over the situation in the capital, asked Soviet troops to move in against the demonstrators. On the morning of April 9, the army violently broke up the demonstration. Hundreds were wounded, and 19 people were killed, mostly women and girls. The events of April 9 were a turning point in the Georgian drama, but they resonated also within the Soviet Union and beyond, dealing a fatal blow to the Communist regime's legitimacy. Virtually minutes after the brutal dispersion of the demonstration, rumors began to spread that the Soviet army had killed demonstrators with sharpened shovels and toxic gas. These rumors found their way into both Soviet and Western media and soon turned into a widely accepted version of what happened. There are good reasons to doubt this version, and I could find no eyewitnesses who actually confirmed the story. Rather, it seems that the victims were trampled to death in the mass panic that emerged when the poorly trained, poorly equipped army units started to clear the square, which was blocked by barricades made from buses.

Whatever the real course of events may have been, the bloodbath of April 9, 1989, destroyed in an instant whatever legitimacy the regime had, with immediate consequences: the national opposition became much further radicalized, and moderate voices were almost completely sidelined. After April 9, the various leaders of the national movement overtly demanded full independence; neither compromise with the authorities nor a gradual approach was an option. Public opinion rallied behind these nationalist demands, while the Communist regime lost all legitimacy and public support. Moreover, as Jonathan Wheatley argued in his authoritative account of the Georgian transition, the events of April 9 also effectively stymied all efforts to create a Popular Front along Baltic lines.[10] In the Baltic, the Popular Fronts were based on a compromise between the so-called reform Communists and the leaders of the broad national movements. It was this compromise that enabled the Baltic states to avoid sharp elite cleavages and internal fragmentation. By contrast, the Georgian national movement was not simply radicalized and internally fragmented; it was also unable to engage in any (even if only tactical) compromise with the state authorities. By default, politics in Georgia became even more deinstitutionalized.

One additional consequence of this was the emergence of paramilitary groups, especially the Mkhedrioni (horsemen, or knights). The Mkhedrioni can be described as a loosely organized paramilitary grouping that successfully combined national-patriotic symbols and rhetoric with lucrative criminal entrepreneurship. It was founded by former bank robber turned playwright Jaba Ioseliani. After April 9, the Mkhedrioni's appeal to protect and defend the Georgian population, especially women and children, from Soviet assaults was answered by many new recruits. The Mkhedrioni would soon have a crucial role in the organization of violence in Georgia.

Moscow reacted to the rapidly unfolding crisis in Georgia as it had some months earlier during the Karabakh crisis by replacing local officials. In this case, it sacked the Georgian Communist Party chief, Jumber Patiashvili, and substituted the chairman of the Georgian KGB, Givi Gumbaridze. The shock of the events of April 9 was so great, however, that the new Communist Party leadership adopted the main demands of the nationalist opposition. Far-reaching concessions were made to the national movement. First, the leaders of the movement—Zviad Gamsakhurdia, Merab Kostava, and Giorgi Chanturia—were freed from jail. In August 1989, the Communist Party–dominated Georgian Supreme Soviet passed a language law that made the use of Georgian mandatory in the public sector throughout the republic, a move that was badly received in Abkhazia (where the majority of the non-Georgian population does not know Georgian) and in South Ossetia.

In September 1989, Gumbaridze demanded before the plenum of the Central Committee in Moscow that Georgia be allowed to regulate its own internal ethnic matters and suggested that it even be allowed to form its own armed forces for this purpose. In November, the Georgian Supreme Soviet proclaimed that it would not recognize Soviet Union laws that were contrary to Georgian interests. It declared Georgia's sovereignty in March 1990, thereby nullifying all treaties concluded by the Soviet government since 1921. Gumbaridze announced that it was the aim of the party to restore Georgian independence. The new Communist Party leader's increasingly nationalistic rhetoric greatly troubled those minorities that had regional autonomy within Soviet Georgia and added to their fears of Georgian dominance.

In March 1990, the Georgian Supreme Soviet legalized all the banned opposition parties and completed its split with Moscow by declaring Georgia to be an annexed and occupied state. In reaction to these unmistakable steps toward Georgian independence from the Soviet Union, the Abkhaz took unmistakable steps toward independence from Georgia. Significantly, the Abkhazian Supreme Soviet unilaterally proclaimed

Abkhazia to be a sovereign union republic and petitioned Moscow to be incorporated into the Soviet Union as a union republic. These steps were declared invalid by the Georgian Supreme Soviet.

After Abkhazia, a second hotspot to emerge was South Ossetia. An autonomous region within Georgia, South Ossetia had a population of just over 100,000, of which 66.2 percent was Ossetian and 29 percent Georgian.[11] About one half of all families in South Ossetia were of mixed Georgian and Ossetian origin.[12] The Ossetian language belongs to the northeastern group of Iranian languages. The majority of the Ossets are Orthodox Christians, while a minority are Sunni Muslims. Between 1918 and 1921, Menshevik-ruled Georgia violently suppressed the Bolshevik revolt of the Ossets. This event has had a significant role in the Ossetian discourse on the wrongs suffered throughout the group's history. In general, however, relations between Tbilisi and Tskhinvali, as well as relations between the Georgians and the Ossets living in South Ossetia, were mostly free of serious tension until the end of 1988. But in 1989, problems between these two groups began to increase. It then became clear that South Ossetia was taking the same path as Abkhazia: one aiming at secession from an increasingly nationalistic Georgia. It wanted to be unified with North Ossetia, an autonomous republic situated in the Russian Federation.

At that time, a war of laws escalated: The Ossets countered the Georgian language law that the Georgian Supreme Soviet had passed in August 1989 by making Ossetian the official language in South Ossetia. In November 1989, the South Ossetian Regional Soviet, the area's highest legislative organ, appealed to the Georgian Supreme Soviet and the Supreme Soviet of the Soviet Union to raise the status of South Ossetia from autonomous oblast (AO) to autonomous republic (ASSR). This appeal contained nothing unconstitutional and was not exceptional during the latter years of perestroika when all AOs and ASSRs strove to have their statuses raised. Nevertheless, the Georgian Communist Party and the national opposition perceived South Ossetia's request as a step toward secession and a threat to the goal of Georgian independence.

The Georgian national movement, the most popular leader of which was now Zviad Gamsakhurdia, made use of increasing tensions with South Ossetia. On November 23, 1989, in reaction to the decision of the South Ossetian legislature to upgrade the area's status to that of a sovereign republic, 30,000 Georgian demonstrators were mobilized and bussed to a protest demonstration in Tskhinvali, the capital of South

Ossetia. Upon entering the city, the demonstrators were obstructed by Soviet security forces. Clashes followed, primarily benefiting Gamsakhurdia, who had demonstrated that he was capable of mobilizing 30,000 people and was able to force his agenda on the Georgian Communist Party leadership. In reaction to this demonstration by the Georgian nationalists, the leadership of the Adamon Nykhas group began to form the first militias in South Ossetia.[13] The Georgian population in South Ossetia began moving its transportable possessions to safety and preparing to flee should it prove necessary.

In August 1990, in preparation for the first free parliamentary elections in Georgia, the Georgian Supreme Soviet passed an electoral law forbidding the participation of groups that were only active on the regional level, essentially excluding any Ossetian party from participating in the elections. The regional South Ossetian Soviet reacted by proclaiming South Ossetia a Democratic Soviet Republic on September 20, 1990, and asked Moscow to allow it to stay within the Soviet Union. On December 9, elections were conducted in South Ossetia. The newly elected Georgian parliament, in which Gamsakhurdia's supporters formed a majority, declared the South Ossetian elections to be invalid and suspended the autonomous status of the region. A state of emergency was imposed on South Ossetia, and Interior Ministry security forces were posted to Tskhinvali.

The Gamsakhurdia government imposed an economic blockade on South Ossetia, cutting off the supply of electricity and gas, and on January 5, 1991, a 5,000-strong Georgian military formation, comprising local militias and members of the recently created Georgian National Guard, entered Tskhinvali, looting and attacking the civilian population. The blockade was maintained throughout the winter, with only sporadic clashes and the looting of a few villages. In early March, Gamsakhurdia outlined his program for resolving the crisis by restoring the "rightful authorities" in Tskhinvali and reducing South Ossetia's status to a "cultural autonomy." South Ossetia refused to participate in the referendum of March 31, 1991, to restore Georgia's independence. Two days before the voting, Gamsakhurdia ordered the newly formed National Guard to take control of Tskhinvali, but the paramilitaries retreated from the area after a couple of weeks of intensive clashes.

The level of hostilities remained low through the summer of 1991. The next escalation started in September, when Gamsakhurdia, facing an increasingly determined opposition, again ordered the National

Guard to move into South Ossetia. He obviously sought to save his presidency by scoring an impressive victory, but the National Guard saw little incentive for engaging in protracted warfare in a province that had no lootable resources. Only a few detachments attempted several attacks, but they were repelled by the better-organized Ossetian militia. In January 1992, Gamsakhurdia was ousted in a military coup (as discussed below), creating an opportunity to deescalate the conflict. Indeed, Georgia's new leader, Eduard Shevardnadze initiated negotiations, seeking to put the blame for the violence squarely on Gamsakhurdia. However, the National Guard attacked Tskhinvali again in June and burned and destroyed up to 80 percent of dwellings in the city. The aim of that "last push" was perhaps not to achieve a decisive victory but to assert a position of strength in the final round of negotiations resulting in an agreement, which was signed on June 24, 1992, by Shevardnadze, Russian President Boris Yeltsin, and representatives from South and North Ossetia. The agreement marked the end of open hostilities and established a cease-fire that was to be monitored by a joint peacekeeping force for which Russia contributed a battalion of 700 lightly armed troops. Political pressure from Moscow, and threatening gestures such as sporadic helicopter attacks on Georgian villages, forced Shevardnadze to agree to a cease-fire. In July 1992, a Russian-Georgian-Ossetian peacekeeping force under Russian leadership began monitoring a negotiated cease-fire.

By the fall of 1990, it was already clear that Georgia was falling apart. Two out of three autonomous entities, South Ossetia and Abkhazia, were largely outside Tbilisi's control. The Georgian national movement was deeply divided, and paramilitary "pro-fatherland" groups were operating largely unchecked. Yet, on April 9, 1991, exactly two years after Soviet troops violently suppressed the April demonstrations in Tbilisi, the Georgian parliament declared Georgia's independence, and on May 26, Gamsakhurdia was elected president with over 86 percent of the vote. Gamsakhurdia lasted less than a year in office. He was ousted after a coup and a subsequent civil war, Georgia's second war.

The starting point of the first Georgian civil war was the August 1991 putsch in Moscow. Gamsakhurdia, surprised by these events, declared that he was neutral in relation to the struggle for power in the Soviet Union, but he complied with the Soviet military commander's demand to integrate the Georgian National Guard into the structure of the Soviet Interior Ministry. The leader of the National Guard, Tengiz

Kitovani, however, resisted this order, which would have meant the dissolution of "his" guard, and withdrew with his troops from Tbilisi in September 1991, leaving the president without an effective military force. Moreover, Prime Minister Tengiz Sigua defected. This left Gamsakhurdia with very few armed men on whom he could rely. Kitovani and Sigua moved against the isolated and increasingly erratic Gamsakhurdia, whose vehement anti-Soviet and nationalist politics could not hide the fact that the Georgian state was falling apart and remained internationally isolated.

On December 22, 1991, approximately 500 National Guard soldiers entered Tbilisi and, after a short siege of the parliamentary building, drove the elected president into exile. On January 6, 1992, Gamsakhurdia fled to Armenia, and the opposition claimed victory. The civil war was by no means over, however. The deposed president mounted a military resistance from his home region in western Georgia against the new authorities in Tbilisi that lasted until the fall of 1993 and only came to an end when Gamsakhurdia's successor traded substantial parts of Georgia's sovereignty to Russia in exchange for military backing.

Zviad Gamsakhurdia is a controversial figure. For many Georgians, he was the messiah of Georgian independence from the Soviet Union; for many liberal intellectuals, he was a dictatorial, even fascist politician who ruined the country. Gamsakhurdia was born in Tbilisi in 1939. His father, Konstantine Gamsakhurdia (1893–1975), was one of the most famous Georgian writers of the 20th century and one of leaders of the National Liberation Movement of Georgia in the 1920s and 1930s. Zviad followed closely in his father's footsteps. Educated as a philologist, he authored a number of critical literary works and monographs, and he translated British, French, and American literature, including works by T. S. Eliot, William Shakespeare, and Charles Baudelaire. He was awarded a professorship at Tbilisi State University and enjoyed membership of the prestigious Writers' Union of Georgia between 1966–1977 and 1981–1992.

Behind the official facade, however, this distinguished man of letters was active in the underground network of samizdat publishers, contributing to a wide variety of political periodicals. In 1955, Gamsakhurdia established a youth underground group, which he called the Gorgasliani (a reference to the ancient line of Georgian kings), that sought to circulate reports of human rights abuses. In 1973, Gamsakhurdia cofounded the Initiative Group for the Defense of Human Rights. In

1974, he became the first Georgian member of Amnesty International, and in 1977 he cofounded the Georgian Helsinki Group.

In 1956, Gamsakhurdia was arrested during demonstrations in Tbilisi against the Soviet policy of Russification and was arrested again in 1958 for distributing anti-Communist literature and proclamations. He was confined for six months to a mental hospital in Tbilisi, where he was diagnosed as suffering from "psychopathy with decompensation," thus perhaps becoming an early victim of what became a widespread policy of using psychiatry as a means of political suppression in the Soviet Union. In 1977, a nationwide crackdown on human rights activists was instigated across the Soviet Union. First Secretary of the Georgian Communist Party Eduard Shevardnadze ordered the arrest of Gamsakhurdia and his fellow dissident Merab Kostava. The two men were sentenced to three years of hard labor plus three years of exile for "anti-Soviet activities."

At the end of June 1979, after serving only two years of his sentence, Gamsakhurdia was pardoned. The circumstances of his release from jail are controversial (Kostava remained in prison until 1987). The authorities claimed that he had confessed to the charges and recanted his beliefs. His supporters, family, and Merab Kostava claimed that his recantation was coerced by the KGB, and although he publicly acknowledged that certain aspects of his anti-Soviet endeavors were mistaken, he did not renounce his leadership of the dissident movement in Georgia. Gamsakhurdia returned to dissident activities soon after his release, continuing to contribute to samizdat periodicals and campaigning for the release of Kostava. When Soviet leader Mikhail Gorbachev initiated his policy of glasnost, Gamsakhurdia soon played a leading role in the national movement. He became the first president of independent Georgia.

During his short career as a politician, Gamsakhurdia capitalized both on his merits as a dissident and on his prestige as an intellectual, and he arguably mixed politics with his convictions about the "mission" of the Georgian nation. For example, in May 1990, in the midst of the political turmoil that the unmaking of the Soviet Union created, he delivered a speech at the Tbilisi philharmonic, in which he developed rather opaque theories about the "spiritual mission of Georgia" and the "ethnogeny of Georgians." Whatever the merits of these theories were, it was quite clear that there was little room in his thinking for those liberal values that may have helped defuse rising tension between various ethnic groups in Georgia. The final stages of Gamsakhurdia's career as a politician were marked by an increasingly authoritarian attitude, populist mobilization, and constant struggles with an opposition that rallied around the National Congress but that was also supported by the old cadres and an urban intelligentsia that increasingly feared the disastrous consequences of Gamsakhurdia's erratic politics. On December 31, 1993, Zviad Gamsakhurdia died under murky circumstances. He was found dead in the village of Khibula in the Samegrelo region of western Georgia. According to British press reports, the body was found with a single bullet wound to the head. A variety of reasons have been given for his death, but most observers outside Georgia accept the view that it was suicide.

With the flight of Gamsakhurdia from Tbilisi in January 1992, what was left of Georgia was de facto governed by the commanders of two militias, Kitovani (commander of the National Front) and Ioseliani (commander of the Mkhedrioni). Kitovani, Ioseliani, and former Prime Minister Sigua formed a triumvirate that went under the name of the Military Council. The new authorities faced considerable challenges: the country was visibly falling apart, and its leaders lacked both domestic and international legitimacy. In a quite surprising move, the new leaders declared their commitment to democracy and signaled their willingness to work together with all political parties and leaders in order to restore order, and they called Eduard Shevardnadze back to Georgia, to be head of state.

Shevardnadze, who had served as Soviet foreign minister during Gorbachev's most innovative phase, commanded a high reputation internationally and within Georgia and was widely seen as a senior statesman who could lead Georgia out of civil war. After his return on March 7, 1992, Shevardnadze was named chairman of a transitional government, the State Council, and entrusted with the task of leading the country out of civil war. In view of the circumstances, this task was extremely complex: in South Ossetia, the war could no longer be won; the conflict with Abkhazia threatened to reescalate at any moment; and deposed President Gamsakhurdia was operating with units loyal to him in western Georgia. In addition, Russia, as the successor state to the Soviet Union, put Georgia under pressure to join the newly formed Commonwealth of Independent States (CIS) and to agree to a Russian military presence in the country. Shevardnadze's only (and very unreliable) backing at this time was his coalition with the entrepreneurs of violence, Ioseliani and Kitovani.

Simultaneous with the deescalation in South Ossetia, a new increase in violence took place in Abkhazia. For several years, the Georgian-Abkhazian conflict had been chiefly a war of laws (issued by the respective parliaments). On August 25, 1990, the Abkhazian Supreme Soviet proclaimed Abkhazia to be a union republic within the Soviet Union. This decision was immediately declared invalid by the Georgian Supreme Soviet. One serious attempt at reaching a compromise was made in August 1991, when Gamsakhurdia reached a power-sharing deal with the Abkhazian leadership in the form of an electoral code whereby electoral districts would be demarcated according to ethnic lines, effectively giving each group a quota of seats in the new 65-seat Abkhazian parliament. Thus, the Georgian population (representing 45.7 percent of the population of Abkhazia in 1989) would receive 26 seats; the Abkhaz (17.8 percent) would receive 28 seats; and the other groups (primarily Armenians [14.6 percent] and Russians [14.3 percent]) would receive the remaining 11 seats. A two-thirds majority was required to make decisions on constitutional issues, thus preventing either of the main groups from pushing through constitutional amendments without the consent of the other.[14] On September 29, 1991, elections were held to the Abkhazian Supreme Soviet on the basis of this law, with a second round of voting held on October 13 and December 1. In the long run, however, the 1991 agreement would not be honored.

One reason that this agreement failed was the collapse of the Gamsakhurdia government, which had several major repercussions. First, because the new Shevardnadze administration was doing everything it could to delegitimize Gamsakhurdia, it was reluctant to lend active support to a power-sharing arrangement forged by him. Second, in response to criticism from Gamsakhurdia's supporters that Shevardnadze's government was "Moscow's puppet," the new government sought to portray itself as an even stauncher defender of national interests than Gamsakhurdia. For this reason, it was tempting for the government to portray the 1991 agreement as a "betrayal of the national interest." Third, the Abkhazian leadership saw a window of opportunity in the breakdown of authority and legitimacy in Georgia, and on July 23, 1992, members of the Abkhazian Supreme Soviet, without attempting to secure a two-thirds majority in accordance with the power-sharing compromise agreement of August 1991, passed a law reinstating the draft 1925 Abkhazian Constitution adopted by the All-Abkhazian Congress of Soviets that declared Abkhazia to be a sovereign state.

Tensions increased once more in August 1992, when troops supporting Gamsakhurdia kidnapped the Georgian minister of the interior and a parliamentary deputy, and were said to have brought their hostages to the district of Gali within Abkhazia. Whatever the truth of this allegation, Georgian troops took it as a justification for entering Abkhazia. On August 14, 1992, some 5,000 soldiers of the National Guard moved into Abkhazia and entered Sukhumi; another 1,000 guardsmen landed in Gagra, blocking Abkhazia's border with Russia. The Abkhazian parliament retreated to Gudauta and declared mobilization against Georgia's "invasion"; its armed forces (no stronger than 1,000) took defensive positions along the River Gumista, with the Russian airbase to their immediate rear.

For the first week of the war, Georgian troops were busy looting Sukhumi and Gagra, but then they discovered that the enemy was serious about protracted resistance. By the end of September, up to 1,000 armed volunteers arrived from the Russian North Caucasus via mountain passes to support the Abkhaz. On October 2–3, a surprise attack was launched on Gagra, where an isolated Georgian grouping was soundly defeated. After restoring the main line of communications with Russia, the Abkhazian de facto government started to build up its forces.

One of the most serious controversies in the Abkhazian war involves the role of Russia. Officially the Russian government tried to mediate the cessation of hostilities on the basis of a compromise, less concerned about the fate of Abkhazia than about its control over the North Caucasus. At the same time, Russian forces deployed in Abkhazia provided direct support for the rebels. The Abkhazians attempted an offensive in mid-July 1993 and launched their decisive attack on Sukhumi in mid September, despite the cease-fire agreement of 27 July, guaranteed by Russia. Sukhumi fell on 27 September, and by the end of the month Abkhazian forces had driven the demoralized National Guard south of the River Inguri, establishing control over the whole territory of Abkhazia and forcing some 200,000 Georgians to flee. That was the end of the war, which was confirmed by the deployment of 3,000 Russian peacekeepers in July 1994 under a CIS mandate and UN monitoring by the 100-strong United Nations Observer Mission in Georgia. That operation, however, has not helped in setting an effective framework for the peace process; negotiations on resolving the conflict remain deadlocked, while fighting occasionally resumes. The most serious clashes occurred in May 1997 and October 2001.

After the defeat in the war in Abkhazia, Georgia was forced to end its opposition to the CIS by becoming a full member and to sign a series of security cooperation agreements. In June 1994, the Abkhazian and Georgian authorities agreed to the deployment of Russian peacekeepers between Abkhazia and the rest of Georgia.

While the war in Abkhazia was still going on, a new Georgian parliament was elected on October 11, 1992. At the same time, a direct election for the chairman of parliament took place, an election for which Shevardnadze stood unopposed. He won 96 percent of the vote on a 74 percent turnout. On November 6, 1992, the new parliament ratified the Law on State Power—making Shevardnadze chief executive, supreme commander of the armed forces, and head of state. Shevardnadze became president after the new constitution was ratified on August 24, 1995, and elections to the post were held on November 5, 1995. Shevardnadze won 74 percent of the vote in 1995, according to official figures.

These elections gave Shevardnadze the democratic and constitutional legitimacy that he had lacked during his assumption of power. After his failure to reestablish control over South Ossetia and Abkhazia, Shevardnadze faced off against Ioseliani and Kitovani, the paramilitary leaders who had called him back to Georgia in 1992 in the expectation that they would be able to control him with their paramilitary groups. Shevardnadze first neutralized the National Guard under Kitovani and gradually integrated it into the state structure. In May 1993, Shevardnadze dismissed Kitovani as minister of defense and in February 1994 Kitovani's protégé, Giorgi Karkarashvili, resigned and was replaced by a Shevardnadze loyalist, Vardiko Nadibaidze. In January 1995, in a last desperate bid for power, Kitovani (with the support of Tengiz Sigua) led a motley force of some 700 lightly armed supporters in a bid to retake Abkhazia. They were stopped by Georgian police and arrested. Meanwhile, in the autumn of 1993 Shevardnadze still had to rely on Ioseliani and his Mkhedrioni to defeat the forces loyal to ousted President Gamsakhurdia. Only in early 1995 did Shevardnadze order his Interior Ministry troops to take on the Mkhedrioni units. In fact, Ioseliani's deputy and the former Georgian minister of internal affairs, Temur Khachishvili, now deputy minister of state security, remained in their posts until the middle of 1995. Not until after the August 1995 assassination attempt against Shevardnadze were Ioseliani and Khachishvili arrested.

Ethnofederalism, Mobilization, and Fragmentation

With hindsight, it is possible to identify the main elements of this highly complex narrative of the Georgian drama, at the end of which one of the most beautiful and prosperous Soviet republics was devastated by a series of internal wars. It was the destructive mechanism of Soviet ethnofederalism, the internal fragmentation of the oppositional nationalist elite, and the unhealthy cooperation between a feeble state and private entrepreneurs of violence that, in the end, unleashed the Georgian wars.

The extent to which the process of mobilization of Georgians, Abkhaz, and Ossets was shaped by the institutions of the Soviet federal system becomes quite clear when contrasting the mobilization of Abkhaz and Ossets to the nonmobilization of other ethnic groups within Georgia. Ossets and Abkhaz are not the only, nor even the largest, national minorities in Georgia. In 1989, some 8 percent of Georgia's population was Armenian and 5.7 percent Azerbaijani. The largest number of both groups lived in relatively compact areas of settlement in southern Georgia, on the borders with Armenia and Azerbaijan. Yet, Armenians and Azerbaijanis living in Georgia did not mobilize, and in contrast to the Ossets and Abkhaz, they demonstrated no separatist tendencies. Decisively, the Abkhaz and Ossets already had their own autonomy and were equipped with political institutions and symbols that facilitated mobilization and secession. Armenians and Azerbaijanis, on the other hand, were not in autonomous regions or republics within Georgia. South Ossetia and Abkhazia, therefore, turned out to be powerful examples of the potentially subversive mechanism of Soviet ethnofederalism.[15] (The third autonomous region within Georgia, Ajaria, did not embark on a secessionist course; the reasons for this are discussed in chapter 7, "Wars That Did Not Happen.")

Soviet ethnofederalism facilitated mobilization and separatism in the autonomous regions in different ways. First and most important, the substantial privileges enjoyed by the titular nations of the autonomous regions in the Soviet Union were threatened by Georgian moves toward independence. This was especially clear in the case of Abkhazia. As a result of demographic shifts in the Soviet period, the Abkhaz made up only 17.8 percent of the entire population of Abkhazia in 1989, while the Georgians comprised 45.7 percent. But because they held the key bureaucratic positions, the Abkhazian elite at that time had disproportionate access to political and economic resources.[16] Moscow's increasing weakness, together with the gradual destabilization of political control and property rights, threatened this system, particularly the privileged position of the Abkhaz.

Consequently, both groups mobilized in response to the new circumstances. The Georgians, hoping that they could take advantage of their position of relative majority, had the goal of abolishing the system of disproportional access to resources for the Abkhaz. The Abkhaz, who hoped for support from Moscow, sought to maintain the status quo or even to improve their political position. From this perspective, it was predictable that the Abkhaz would campaign for their autonomous republic to be directly subordinated to the Soviet Union. The demand for independence arose when the Soviet Union perished, depriving the Abkhaz of this potential umbrella. For the Georgian national movement, in contrast, Abkhazian loyalty to Moscow, inspired initially by predominantly economic interests, proved that they were the "servants of the Soviet empire," thus threatening Georgia's national struggle for independence. In this way, a conflict over resources was ethnically reinterpreted and harnessed to aid mobilization.

In addition, mobilization for separatism was favored by the fact that groups with autonomous entities, in contrast to national groups without their own territory, had political institutions that elites could exploit. In Abkhazia and South Ossetia, the national movements quickly gained ascendance in the context of a general crisis in the Soviet political system. In both entities, there was fierce competition for control over the local state structures between national elites. Communist officials participated in the rallies in Abkhazia and South Ossetia, putting their state and party resources at the disposal of their own national movements. Similarly, both the Ossetian and the Abkhazian elites embodied a "personal union" of the national intelligentsia and Communist Party officeholders. In both cases, the separatist activities soon shifted to the legislative bodies (soviets). Both the South Ossetian and the Abkhazian soviets turned repeatedly to Moscow with the request to be directly subordinated to the Soviet center. Both legislatures initially followed Soviet procedures, thus gaining a certain degree of formal legitimacy that was difficult for the government in Tbilisi to contest, particularly when Georgia had itself ceased to play by Soviet rules.

Moreover, the Soviet central government encouraged the separatist aspirations of the autonomous entities within the various union republics—sometimes deliberately, sometimes involuntarily. The principle of divide and rule had been a core element of Soviet nationality policy since the Stalin era. In some cases, the autonomous units in the union republics were then used as a counterbalance to nationalist stirrings of the titular nation of a union republic. The titular nations of subordinated autonomies particularly profited from this arrangement, gaining a disproportionate access to resources, at least as long as their loyalty to Moscow was not questioned. In the late perestroika period, Moscow reverted to this procedure and largely supported both South Ossetia and Abkhazia against Georgia politically and, after the outbreak of hostilities, militarily as well. The Georgian side, struggling to explain away its two military defeats, often exaggerated this assistance. But South Ossetia and Abkhazia, before the outbreak of war, almost certainly overestimated Moscow's real levers of influence. Distorted assessments doubtless did shape the separatist agendas in South Ossetia and Abkhazia.

Along with the drive of ethnonational mobilization and the enabling institutions of Soviet ethnofederalism, internal divisions among the new Georgian elites also paved the way for organized violence by preventing the consolidation of newly won independence.[17] The story of Georgia's national movement is a story of increasing radicalization and fragmentation.[18]

Surfing the wave of national mobilizations, the various nationalist groupings had already proved that they could mobilize hundreds of thousands of demonstrators in 1988. The traumatic events of April 9, 1989, strengthened the radical leaders over the moderates and turned the national movement into a serious political force—but a force that was internally fragmented and unwilling to engage in a tactical compromise, not to speak of cooperation, with the Communist regime. The first visible split within the movement related to the tensions in South Ossetia. Gamsakhurdia, by far the most popular leader, and seen by many of his followers as a sort of Georgian messiah, had a long record of defending what he perceived as the interests of Georgians within Georgia. Predictably, he took a radical stance toward the Ossets' separatist aspirations, as he regarded them to be "guests"—as relatively new migrants—in Georgia anyway. In November 1989, he organized a protest march to South Ossetia's capital, Tskhinvali, which was blocked only by Soviet Interior Ministry troops, thus preventing a probable bloodbath. Other leaders of the national movement, among them the leader of the National Democratic Party, Chanturia, thought Gamsakhurdia's preoccupation with the issue of ethnic minorities within Georgia was far less important, and even damaging, to the overall objective of Georgia's independence from the Soviet Union.

A second blow to the internal cohesion of the national movement came with the elections to the Supreme Soviet of Georgia, which were planned for March 1990. Initially, most groupings agreed to boycott these elections to, as they saw it, a Soviet institution and planned instead to hold elections to an alternative parliament, the National Congress. To this end, the various groupings formed a National Forum, which was meant to plan for the elections to the alternative parliament. But Gamsakhurda, facing criticism over his attitude toward Ossetia, walked out of the National Forum and set up a new loose coalition, the "Round Table," which eventually participated in the election to the Supreme Soviet. These elections took place on October 28, 1990, and saw Gamsakhurdia's Round Table winning an overwhelming majority with 54 percent of the votes and 155 out of 250 seats.[19] On September 30, shortly before the election to the Supreme Soviet took place, the National Forum went ahead with the elections to the alternative parliament. Although voter participation was not particularly high, it was sufficient to pass the 50 percent threshold the organizers had set. The National Independence Party and Chanturia's National Democratic Party came out first and second, respectively. The alternative parliament was also supported by Jaba Ioseliani, commander of the paramilitary Mkhedrioni, who even got himself a seat in the assembly.

Thus, by fall 1990, there were two "parliaments" in Georgia, the "Soviet" and the alternative, both dominated by radical nationalists although the most powerful armed grouping supported the latter. Influential patronage networks, old cadres, and the urban intelligentsia were not represented in either of these assemblies. The new legislature was thus never in a position to halt the erosion of the state. In particular, it was not able to mobilize the economic and political resources of the old cadres and patrons. Almost by default, Gamsakhurdia and his new parliament fell back on ethnonational mobilization as a means of retaining power. However, although nationalist mobilization led to electoral victory, it could not create state unity.

Organization of Violence and the Human Costs of War

The three Georgian wars had remarkably different patterns of organization, but in all three the paramilitary forces had to be built from scratch since the military structures of the Transcaucasus Military District remained under Russian control. While the spontaneous meltdown of Soviet law-and-order institutions created tempting opportunities for political actors to get access to the instruments of power, the rapid growth of militias can be explained only by a sharp decrease in recruitment costs. What emerged in Georgia in 1990–1991 as a result of the collapse of the institutional framework was a market of violence in which the demand was shaped by competing political platforms, with their various mobilization techniques, and the supply was basically the function of three parameters: the availability of young men, the availability of weapons, and the availability of financial resources.

In Georgia, the main armed groups were the National Guard (which was meant to be the core of a future national army) and the paramilitary Mkhedrioni. One of the first laws adopted by the new Georgian parliament declared the conscription of Georgians into the Soviet Armed Forces illegal—and this provided a potential pool of young men for a proto-army, the so called National Guard. The corresponding legislation was approved in January 1991 and authorized the buildup of a 12,000-strong force on the basis of conscription. Moscow reduced its financial transfers to the mutinous republic, so the Georgian government was unable to support its demand for the National Guard with meaningful resources. Instead of conscription, it had to rely on volunteers who enlisted to serve with their own weapons, and these volunteers had to rely on their weapons in order to feed themselves. Only in July 1992 did the National Guard receive a large amount of heavy armaments, including some 50 tanks, from the former Soviet arsenals in Georgia, controlled by Russia.[20]

Tengiz Kitovani, a close supporter and friend of Zviad Gamsakhurdia, was appointed first commander of the guard and also minister of defense. In the 1970s, Kitovani (born in 1939) served a prison sentence for armed assault, and in prison he had made the acquaintance of nationalist dissidents. Beginning in the early 1980s, he was very close to Gamsakhurdia. An artist by profession, Kitovani had neither military training nor experience, but he proved himself to be a very efficient fundraiser. Since state funds for the new National Guard were virtually unavailable, Kitovani engaged in targeted taxation of various shadow businesses, thus building his forces through a soft extortion racket. Later on, the guard also controlled a lucrative arms trade. Many fighters motivated by the opportunity to loot joined its operations. In particular, the campaign against Abkhazia was clearly driven by the National Guard's economic motives, including a desire to control key sectors of the region's shadow economy.

The National Guard never came close to the targeted 12,000 men; until the summer of 1991, it had around 1,000 armed men. Although the pool of sympathizers, which could be mobilized when necessary, was far larger, they were untrained and undisciplined weekend soldiers, with a general motivation for looting. In its highly unsuccessful campaigns against South Ossetia and Abkhazia, approximately 5,000 to 6,000 men were involved, fighting under the umbrella of the National Guard, but many of them were these de facto weekend fighters and volunteers.

The founder of the other group, the Mkhedrioni, Jaba Ioseliani (1926–2003), was a former patron of the Soviet underground (a so-called thief in law—a criminal observing a code of honor and commanding respect from other criminals). Born in Khashuri, Georgia, Ioseliani majored in Oriental studies at Leningrad University but did not graduate. He staged a bank robbery in Leningrad in 1948, for which he served 17 years in a Soviet jail. Released in 1965, he later served another sentence for manslaughter. He eventually returned to his native Georgia and graduated from the Georgian Institute of Theater Arts, where he became a professor. He wrote a number of popular plays and enjoyed membership in the Writer's Union of Georgia.

The Mkhedrioni funded its activities from criminal dealings, including extortion and racketeering. In 1992, it also gained control over lucrative sectors of the economy, such as the gasoline trade.[21] The Mkhedrioni saw itself as a patriotic society for the protection of Georgia, and its members often played with patriotic and religious symbols. Many displayed a large amulet with a portrait of Saint George on their chests. Essentially, the Mkhedrioni was the weapons-bearing arm of successful patriot-businessmen who put their private army at the service of the state when it waged war against secessionist minorities.

The Mkhedrioni had only very loose connections to any of the political parties or groups, but its leader, Ioseliani, had a personal antipathy toward Gamsakhurdia and treated him with the disregard that a renowned criminal authority thought appropriate for a bookish and weak intellectual. By mid 1991, the Mkhedrioni had about 1,000 fighters and around 10,000 associate members and focused their attention on getting access to arms, buying or seizing them from Soviet military garrisons. According to Ioseliani himself, he had around 800 to 1,000 men in Tbilisi alone and around 4,000 in Georgia.[22] The heyday of the Mkhedrioni came when, in 1993, Shevardnadze entrusted them with fighting supporters of the overthrown President Gamsakhurdia in West Georgia. In many respects, this war was similar to an organized looting campaign by weekend fighters, who were attracted by the calls for volunteers uttered by Ioseliani and other Mkhedrioni leaders on television. In general, volunteers formed small groups on a neighborhood basis and then obtained automatic weapons from the Mkhedrioni enlistment offices. At the height of the escalation, up to 3,000 fighters were engaged on each side. Up to 2,000 were estimated to have been killed in the fighting.

Neither the Mkhedrioni nor the National Guard was at any time under the control of the state. The Mkhedrioni opposed President Gamsakhurdia from the time it was established, and the National Guard resisted incorporation into the state structure and refused to pledge loyalty to the president. Gamsakhurdia's attempts to gain control over both organizations by means of patriotic mobilization led to an escalation of the war in Ossetia in the fall of 1991, and, in the final analysis, failed. Neither the Mkhedrioni nor the National Guard were interested in a campaign against the impoverished and already looted Ossetia. Both organizations were still less interested in coming under the control of the state because it threatened the basis of both organizations: their lucrative activity on the Georgian market of violence—in particular, the protection-racket business.

When the government attempted to establish firmer control over the National Guard and suppress the Mkhedrioni, the struggle for power in Georgia degenerated into a civil war. The warlords opted to seize political power directly, seeing the need to secure their monopoly on the extortion racket in order to sustain their paramilitary structures; they also recognized the need to find new loot. Gamsakhurdia's fate was sealed in the fall of 1991 when Kitovani and the National Guard turned against him. The battle for power in Tbilisi ended quickly after Gamsakhurdia's expulsion.

The successful coup still left the National Guard and the Mkhedrioni with the problem of a rapidly shrinking resource base that undermined their sustainability. It was a remarkable achievement that a brewing clash between them was avoided by carefully dividing the spheres of control so that the Mkhedrioni got the monopoly over the distribution of fuel and the National Guard got the profit from the arms trade. After Kitovani and Ioseliani agreed to bring Shevardnadze back, both armed groupings were "promoted": the National Guard became the "official army" (with Kitovani as the defense minister), and the Mkhedrioni became the interior forces (Temur Khachishvili, one of Ioseliani's lieutenants, became the interior minister).

It was only the defeat of the National Guard in Abkhazia, as personally painful as it was, that provided Shevardnadze with a chance to eliminate the warlords from Georgia's political arena. In late 1993, relying on assistance from Russia, Shevardnadze started to build a new security force, answerable to State Security Minister Igor Giorgadze, and was soon able to take assertive steps. In February 1994, the weakened Mkhedrioni was formally transformed into a so-called Rescue Corps. The next year, it was ordered to surrender its arms; and after the August 1995 assassination attempt on Shevardnadze, it was disbanded and its leadership arrested. Before that, in February 1995, Kitovani had been provoked into attempting a new march on Abkhazia, which was presented as a mutiny and suppressed by the security forces. In autumn 1995, relying on rehabilitated police and Interior Minister Shota Kviraia (a former KGB general), Shevardnadze also managed to get rid of Giorgadze, which left him as the undisputed leader of Georgia's armed agencies.

In Abkhazia, the capacity for the organization of violence started much later than in Georgia. Interestingly, until 1992 there was astonishingly little organized violence between local ethnic groups in Abkhazia. The ethnic balancing and functional multiculturalism of Soviet making was defended by all groups over a period of time and only destroyed by the intrusion of "foreign" paramilitary groups from Tbilisi. The escalation was a consequence of the overspill of the Georgian civil war.

When in August 1992, Kitovani's National Guard started its military campaign in Abkhazia, the Abkhazian government fled to Gudauta and called for a general mobilization. The Abkhazian National Guard, at this point around 1,000 strong and mostly equipped with light weapons, took up defensive positions along the Gumista River near the Russian air base. The war was financed primarily by Abkhazians with budget funds of the Abkhazian ASSR, with money from the local populations, and with contributions from the Turkish diaspora and Abkhazian businessmen in Moscow. The Abkhazians gained support from volunteers from the North Caucasus. Hundreds of volunteer fighters arrived, trickling through the mountain passes in small groups. Most of their weapons were from Chechnya.

Instrumental in the recruitment of these volunteer fighters was the Confederation of Mountain Peoples of the Caucasus. This was a pannationalist movement founded in August 1989 by activists from Adygea and Karachai-Cherkessia (both autonomous regions in the North Caucasus within the Russian Federation) and Abkhazia. In the early 1990s, the Confederation of Mountain Peoples of the Caucasus evolved into an insurgent political movement seeking independence for the states of the North Caucasus. While independence from Russia remained an elusive goal, the confederation was nonetheless able to build up a volunteer armed force that proved to be important during the war in Abkhazia. Later, in 1994, parts of this force became the core of the Chechen resistance against Russia.[23]

The numerically disadvantaged Abkhazians found further support from the Russian army. Officially, Russia was endeavoring to find a peaceful settlement in Abkhazia and denied any involvement in the war. But its policy of divide and rule included military support to both sides in the conflict, which, over the course of the conflict, increasingly favored the Abkhazians. The Abkhazian National Guard received weaponry from a battalion of Russian forces stationed in Sukhumi, and some volunteer training camps were under the leadership of Russian instructors.[24] Furthermore, Russia supported the Abkhazians logistically, provided them with weapons, and occasionally leveled air strikes on Georgians from an airbase in Abkhazia. The Georgian side tended to inflate the Russian contribution to the war, underplaying the fact that it also obtained its weapons exclusively from Russian supplies.

Over the course of the year, while reinforcements from the North Caucasus and Russia constantly increased the fighting strength of the Abkhazians, on the Georgian side the opposite was true. The Georgian army of fighters and plunderers started to fall apart. On September 27, 1993, the Abkhazian fighters drove the last of the Georgian troops out of Sukhumi and a few days later were in control of the entire territory of Abkhazia. The remaining Georgian population in Abkhazia, totaling around 200,000 people, fled the region.

In Ossetia also, it was the challenge from Tbilisi that sped up the mobilization of the Ossets around the Adamon Nykhas (People's Assembly), created as a political platform for advancing the claim for more autonomy. This organization, operating on a very limited manpower base and an even more limited resource base, was hard pressed to build a paramilitary structure. The main source of small arms was the Soviet army helicopter regiment based in Tskhinvali. In response to that mobilization, in the neighboring Georgian villages a self-defense force known as the Merab Kostava Society began to grow and engaged in sporadic, low-profile clashes.

In early 1990, South Ossetian forces had only 300 to 400 poorly armed fighters, who were able to hold the second line of defense behind some 500 Soviet Interior troops. But in just six months, that force grew to about 1,500 full-time fighters plus some 3,500 quick-to-mobilize volunteers; it was able to resist more determined attacks without any direct help from Moscow. The better organization of forces on the South Ossetian side was largely the result of direct material support from North Ossetia (a part of the Russian Federation). Some 320,000 Ossets lived there (out of a total population of 630,000), compared with just 60,000 in South Ossetia, so the arrival of a few hundred volunteers made a big difference when the fighting around Tskhinvali came to a head. North Ossetia had several large Soviet army garrisons, which were "leaking" arms to local militias who then delivered them to the conflict area. It should also be noted that for South Ossetia the costs of mobilizing the force were further lowered by the flow of Ossetian refugees from the rest of Georgia.

Assessing the human costs of the Georgian wars is difficult because the available data is even poorer than those for the wars in Chechnya and Karabakh, and it is hard to distinguish between civilian and noncivilian casualties.

With regard to the war in South Ossetia, most sources speak of between 500 and 600 dead.[25] Around 12,000 Georgians (out of approximately 30,000 Georgians living in South Ossetia) left the region in several waves between 1990 and 1992. At the same time, approximately 30,000 Ossets living in Georgia left for North Ossetia in response to Gamsakhurdia's nationalist urgings.

The violent struggle for power in Tbilisi (from October 1991 to November 1993) took place in two distinct locations. The actual coup against Gamsakhurdia in Tbilisi in December 1991 cost around 120 lives. The further confrontations between the opponents and supporters of Gamsakhurdia took place mainly in West Georgia, Gamsakhurdia's home. In this war approximately 2,000 were killed.[26]

The third war in Georgia was fought over the secessionist Abkhazia (August 1992–October 1993). This war was by far the bloodiest of the three Georgian conflicts, taking up to 10,000 lives, of which at least three-quarters were civilians.[27] Almost the entire Georgian population, between 230,000 and 250,000 people, were forced to leave Abkhazia.[28]

Georgian Lessons

The story of the Georgian wars highlights once again the pivotal role of the Soviet ethnofederal system. The Georgian drama resulted from the disintegration of this structure, where each level of governance was ordered hierarchically—with the union center (Moscow) at the top, the union republic (Georgia) in the middle, and finally, the autonomous republic of Abkhazia and the autonomous oblast of South Ossetia at the bottom. Over the course of events, hierarchical top-down control became increasingly loose, and secessionist pressures at lower levels gathered strength. The emergence of a sovereign Georgia was paralleled by the growing determination of forces in South Ossetia and Abkhazia to achieve their own sovereignty.

Mobilization in the third-tier units (ASSRs and AOs) was facilitated by the political institutions that these units provided to their titular groups. In Abkhazia and in South Ossetia, the national elites quickly put state and party bureaucracies at the service of the national cause. In particular, the Supreme Soviets, until 1988 little more than a simulation of representative bodies, increasingly changed into seats of political power and legitimacy that advocated and legitimized a separatist course for Tbilisi. Initially, both the Osset and the Abkhaz Soviets turned repeatedly to Moscow with the request for the respective autonomous region to be uncoupled from Georgia and directly subordinated to the Soviet Union. Formally, both legislatures initially retained the Soviet procedures, which lent their concerns a certain degree of legal legitimacy.

The separate waves of mobilization in Georgia, Abkhazia, and South Ossetia soon grew into a highly interdependent process in which each action produced a counteraction, thus further adding to the mobilization spiral. There are two elements to this spiraling. First, as Mark

Beissinger's seminal study convincingly argued in relation to mobilization processes throughout the Soviet Union, events in Georgia were interdependent and linked by what may be called the demonstration effect of successful nationalist mobilization.[29] Publics and elites closely monitored the efforts of other national movements, and every wave of mobilization that went unpunished by Moscow added energy to other national movements. In that sense, the spiral of ethnonational mobilization within Georgia was fueled not only by the rival movements of Georgians, Ossets, and Abkhaz but also by the national movements among the Baltic nations and the Armenians. Second, Georgians, Abkhaz, and Ossets mobilized in reaction to the national project of the other groups, which was perceived as a threat to their own national project. Each of these three groups came to see the ethnonational claims of the other group as mutually exclusive, and they mobilized in reaction to the other group's mobilization.

Neither the Abkhaz nor the Ossets had national independence high up on their agenda in 1988 or even 1990. Both entities actually opted to remain a part of the Soviet Union, with the status of a sovereign republic. This is arguably quite different from a national project that seeks to establish a fully independent, sovereign nation-state. One could then argue that the national project of the Ossets and Abkhaz was not so much defined by what they wanted to become but, rather, by what they did not want to be: a minority group within a rapidly nationalizing Georgia that clearly did not intend to honor the status quo that the Soviet Union had guaranteed to Ossets and Abkhaz. As a titular nation of an ASSR and an AO, each had profited from the "affirmative actions" of the Soviet Union. The Abkhazians in particular, who were only a minority within their autonomous republic, were set to lose these privileges within a nationalist Georgia. Yet, for a time, the competition between ethnonational discourses remained purely a war of words. Then it turned into a war of laws: beginning in 1989, many of the nationalist positions were turned into laws and proclamations by the revitalized Soviet legislatures, in which each authority claimed to be sovereign. But despite the fact that by now mutually exclusive claims were codified as laws, violence had not yet occurred, and the ethnically mixed communities within Abkhazia and Ossetia still avoided violence. As in the war in Bosnia, interethnic ties only broke down when the center unleashed its paramilitary forces to invade.

Violence in South Ossetia started only when Zviad Gamsakhurdia, long a champion of the rights of ethnic Georgians within the autonomous republics, unleashed the recently created, paramilitary National Guard. Whatever the personal beliefs of Gamsakhurdia, it is clear that the war was a tactical move by a nationalist populist politician who was constantly threatened with being outflanked by an extra-parliamentary radical nationalist opposition. Furthermore, the move was based on a woeful miscalculation of the costs and benefits of this war, which was quickly lost on the battlefield.

The war in Abkhazia started when the commander of the National Guard decided to move beyond his military objective (which was to free hostages and unblock railroad barricades) and attacked the capital of Sukhumi. Here again, the National Guard proved to be effective at looting and plundering but was soon defeated on the battlefield. Earlier, a power-sharing arrangement that Gamsakhurdia (perhaps while under the impression that Ossetia had been defeated) and his counterpart Ardzinba had worked out, broke down, because Gamsakhurdia lost power in a coup where his own National Guard had turned against him.

In this light, war was neither inevitable nor the direct result of mutually exclusive national projects. Rather, what transformed competing mobilization and then the war of laws into shooting wars was the inability of the new Georgian nationalist leadership to close its ranks, to co-opt paramilitary forces into state control, and to consolidate state power.

One reason for the failed consolidation of Georgian statehood is that politics in Georgia was traditionally very highly personalized and dominated by many personal rivalries and animosities, especially within the national movement. Gamsakhurdia's awkward personality was also not suited to uniting an already divided national movement. After April 9, 1989, when Russian army units killed 19 demonstrators and wounded hundreds more, the national movement became even more radicalized, opposed to any compromise with the Soviet establishment, but at the same time remained internally fragmented.

Yet another step toward fragmentation was taken when parts of the national movement boycotted the elections to the Supreme Soviet but elected an alternative national assembly. As a result, there were two "parliaments" in Georgia: one, the Supreme Soviet, was dominated by Gamsakhurdia and national populist followers; the other was dominated by an equally nationalist opposition and by the commander of the only meaningful armed group, the paramilitary Mkhedrioni. In neither assembly were the liberal intelligentsia represented. Perhaps more significant, there were no representatives of the influential nomenclature patronage-networks, which had shaped politics in Georgia over the previous decades and which commanded the large shadow economy. Hence, Gamsakhurdia, who dominated the parliament, could never tap into the economic or organizational resources of the old elite. He could only fall back on ethnonational mobilization as the key resource for retaining power, with, as it was to become clear, disastrous consequences.

Radical nationalist discourse, the factual loss of the state monopoly of violence, and the clear tendency of the Georgian "rump state" to employ the services of private violent entrepreneurs paved the way for the ascendance of paramilitary groups with obvious criminal-economic interests. Both the National Guard and the Mkhedrioni "taxed" the economy, engaged in criminal activities, and, when sent to war, did more looting than fighting. Both groups de facto operated beyond the control of the state and remained undisciplined paramilitary organizations, loyal only to their commanders, who combined "patriotic" with purely profit-seeking motivations. The escalation of the wars in Ossetia and Abkhazia was related less to a Georgian "grand policy" than to the fact that the Georgian rump had to rely on these loot-seeking groups, which it never could control.

This narrative of the Georgian wars has very much focused on domestic politics and especially on the fragmentation and radicalization of the national movement. The period was dominated by the very clear primacy of domestic policies, and events were shaped by local institutional structures and their interaction with the center in Moscow. None of the political actors normally thought to have an interest in the South Caucasus—Turkey, Iran, Armenia, Azerbaijan, the United States, and the European Union—significantly influenced Georgian domestic conflicts between 1988 and 1993.

An exception is obviously the Soviet Union and—after its dissolution —Russia. It would be wrong to deny the influence of Moscow on the events in Georgia, but it is equally wrong to attribute all of Georgia's misfortunes to a malicious, well-planned imperial policy, as many Georgians and some Western observers did and still do. In fact, from at least the summer of 1990 on, Moscow was not capable of formulating a coordinated policy, let alone implementing one, due to the country's accelerating economic collapse and the ongoing power struggles in the Kremlin. In the Caucasus, poorly planned and executed operations to "restore" peace multiplied, such as the actions taken against demonstrators at Yerevan Airport in July 1988 and in Tbilisi on April 9, 1989. In the final analysis, these operations served only to speed the erosion of the Soviet monopoly of violence and the collapse of statehood, and to give momentum to the national movements. All this, in turn, added fuel to the conflicts within Georgia but certainly was not the intended consequence.

In its struggle against the secessionist union republics, it is undeniable that the Soviet central government sought a tactical alliance with national movements in autonomous regions and republics. It thus provided incentives for South Ossetia and Abkhazia to push for their own independence from Georgia. However, a prominent role for Soviet or Russian politics is not visible in any of the crucial watershed decisions on Georgia's road to war, and neither the fragmentation of the national movement nor Gamsakhurdia's radical nationalist populism and the emergence of national-patriotic paramilitary forces can be blamed on Russia. Once war started, the Russian army enforced a cease-fire in South Ossetia, and it militarily supported the Abkhazians against the Georgian forces. Thus, while Russia cannot be blamed for the wars in Georgia, it does bear some responsibility for the outcomes of these wars.

The story of the Georgian wars is the story of a weak transition state quickly degenerating into a failed state. However, Georgia's fatal state weakness is not a direct consequence of the Soviet collapse. Rather, it is the consequence of a transition that could not be managed because the new ruling elites could not rule: they were internally too fragmented, they were challenged by two separatist national movements, and they could neither compromise with the old *nomenklatura* nor use the remaining state structures because their fierce anti-Soviet politics had deinstitutionalized what was left of the Soviet institutions.[30] Deprived of any meaningful tools for ruling, the new Georgian elites relied on their only resources—nationalist populism. The power of nationalism that had mobilized hundreds of thousands to demonstrate in the main squares of Tbilisi, Sukhumi, and Tskhinvali, and that had swept away the Communist *nomenklatura,* was not powerful enough to unite the national movement or to consolidate statehood. The national movement remained loosely organized, highly fragmented, without a broad social base, and plagued by bitter quarrels among charismatic patrons and their clientele. As a result, paramilitary forces that were equally good at tapping into nationalist sentiments and into the shadow and criminal economy emerged. The Georgian rump state gladly embraced the offers of these groupings to add muscle to the national cause.

Georgia has no lootable natural resources, and hence the various armed groups in Georgia needed to finance themselves in other ways. The Mkhedrioni, but also the National Guard, engaged in lucrative criminal activities: they dealt in arms and weapons, smuggled tobacco and alcohol, "taxed" the formal and even more so the informal economy, manned roadblocks and extorted road fees, and took control over legal segments of the economy, such as the gasoline trade. The main entrepreneurs of violence were no newcomers to this business; they all had a track record as criminal entrepreneurs within the Soviet shadow economy. Once war started, all groupings started to loot and plunder. One factor that may explain the relatively short duration of the wars in Georgia was that the base for looting was small (especially since Ossetia was poor) and diminished quickly, which greatly reduced incentives for fighting.[31]

Diaspora groups and ethnic kin groups certainly helped to sustain the secessionist wars in Abkhazia and South Ossetia. The Ossets received substantial financial assistance and, more important, supplies and manpower from their ethnic kin across the High Caucasian Mountain Range in North Ossetia.[32] The Abkhazian fighters were helped by fighting units of North Caucasian volunteers and received further support from the Abkhaz diaspora in Turkey. Among the most prominent and effective of these units was the Abkhaz battalion of Chechen rebel leader Shamil Basayev. Basayev and his approximately 300 fighters—who later became the most formidable of the Chechen secessionist forces—actually gained their first combat experience in Abkhazia fighting the Georgians.

Demography and ethnic settlement patterns are also significant factors. Within Georgia, the Georgians made up the absolute majority, 70 percent of the population in 1989. The nationalist rhetoric and a whole raft of legal acts, which the Georgian Supreme Soviet passed before 1990, led the Abkhazian and Ossetian minorities to conclude that the Georgians in an independent Georgia would use their numerical superiority to change the status of the minorities, which had until then been privileged and had enjoyed protection from the Soviet Union. In reaction to this, they strived to secure control over the state in their autonomous regions of South Ossetia and Abkhazia, initially through an increase in the status of these regions, then by means of a transfer to Russia, and finally with the attempt to establish an independent state. The increasingly strong, secessionist tendencies of the autonomous regions were regarded in Georgia as a threat to the newly won state sovereignty. Consequently, both sides radicalized their discourses. This spiral of ethnic mobilization led to the organized violence in Ossetia and Abkhazia.

This analytical narrative offers little support for the preferred factor in the classical script, the "history of wrongs suffered." Until 1988, when the construction of antagonistic nationalist discourses started, relations between Georgia and Abkhazia or Ossetia were to a large extent untroubled by stories of wrongs suffered. Although during the Soviet period competition for resources between Tbilisi and Sukhumi, as well as the Abkhazians' fear of Georgian demographic and political dominance, had repeatedly caused political friction, but over a long period of time, this had no effect on the notably relaxed relations between the local Georgian and Abkhazian populations. The Abkhazian elite had requested the transfer of Abkhazia from Georgia to Russia several times (in 1956, 1967, and 1978). Each time the Soviet center turned down this request but compensated the region with a package of concessions and investments, which the Georgians then viewed as discrimination against the Georgian majority in Abkhazia. After glasnost allowed a public sphere to unfold, the Abkhazian national discourse thematized, among other things, the conflicts between the Georgians and the Abkhaz in the early 19th century, and the illegal, in the eyes of the Abkhaz, incorporation of Abkhazia into the short-lived Georgian republic of 1918–1921. In the final analysis, however, it must be remembered that the nationalist discourses of Georgians and Abkhaz were situative, conditioned by the looming dissolution of the Soviet Union. The Georgian national discourse was anti-Soviet; hence, in view of the feared Georgian dominance of an independent Georgia, the Abkhazian discourse was to be pro-Soviet.

Until 1988, the history of Georgian-Ossetian relations was also largely free of tension. Only with glasnost did the Ossetian nationalist discourse begin to thematize the suppression of the Bolshevist uprising of the Ossets against Menshevist Georgia between 1918 and 1921. The nationalist Georgian discourse described the Ossets as guests in Georgia and disputed their status as an autochthonous people. But the emergence of this discursive friction also was not relevant for the organization of ethnic violence.

Finally, and contrary to one of the statistically most robust findings of mainstream conflict theory, geomorphological factors, such as mountainous terrain and woodlands, played no obvious role. Mountainous terrain makes up 65 percent and 85 percent, respectively, of Abkhazia and South Ossetia.[33] The character of the terrain obviously did not matter much at the start of the struggle for power, as the conflict was centered around the capital, Tbilisi. Terrain became important only when the western province of Mingrelia became the key theater of violence. Terrain was also not particularly relevant in the South Ossetian war, which was fought primarily around the capital, Tskhinvali. In fact, high mountains were more of a problem for the rebels since their vital connection with North Ossetia was blocked during winter. Even the war in Abkhazia was not influenced that much by the mountains and forests since it was fought primarily in the narrow corridor along the coast, with very little guerrilla activity.

After the Wars

Soviet ethnofederalism no longer exercises its destructive energy, but it has left open wounds. After a decade of stalled negotiations, a solution to the Ossetian and Abkhazian conflicts is still not yet in sight. In September 2003, Abkhazia celebrated the tenth anniversary of the victory in its "war of independence"—a "victory" that came at the price of heavy political and economic dependence on Russia and international isolation. Most Abkhazians have applied for Russian citizenship, which is widely perceived as a viable gateway to some social and political security. Violence erupts periodically, and dozens of Russian peacekeeping troops, Abkhazian officials, and civilians from the different national communities have been killed since the end of war. At present, Moscow controls the situation in Abkhazia through its military presence and its economic and political support—none of which can be matched by Georgia.

The situation in South Ossetia seems more fluid. Like Abkhazia, this tiny quasi-state has become a hub for informal trade, mainly in alcohol and tobacco. Its political elite is centered around one or two powerful political clans that exploit what is a quasi-private free economic zone. In contrast to the situation in Abkhazia, Georgia and South Ossetia did take practical steps to mend their relationship after 1992. Nonetheless, a final settlement to the conflict remains out of reach. In May 2004, Georgia closed the huge and famous Ergneti Market in South Ossetia, where all sorts of goods were traded, most of them smuggled from Russia. Some analysts estimate that the Ergneti Market, essentially an illicit free economic zone, had yielded as much as US $35 million annually, a substantial portion of which ended up in the hands of the South Ossetian political elite.[34]

In short, both South Ossetia and Abkhazia remain unresolved conflicts. A solution still seems distant, given that Georgia has little to offer to the breakaway entities politically or economically and is too weak militarily to alter the situation by force. Furthermore, Russia has an interest in maintaining the status quo and in keeping its position as the veto player in the region.

6

The War over Karabakh

Background

In October 1987, the regional administration of the small Azerbaijani town of Chadakhly took the decision to transfer some land from one *kolkhoz* (collective farm) to a neighboring one; the former *kolkhoz* was administered by Armenians, the latter by Azeris. When the Armenian workforce refused to comply, the regional committee of the Communist Party fired the Armenian director of the *kolkhoz*. This measure led to demonstrations by Armenian farmers and escalated into a violent confrontation with security forces from the Azerbaijan SSR. When the news broke, public demonstrations took place in Stepanakert (in Nagorny-Karabakh) and Yerevan, demanding the transfer of Nagorny-Karabakh and Nakhichevan to the Armenian SSR. This conflict between two Soviet state farms about a piece of land marked the beginning of the conflict over Nagorny-Karabakh, an autonomous region within the SSR of Azerbaijan with a predominately Armenian population (77 percent).

The former Autonomous Oblast of Nagorny-Karabakh (NKAO) is situated in the southwest section of Azerbaijan. Its territory comprised 4,400 km^2 and in 1989, it had a population of 189,085, of which 77 percent were Armenians and 22 percent were Azerbaijanis. Approximately half of the territory of Nagorny-Karabakh is mountainous. The smallest distance between Karabakh and the eastern border of the Armenian SSR is only 6 km. After it unilaterally declared independence from Azerbaijan, the republic of Nagorny-Karabakh, which is not recognized by any state, including Armenia, laid claim to a territory of 5,001 km^2, which also includes the Shaumian region in the north.

As are all conflicts in the former Soviet Union, the Karabakh problem is closely connected to the political cartography of the early Soviet Union. From 1918 to 1921, as the South Caucasus was incorporated

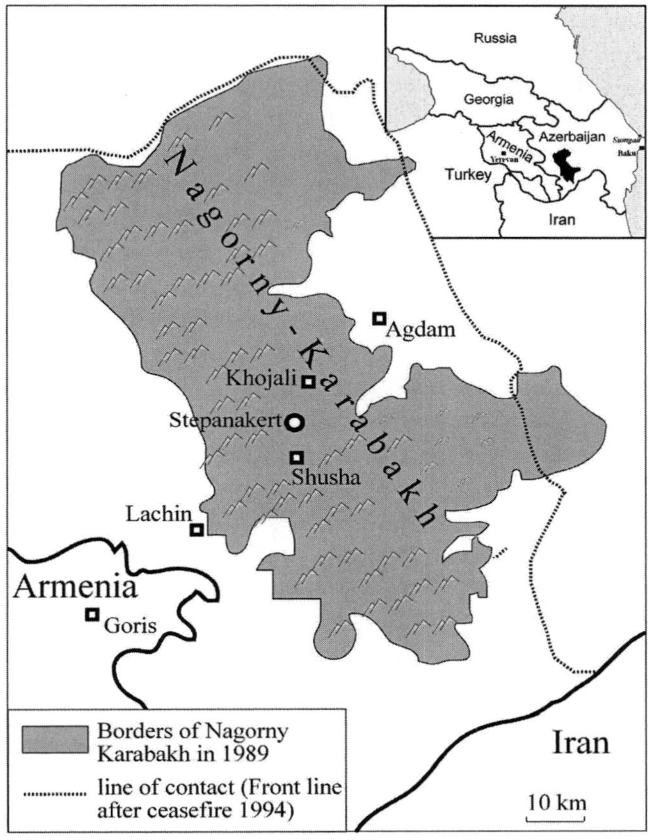

into the Soviet Union, the region of contemporary Karabakh had been de facto independent. These three years were marked by constant attempts of the Armenian population to defend this factual independence against the young Azerbaijani republic. When the Red Army entered Baku at the end of April 1920, the phase of Soviet Karabakh politics began. Initially, this seemed to herald a turn for the better for the Karabakh Armenians. On July 3, 1920, the Kavbiuro (the Caucasian section of the Russian Communist Party) decided at a sitting in Tbilisi, at which Stalin was in personal attendance, to assign Karabakh to Soviet Armenia. But only two days later, the Kavbiuro reversed this decision and decided to assign Karabakh to Azerbaijan. This decision was justified with reference to the economic dependency of Karabakh on the surrounding

Azerbaijani territory.[1] Up to the present day, the real reason for this so consequential a decision has never been fully clarified.[2]

In July 1923, Karabakh became an autonomous oblast within Azerbaijani borders, without a link to the territory of Soviet Armenia.[3] For the next 70 years, Karabakh remained an AO within Soviet Azerbaijan, with correspondingly few cultural and political rights. Karabakh Armenians did not enjoy higher education in their native language, the region had no Armenian-language electronic media and no national symbols, and the area clearly lagged behind Armenia in terms of economic development. Many Karabakh Armenians put this down to a deliberate anti-Armenian policy on the part of Baku. These unfavorable conditions led to emigration from Karabakh. Especially the better-educated Armenians left the region. In Baku, Yerevan, and Moscow, communities of émigré Karabakh Armenians were formed. At the same time, the immigration of Azerbaijanis was on the rise.[4]

After the Stalin era, the Karabakh Armenians began to make public their discontent, becoming the first national group in the Soviet Union to do so. In 1963, some 2,500 Karabakh Armenians had already signed a petition calling for Karabakh either to be put under Armenian control or to be transferred to Russia. In the same year, there were violent clashes in Stepanakert, the capital of Karabakh, which led to the death of 18 Armenians.[5] In 1965 and 1977, there were again large demonstrations in Yerevan, at which calls for the unification of Karabakh with Armenia were also made.

With the advent of perestroika, the Karabakh issue duly came back into the public eye. The conflict over Karabakh was the first large-scale ethnopolitical conflict that openly emerged in the Soviet Union, and the decaying Soviet Union failed to manage it on a grand scale. The escalation of violence is closely connected with the rapid degeneration of the state's power to enforce its will, and, still more important, with the Soviet state's loss of legitimacy. It is seen even more clearly than in other cases how, in Nagorny-Karabakh, Soviet policy, oscillating between half-hearted concessions and the erratic application of violence, in the shortest period of time convinced all conflict parties that the Karabakh question could not be solved with, but only against, the Soviet Union. The politics of the center repelled all conflict parties equally and only accelerated the construction of alternatives to Soviet rule in Armenia and Karabakh.

The question of a starting point in space and time for the conflict became as disputed as the question of what the conflict is over. From the Azerbaijani perspective, Armenian inhabitants of Nagorny-Karabakh AO started the conflict in February 1988 by unilaterally demanding the transfer of the oblast to the Armenian SSR. Armenians, in contrast, consider the pogrom against their ethnic compatriots in the industrial town of Sumgait some 30 km north of Baku at the end of February 1988 to be the immediate starting point of the conflict. In the course of seeking ultimate justification for their objectives, the ideologists of the conflicting parties pushed the question of when the conflict was started decisively backward in time. It has been increasingly linked to the question of "who was first to settle in the territory of Nagorny-Karabakh." This question gained importance in the dispute over the legitimacy of borders and administrative statuses established in the early days of Soviet rule.[6] While this issue touches on the general problem of the legitimacy of borders decided by colonial powers, "who was first" has been raised by both sides as a fundamental claim to ethnically defined ownership of land and tended to drift from population statistics around the turn of the last century backward via pre-Russian, pre-Ottoman, and pre-Persian history to prehistory itself. Volker Jacoby's view on the sometime absurd dilemma of the intellectual game of "who was first, wins" cuts through the futile debate:

> The territorilization of questions of origin is in any case highly problematic. The argument that "we were here before you" does not decide the question of origin; the latter depends on the time frame applied in order to assess autochthony or allochthony. Is the frame of reference 100 years, 200 years, 4,000 years, or 1.5 million years? In the end even zoological evidence needs to be consulted to prove a point.[7]

Against the background of the genocide of 1915, Armenians were quick to interpret the rising tensions and the intercommunal violence as a continuation of the genocide, thereby equating the "Turks" of Azerbaijan with those of the Ottoman Empire. The effectiveness of the Armenian nationalist discourse turned the Karabakh conflict into a question of the life or death of the nation. The cornerstone of these discourses was the latent danger of a fresh genocide at the hands of the "Turks" (in this case the Azeris), the fear of being abandoned again by a presumed ally (in this case the Soviet Union), and the demographic threat to Karabakh, where the ethnic proportions had shifted slightly in favor of the Azeris due to migration and a higher birthrate.

One of the many peculiarities of the Karabakh conflict is the pervasiveness of this particular interpretative routine in Armenia, and how it soon structured the discourse of the national movement in its struggle against the Soviet regime. "Genocide" became a key word, which had several connotations. "White" genocide or "white" massacre denoted the repression, assimilation, or forced migration of Armenians from their historical lands (which were supposedly far larger than Soviet-Armenia and included Karabakh, as well as areas belonging to contemporary Turkey). "Biological" or "ecological" genocide denoted the environmental damage that Soviet industry caused in Armenia. "Physical" genocide referred to the conflict with Azerbaijan over Karabakh. By February 1988 at the latest, when at least 26 Armenians were killed in the course of anti-Armenian pogroms in the Azerbaijani city of Sumgait, the ghost of a new genocide had become omnipresent in Armenian public discourse.

A wide consensus among Armenians was that, first, the security of the nation required that Karabakh was no longer part of Azerbaijan but united with Armenia, and, second, there were no grounds for Azeris and Armenians to live together. In the context of the Soviet Union, which had, after all, provided many examples of relaxed mutliethnic environments, the almost totalitarian refusal of Armenian society to share territory made a conflict likely. The fact that the Soviet Union was decaying made it, much to the surprise of many key protagonists, a reality.

The Karabakh conflict has crucially shaped domestic politics and national identity in Armenia and in Azerbaijan, albeit in different ways. In Armenia, the Karabakh question became the crystallization point for the mass movement and thus also the driving force of change for the political system. In Azerbaijan, by contrast, Karabakh only became the dominant theme of political competition between regime and opposition in response to the Armenian mobilization. In Armenia, Karabakh has helped to overcome elite fragmentation: Karabakh became the glue to bind together incumbent and oppositional elites. However, unlike Georgia and Chechnya, where the occurrence of wars were linked to elite fragmentation, the elite unity in Armenia did not bring peace; rather, it helped organize a successful national war. In Azerbaijan, oppositional elites instrumentalized the Karabakh question in their conflict with the Communist regime. In Azerbaijan, the Karabakh question had no uniting force but was instead a political playing field, on which ever more irreconcilable divergences manifested themselves between the Moscow-oriented Communists on the one hand and the national-democratic opposition on the other. This domestic political fragmentation hindered the organization of state-run military violence and explains, to a large extent, the defeat of Azerbaijan on the battlefield.

Sequence of Events

Beginning in 1988, the conflict over Karabakh developed on four different political levels—Moscow, Karabakh, Armenia, and Azerbaijan. Additionally, on each level, a power struggle took place between Soviet officials and national-democratic challengers, the course of which was shaped by the Karabakh question. This narrative, therefore, describes the interdependencies between the events at the Moscow center, as well as in Armenia, in Nagorny-Karabakh, and in Azerbaijan. All four levels are closely connected: on the one hand, by the vertical hierarchies of the Soviet Union, functional up to the beginning of 1990, which made Moscow *nolens volens* an arbitrator in this conflict; on the other hand, by the fact that Armenians, Karabakh Armenians, and Azerbaijanis observed mistrustfully the political events on the other levels and interpreted them according to their respective nationalist discourse.

In Armenia, the public political agenda (called into being with the onset of glasnost and perestroika) was shaped initially by three groups of issues. The first issue was the fears about threats to the environment from a chemical plant in Nairit and an atomic power station in Metsamor, near Yerevan. The second issue was the criticism of Armenian Party Secretary Karen Demirchian's leadership, as he was increasingly made responsible for the stagnation and deep-seated corruption in Armenia. The third issue, and by far the most important, was the future of Nagorny-Karabakh. On October 17, 1987, several thousand demonstrators took to the streets of Yerevan to call for the closure of the chemical plant in Nairit and the nuclear power station in Metsamor. The next day, a splinter group from these demonstrators held the first demonstration calling for the self-determination of Karabakh. Only four months later, "Karabakh" had become a rallying cry for the opposition, and the Karabakh movement became the driving force of system change in Armenia. The period between October 1987 and February 1988 was a time of historical compression, in which the range of possibilities narrowed, until in February 1988, organized violence had become almost unavoidable.

In January 1988, the Armenians dispatched a petition to Moscow, which tens of thousands had signed, to demand a referendum on the status of Karabakh. Prominent Armenians in Moscow and abroad began to put the Karabakh question on the agenda, through interviews and public discussions, and expressed the hope that perestroika would lead to a just (from the Armenian point of view) solution to the Karabakh question. In Stepanakert and in Yerevan, demonstrations became increasingly frequent.

The "movement," up to that point euphoric, suffered a severe setback, when, on February 13, 1988, the Politburo of the CPSU at a special session in Moscow decided not to change the status of Karabakh, since a change of border ran "contradictory to the interests of the working class in Armenia and Azerbaijan and would damage interethnic relations."[8] In Yerevan, up to a million people took to the streets in the following days. The demonstrators carried portraits of Gorbachev and the flags of Soviet Armenia and thus made it clear that their protest was to be understood as a vote for system-internal reform.

The Karabakh question resulted in a new dimension on February 20, 1988: impressed by the mass demonstrations in Yerevan and Stepanakert, the Karabakh regional Soviet passed a resolution at a special sitting, calling for the transfer of the region to Armenia. The Azeri deputies did not take part in the special sitting. A day later, the party leadership in Karabakh accepted the resolution with a vote of 80 to 10.[9] Thereby, both of the the most important political institutions of Soviet power—the Communist Party and the Soviet parliament—had, for the first time, taken an unambiguous stance, and one not aligned with the Moscow center, but, instead, with the demonstrators on the streets of Yerevan and Stepanakert. Formally, this was the regional Soviet and the party's perfectly legal right; de facto, however, it was unheard of for a Soviet parliament and a local party branch to actually make use of the rights they enjoyed on paper. Much to the concern of Moscow, these bodies had been brought to life by hundreds of thousands of demonstrators.

In Stepanakert and Yerevan, the tension mounted. Rumors of looming violence against Armenians circulated, and the first bloody clashes occurred in Karabakh, taking the lives of four Armenians.[10]

Moscow reacted on February 25, 1988, by dispatching the army to Yerevan, to bring the city back under control. At the same time, Gorbachev attempted to halt escalation of the conflict by meeting with the leading representatives of the protest movement in Yerevan. They had given themselves a loose organizational form on February 24, 1988, through the founding of the Organizational Committee for the Reunification of Soviet Armenia with Karabakh (hereafter referred to as the Karabakh Committee) and thus laying the first stone in the construction of a dual authority in Armenia, which only ended in the summer of 1990, when the opposition came to power.[11] Gorbachev succeeded in securing a four-week moratorium on demonstrations in Yerevan. His only real concession to the Karabakh Armenians, however, was the replacement of the party leader of many years, Boris Kevorkov, with Henrik Pogosian, who soon proved to be a fierce supporter of the Karabakh Armenians.

Only two days later, on February 27, 1988, violence broke out in Sumgait, an Azerbaijani industrial city on the Caspian Sea, the fierceness and suddenness of which surprised most Armenians and Azeris alike, despite all the tension of the previous months. For two days, an anti-Armenian mob raged in the streets, until Soviet security forces moved in. According to official sources, 26 Armenians and 6 Azeris lost their lives in these pogroms, dozens were raped or robbed, and 200 Armenian apartments and cultural institutions were ransacked.[12] The background of the attacks was never fully explained. The dominant Azerbaijani narrative refers to "outsiders," provocateurs or even Armenians, who had staged the disturbances. On the Armenian side, "Sumgait" was immediately viewed as a new stage of the genocide. The riots seem to have been triggered by a radio report in which a Moscow lawyer reported on the murder of two Azeri youths in Agdam. It is not disputed that in Sumgait (as well as later at the pogrom in Baku in January 1991), Azeri refugees from Armenia played a leading role.[13]

The Armenian Communist Party, under Karen Demirchian, reacted mildly to the events in Sumgait. The events were condemned, and a vague list of measures was announced to improve relations between Azeris and Armenians on the basis of Leninist Internationalism.[14] The

Karabakh Committee, however, condemned the Sumgait pogrom severely and made a direct connection to the genocide of 1915.

Sumgait marked the end of the first phase of the Karabakh conflict; a peaceful solution to the Karabakh problem after the events of February 1988 was not a real prospect. Furthermore, Sumgait had two important consequences. First, the obvious inability of Moscow to protect the Armenians living in Azerbaijan, or at least to put those responsible on trial, irreparably damaged Moscow's legitimacy in Armenia. Second, the Karabakh Committee, in contrast to the Armenian Communist Party, had labeled Sumgait immediately and explicitly, due to deeply rooted beliefs and the usual terminology, a genocide, and thus gained social legitimacy at the cost of the party.

Soon after the events in Sumgait, on July 18, 1988, the newly installed first secretary of the Regional Committee of Karabakh, Henrik Pogosian, addressed the presidium of the Supreme Soviet of the Soviet Union and demanded the separation of Karabakh from Azerbaijan. Interestingly, in his speech he deviated from the usual routine of stressing the economic discrimination against Karabakh within Azerbaijan. Instead, he pointed out that Karabakh was actually a productive region within the Republic of Azerbaijan: "We have not benefited from subsidies; on the contrary we have furnished essential products to the Republic." But then Pogosian set out to explain that there could be no future that entailed the two ethnic communities living side by side. Karabakh, said Pogosian, has always been inhabited by Armenians and constituted a part of their homeland, but

> for the Armenian population of the Autonomous Region, these sixty-five years of supposed "autonomy" were years of oppression. In general, all important positions in the leadership of the Autonomous Region were preserved for emissaries from Baku. . . . I would like you to understand me well: the Armenian population of Mountainous Karabakh cannot be satisfied with material goods at the expense of its national, cultural and spiritual development. . . . It is no longer a secret that a serious break has been created in the good relations between Armenians and Azerbaijanis. It will take time to bandage the wound; despite our efforts, it will require years for the wound to heal, for the bitterness and offences of both sides to be forgotten, for Sumgait to be forgotten. The representatives of the two communities are *obliged to have innumerable daily contacts*. Today these *contacts are impossible* [my

> italics] and, being realistic, they cannot be renewed soon. It is beyond the means of administration to control everyone's behaviour and to encourage expressions of understanding and the spirit of compromise. In the existing situation, the only just solution is the separation of Mountainous Karabakh from Azerbaijan. I see no other alternative.[15]

In essence, Pogosian postulated that, after Sumgait, there was no more ground for daily contact between the two communities. Given the fact that Karabakh had a multinational population, such a program, if implemented, almost inevitably would lead to ethnic cleansing.

In the aftermath of Sumgait, the formation in Armenia and Karabakh of oppositional groups accelerated. In the Karabakh Committee, a change of leadership and a tightening of the loose organizational structures took place. Previously relatively unknown people took over the leadership roles, among them orientalist Levon Ter-Petrossian, mathematician Vazgen Manukian, teacher Ashot Manucharian, mathematician Babken Ararktsian, writer Vano Siradeghian, television journalist Samvel Gevorgian, teacher Samson Khazarian, and historians Aleksan Hakobian and Hambarzum Galustian.[16] Three years later, in 1991, all these men would hold important state posts in Armenia. The steepest career of all was Levon Ter-Petrossian's. Like Zviad Gamsakhurdia in Georgia and Abulfez Elchibey in Azerbaijan, his is yet another story of an intellectual swept to presidency by the tide of nationalist mobilization.

Levon A. Ter-Petrossian was born on January 9, 1945, in Aleppo, Syria. In 1946, his family came to Armenia. In 1968, Ter-Petrossian graduated from the Oriental Studies Department of Yerevan State University and subsequently worked for four years as junior researcher at the Literature Institute of Armenia. In 1985, he began work at the Yerevan Matenadaran Institute of Ancient Manuscripts as a senior researcher. During his career as a researcher, he authored more than 70 scientific publications in Armenian, Russian, and French.

In February 1988, on the tide of national mobilization, Ter-Petrossian founded and led a section of the Karabakh Committee within the Matenadaran Institute of Ancient Manuscripts and soon became a leading figure within the National Movement. From December 10, 1988, to May 31, 1989, he was placed under house arrest, with other members of the Karabakh Committee. But in 1989, Ter-Petrossian was elected member of the board of directors of the Armenian National Movement.

Later, he became chairman of the board. On August 27, 1989, he was elected deputy of the Supreme Soviet of the Armenian SSR, and on August 4, 1990, he became chairman of the Supreme Soviet of the Republic of Armenia. Ter-Petrossian was elected the first president of the newly independent Republic of Armenia on October 16, 1991, and reelected on September 22, 1996. His popularity waned during his rule, as he sold Armenian electrical capacity to Georgia while limiting the availability of electricity in Armenia to four hours per day in order to fund the war with Azerbaijan. He was forced to step down in February 1998 after advocating additional concessions to Azerbaijan in the resolution of the conflict over Nagorny-Karabakh, a move that was opposed by the military leaders of Karabakh, whose influence over Armenian politics was so great that they forced him to resign.

Within Nagorny-Karabakh, in the spring of 1988, political organizations began to emerge that started to compete with the Soviet political institutions for control over local politics. In March, *Krunk*[17] was founded. Arkadiy Manucharov, Arkadiy Karapetian, Robert Kocharian, Henrik Pogosian, and Armenianorii Balayan were the leaders. *Krunk* was soon banned—on March 23, 1988. As an alternative, a Council of Factory Directors was formed, but this structure, despite its harmless Soviet-sounding name, was dissolved as well, when Karabakh was directly subordinated to Moscow on January 12, 1989. *Miatsum* ("Unification") was then founded as the successor organization for both *Krunk* and the Council of Factory Directors. The leaders of this organization were Robert Kocharian, Henrik Pogosian, Levon Melik-Shakhnazarian, Henrikh Grigirian, Serzh Sargsian, and M. Petrosian.[18] Soon many of these actors would form the first de facto government of Nagorny-Karabakh.

At that time, the request for unification with Armenia made by the Karabakh regional Soviet was still under official consideration. On June 13, 1988, the Azerbaijani Supreme Soviet declined the transfer of Karabakh to Armenia. But on June 15, the Armenian Supreme Soviet assented to the request and thus made a decision contrary to the explicitly expressed will of Moscow. It was not possible to effect a transfer of territory by constitutional means against the will of Moscow and Baku, however. In an attempt to overcome this stalemate with a compromise, the deputies of the Karabakh Soviet sent a formal request to the Supreme Soviet of the Soviet Union on June 21, 1988, demanding that Karabakh be temporarily directly subordinated to Moscow. The hopes and expectations of the Armenians rested now on the 19th All-Union Party Conference, where an initiative toward solving the Karabakh problem was expected. However, the actual results of the 19th All-Union Party Conference disappointed these hopes. In his speech on June 28, 1988, the general secretary of the CPSU, Mikhail Gorbachev, categorically ruled out any prospect of a change of borders again.

In response to this, the Karabakh Soviet unilaterally announced the transfer of Nagorny-Karabakh to a union with the Armenian SSR on July 12, 1988. Azerbaijan reacted by imposing a blockade on the land corridor between Karabakh and Armenia. In Yerevan, thousands took to the streets to force the Armenian Supreme Soviet to accept the transfer of the territory and to give legal endorsement to the unification of Karabakh and Armenia. The Karabakh Committee called for a general strike. When demonstrators occupied the airport, the Soviet army and Soviet security forces moved in and cleared it, leaving 63 persons injured. This created a total break between the national opposition led by the Karabakh Committee and the Soviet system.[19] In the summer of 1988, the Armenian Communist Party had lost all authority, and regime collapse was looming. At the same time, the Karabakh Committee had grown into a mass national movement whose protests were no longer those of a reform movement loyal to the system; instead, it unambiguously demanded that the Soviet system be abolished.

On July 18, 1988, a session on nationality questions took place at the Presidium of the Supreme Soviet of the Soviet Union. The session was broadcast live, and again Armenians waited in suspense for the decisions from Moscow. The session ended with fresh disappointment. Yet again, Gorbachev and the Supreme Soviet spoke out against any change in borders or status. That made it clear that the Karabakh problem was not to be solved to the Armenians' satisfaction within the framework of the institutions and procedures of the Soviet Union. The consequence was a further radicalization of the Karabakh movement. Power was now increasingly shifted to the national movement.

In the summer of 1988, violent clashes between Azeris and Armenians became frequent, and the euphemistic "forced exchange of populations" increased—omens of ethnic cleansing. Tens of thousands of Azeri refugees left Armenia and went to Russia or Azerbaijan, with thousands fleeing initially to Azeri villages in Karabakh. This fanned the violence in Karabakh, which by now had escalated to a small-scale interethnic war. Both communities began to use whatever weapons they could find, and the Armenians exploited their greater force of numbers. In the late summer of 1989, local militias, so-called self-defense groups, were formed in villages and city districts in Karabakh.[20] In November and December, there were mass expulsions of Azeris from Armenia and of Armenians from Azerbaijan, especially from Baku and Kirovobad. In the course of a few weeks, 160,000 Azeris left Armenia and 180,000 Armenians left Azerbaijan.[21]

In November 1988, the Karabakh question finally reached the heart of politics in Azerbaijan, too. Large demonstrations took place in Baku, Kirovobad, and Nakhichevan. On November 25, 1988, some 500,000 persons demonstrated in front of the government building in Baku, demanding the restoration of factual control by Azerbaijan over Karabakh and security for Azeris in Armenia. On the fringes of these demonstrations, violence flared against Armenians in Baku.

This escalation, now moving more quickly in both republics, was interrupted by a natural catastrophe of enormous proportions. On December 7, 1988, there was an earthquake in Armenia. The cities of Spitak and Stepanavan were almost completely destroyed. Hundreds of thousands were left homeless, and 25,000 died. This catastrophe brought forth an unexpectedly large wave of solidarity in the Soviet Union and worldwide. At the same time, however, the earthquake gave the CPSU a chance to restore its influence over the region. On December 10, 1988, when Gorbachev visited the stricken region, five members of the Karabakh Committee were arrested; then, on January 7, 1988, the rest of the members were detained. This step was justified with the claim that the nationalist politics of the committee hindered the efficient organization of aid work—a claim that was anything but true, since the Karabakh Committee had proved itself to be extremely efficient both in raising humanitarian assistance and in the organization of aid on the ground.

On January 12, 1989, Karabakh was temporarily directly subordinated to Moscow's control by a decree of the Presidium of the Supreme Soviet of the Soviet Union. The direct administration was carried out by the Committee of Special Administration of Nagorny-Karabakh under the leadership of Arkadiy Volsky, the personal representative of Gorbachev. Volsky became, as Tom de Waal described, "a kind of governor-general, responsible, in his own words, for everything from inseminating cows to military issues."[22] However, this measure also backfired. Despite the heightened presence of Soviet security forces, the low-scale war between Armenian and Azeri militias continued almost unimpeded, and the legitimacy of the direct administration quickly shrank in the eyes of both sides.

When the Special Administration suspended all political institutions, the Karabakh Armenians started to create their own political structures. In the summer of 1989, the Karabakh Armenians elected a Congress of Authorized Representatives of the Population of the NKAO. The Armenian National Movement supported the elections logistically, and the Special Administration did not obstruct it. The congress was made up exclusively of Armenian deputies, elected by local soviets or by village councils.[23] The deputies were mostly functionaries and representatives of the intelligentsia. On August 24, 1989, the congress elected a National Council, comprising 78 members, and its Presidium became the de facto government of Karabakh. Hence, from the summer of 1989 on, the Karabakh Armenians possessed a representative body, which, although unconstitutional, had been legitimated by a very high degree of acceptance, and a de facto government. The Karabakh National Council was immediately recognized by the Supreme Soviet of the Armenian SSR as the only legitimate representative body of Armenians in the NKAO.[24] The Supreme Soviet explained this measure as being necessary because the National Council filled a political vacuum, which developed after the establishment of the Special Administration and the suspension of local soviets.

These developments once again led to mass mobilization in Azerbaijan. The anger of the demonstrators was, first and foremost, aimed at their own Communist leadership, who had agreed to the Special Administration, and hence, in the eyes of many Azerbaijanis, taken a step toward the loss of Karabakh. The Popular Front of Azerbaijan stepped up the pressure on the Communist regime through strikes and mass demonstrations, in which up to half a million people participated. Toward the end of 1989, the Armenian National Movement and the Azerbaijani Popular Front had become legal mass movements dictating to their respective Communist regimes the political agenda on the Karabakh question.

In Armenia, the national movement was quickly gaining the upper hand over the Soviet *nomenklatura*. The founding of the Organizational Committee for the Reunification of Soviet Armenia in Armenia" back in February 1988 had marked the beginning of dual authority in Armenia, However, and unlike in Azerbaijan, Georgia, and Chechnya (but similar to the Baltic states), the struggle for power was hardly ever confrontational. Instead, the committee gradually took over the soviets and "nationalized" them, while, at the same time, the old elites, after some slight hesitation, adopted the positions of the opposition. The Armenian "revolution" was—internally—a peaceful one.[25] On the most important (and soon the only) political question—that of Karabakh—after Sumgait, there was no strategic difference between incumbents and challengers. The national-democratic movement set the pace and exerted pressure with its capacity for mass mobilization, until the Supreme Soviet assented to and sanctioned their demands according to Soviet rules, which were still valid. In the first free elections to the Supreme Soviets of the Republics, which took place in the summer of 1990, the Armenian National Movement, legalized in May 1989, won the majority, and Levon Ter-Petrossian was elected chairman of the parliament in July. The march through the institutions was thereby almost complete for the Karabakh Committee, but they took over a state in decay. In the summer of 1990, Armenia was already indirectly involved in a partisan war in Karabakh, the economic blockade imposed by Azerbaijan had paralyzed the country, and private militias competed with the remaining Soviet security services.

In Karabakh in the autumn of 1989, the rapidly escalating violence, as well as the threatened position of the Communist regimes in Baku and Yerevan, prompted Moscow to make another U-turn in its Karabakh policy. On November 28, 1989, the Supreme Soviet of the Soviet Union voted by 340 votes to 5 to end the Special Administration and to subordinate Karabakh once more to Azerbaijan, thereby returning to the status quo of 1988. This again was an ill-fated decision and was one further step toward a fait accompli. In response, the Supreme Soviet of the Armenian SSR and the National Council of Karabakh at a joint session proclaimed the Autonomous Oblast of Karabakh to be part of the Armenian SSR. The Soviet central authorities, openly challenged, reacted by introducing an occupational regime, stationing 6,000 Soviet security forces in Karabakh. By this point, the spiral of violence was out of control, however.

On January 13, 1990, some 250,000 people demonstrated in Baku against the Communist regime and against the independence movement in Karabakh. A small group of demonstrators, supposedly mostly Azeris driven out of Armenia, broke off from the main demonstration and began to beat Armenians in the streets of Baku. The attacks escalated into a pogrom against those Armenians who had not yet left Azerbaijan. Hundreds were injured, and dozens lost their lives.[26] After this massacre, 13,000 Armenians left Baku. Around 175,000 had already left the city after the pogrom at Sumgait in February 1988. Although a state of emergency was declared on the same day, the Soviet army intervened only after some days had elapsed. When, on January 19, 1990, Soviet troops marched into Baku, most Armenians had already left the city. In the following days, the Soviet army broke up all mass demonstrations and suppressed the activities of the Azerbaijani Popular Front. Hundreds of activists were arrested.

This violent restoration of the Communist regime in Azerbaijan caused more than 100 deaths, and over 1,000 people were injured.[27] Ayaz Mutalibov was appointed the new Communist Party leader. Mutalibov attempted to stabilize his regime through concessions to the Popular Front, and he declared that he would hold elections to the Supreme Soviet. The elections brought Mutalibov and the party an overwhelming victory, but the results were obviously manipulated. As a consequence, the Azerbaijani Supreme Soviet never developed into a legitimate locus of power, as had happened in the Baltic countries and in Armenia after the first free elections. Only a year after these elections, Mutalibov was forced to incorporate the national-democratic opposition into his regime. He did this by transferring the legislative authority of the Supreme Soviet to a new ad hoc body, the Milli Shura, to which 25 Communist Party members and 25 members of the democratic block belonged.[28] In this way, Mutalibov had infringed democratic principles twice—once by the manipulation of the elections, and once by abolishing the "elected" body in favor of a body bearing his own signature.

The results of these politics, which were no longer shored up by a strong security apparatus, were predictable: the opposition formed mostly outside the (greatly devalued) political institutions, as a mass protest movement, and instrumentalized "Karabakh," knowing that the government was very vulnerable over this issue, due to the unfavorable course of the war. The Karabakh question in Azerbaijan did not become a dominant political theme because of its existential significance for the nation but, instead, because it was the most suitable playing field on which to score political points off opponents. In May 1992, Mutalibov was finally overthrown by the Popular Front, in a bloodless, and to a large extent peaceful, coup, and the leader of the Popular Front, Abulfez Elchibey was elected president.

When Moscow declared a state of emergency in Karabakh on January 15, 1990, Azerbaijani security forces and Soviet troops were dispatched to Karabakh with the task of stopping the low-intensity war between Azeri and Armenian militias. The security forces were in no way up to this task. Instead of putting an end to the war, as an impartial state power, there was arbitrariness, and attacks on the Armenian civilian population, while the militias on both sides remained largely unimpeded. The Soviet forces were quickly viewed as accomplices of the Azeri militias by the Armenian militias, and thus as party to the conflict. In 1990 alone, there were more than 100 attacks on Soviet army patrols in Karabakh.[29] Almost the entire male Armenian population of Karabakh participated in the partisan war now being openly waged against the Soviet security forces.[30] The Karabakh Armenians were additionally supported by militias from Armenia.

The partisan war between Karabakh Armenians and the Soviet army, along with the intercommunal violence between Armenians and Azerbaijanis, constantly increased in intensity. In what turned out to be a final attempt to bring the situation under control through military methods, Soviet and Azerbaijani security forces launched Operation *koltso* (Ring) on April 30, 1991. The military goal was the disarmament of the Armenian militias; the political goal was very much the punishment and suppression of independence-minded Armenians.[31] Right up to the summer of 1991, military units of the 23rd Division of the 4th Soviet Army, in cooperation with troops of the Azerbaijani Interior Ministry, time and again sealed off Armenian villages, combing the settlements for partisans. Subsequently, the Armenian population of the "cleansed" village would be deported to Stepanakert, and Azeri refugees from Armenia settled in their place. Operation *koltso,* in all probability, would have failed anyway: the Soviet and Azerbaijani forces had seriously underestimated the resistance that the Armenian irregulars were able to mount, and the brutal actions against civilians swelled the ranks of the Armenian forces with highly motivated volunteers. However, the collapse of the Soviet Union also brought an end to Operation *koltso* and the Soviet army. In August 1991, the Soviet Union imploded. Armenia and Azerbaijan found themselves, almost overnight, independent sovereign states. On September 2, 1991, Karabakh declared its independence and underlined this on December 10 with a referendum.[32] In this way, the Karabakh conflict had become an international conflict.

The War

Between February 1988 and the summer of 1991, a low-intensity war had been fought in Karabakh between private militias lacking heavy weaponry, but this war had still cost around 1,000 lives.[33] In 1991, with the end of the Soviet Union and the de facto independence of Armenia, Azerbaijan, and Karabakh, the character of the war changed. The warring parties acquired heavy weaponry from the arsenals of the withdrawing Soviet army: initially automatic weapons and Soviet rocket-propelled grenades (RPGs), then mortars and GRAD multiple rocket launchers, armored personnel carriers and then finally tanks, combat helicopters, and fighter planes. Recruits, soldiers, and officers flooded back to their native republics from the disbanded Soviet army, and many of them were involved in the construction of the national army. To enable the efficient organization of the war, state organs were now brought into being to take care of recruitment and supplies. The "nationalization" of the military leadership in Azerbaijan, however, worked poorly, and, correspondingly, the war went badly for Azerbaijan.

In Karabakh proper, where fighting started as violence, demographics played against Azerbaijan. Azeris made up only 22 percent of the population in 1989, and the pool for the recruitment of self-defense units in Karabakh was accordingly small. Recruiting volunteers in the Azerbaijani mainland was difficult because the enthusiasm for the war in Karabakh was very limited, and, in contrast, the hard-pressed Communist regents (Vezirov and, from 1990 on, Mutalibov), did not encourage the formation of paramilitary groups by the national-democratic opposition, out of a perhaps well-founded fear that these groups could be used against the regime. Furthermore, the regular state troops of the Interior Ministry and the KGB were poorly motivated, and coordination with volunteer groups seldom functioned. Finally, there were also far more Soviet-trained officers on the Armenian side, due to the fact that, in the Soviet armed forces, Muslims had poorer career opportunities than non-Muslims.

In early 1992, Armenian forces began to break out of the capital of Stepanakert, capturing the Azeri villages that surrounded the town and expelling the Azeris who remained. In February 1992, Armenian forces attacked the Azeri-populated village of Khojali in Nagorny-Karabakh, which was situated near the region's airport. The assault began on February 25, four years to the day after the pogroms in Sumgait. Armored vehicles from the 366th Regiment of the Soviet army (a regiment that was still in Karabakh but had no more than 300 soldiers left) participated in the assault, which turned into a massacre. At least 485 Azeris were killed, most of them civilians.[34] Serzh Sargsian, a Karabakh military leader, is quoted by Tom de Waal to have said later on the events:

> Before Khojali the Azerbaijanis thought that they were joking with us, they thought that the Armenians were people who could not raise their hands against the civilian population. We were able to break that [stereotype]. And that's what happened. And we should take into account that amongst those boys were people who had fled from Baku and Sumgait.[35]

In May 1992, Karabakh Armenian forces took the town of Shusha, strategically located in the mountains overlooking Stepanakert, and extended control over the Lachin corridor linking Karabakh and Armenia. In June 1992, Azerbaijani forces launched an offensive in Mardakert, in northern Karabakh, and the neighboring Geranboi-Shaumian district of Azerbaijan, displacing some 40,000 Armenians, but by June 1993, Armenian forces had retaken Mardakert and gone further, to Kelbajar. By early 1993, the Armenians had secured a land link between Armenia and Karabakh and thus effectively won the war for Karabakh. In May 1994, the Bishkek Protocol was signed and a cease-fire began. To the present day, Armenian forces control an area that is far larger than the territory of the former NKAO. Around 16 percent of the territory of Azerbaijan remains occupied.[36]

The prewar conflict over Karabakh decisively shaped the Armenian national "revolution"; now, the war over Karabakh backfired on Azerbaijani politics. Unlike the situation in Armenia, in Azerbaijan there was neither a ready nationalist discourse nor a generally accepted interpretive routine. "Karabakh," therefore, never became an existential threat in Azerbaijan as it did in Armenia. Precisely for this reason, however, "Karabakh" also did not become a factor of integration, which could facilitate the reconstruction of statehood. Instead, the conflict over Karabakh was, in the contest between regime and opposition, a playing field on which decisive domestic political points could be won—but were usually lost.

Between 1991 and 1993, defeats at the front in Karabakh always had decisive consequences for politics in Baku. The fall of Shusha in May 1992 led to the overthrow of Mutalibov and to the assumption of power by the leader of the Popular Front, Abulfez Elchibey. He lasted barely more than a year before losing office. Elchibey fell partly because he and his group of politically inexperienced intellectuals and former dissidents did not manage to win the loyalty of the old professional bureaucrats and, especially, of the security apparatus. But he lost his presidency also partly because of the continued unfavorable course of the war in Karabakh. Elchibey and his administration were not able to keep their election promises regarding an efficient and successful prosecution of the war.

In the absence of a functioning state apparatus, the Popular Front war effort relied on the organized militias, which were, in turn, to a large extent dependent for financial support on local patriot-businessmen, such as, for example, Iskender Hamidov (leader of the Grey Wolves "*Bozkurt*") and Surat Husseynov (former director of a wool plant in Yevlakh in the Ganja region), but these men proved to be neither particularly loyal nor particularly efficient allies. When, in early 1993, Armenian forces took the strategically important corridor of Kelbajar, Husseynov, who was responsible for the defense of this area, was preoccupied with organizing a putsch against Elchibey.[37] The president, under great pressure, called for help from the gray eminence of Azerbaijani politics, Heydar Aliyev, former member of the Politburo, longtime chairman of the Central Committee of the Azerbaijani Communist Party. Aliyev initially let himself be co-opted as 51st member of the 50-strong parliament and was then elected chairman. He organized a plebiscite against Elchibey, which ended with a clear vote of no confidence in the president. Aliyev won the following presidential elections with a solid Soviet result of 98.8 percent, with a turnout of 90 percent. Thus began the Aliyev era, which brought Azerbaijan a stable, yet undemocratic, regime.

Organization of Violence

Between 1988 and 1990, two overlapping wars were being waged on the territory of Nagorny-Karabakh: first was a low-intensity war between local Azeri and Armenian militias in Karabakh; second was a partisan war that Armenian irregulars fought against the Soviet forces that were tasked with bringing the unruly province back under Soviet Azerbaijan's control. After the collapse of the Soviet Union in August 1991, the war developed quickly into an interstate war between Azerbaijan and Karabakh Armenia, in which both sides employed heavy armaments from the arsenals of the collapsed Soviet Union. The war efforts were now increasingly organized by the emerging state bureaucracies in Karabakh Armenia and Azerbaijan.

During the first phases of the intercommunal violence, the number of fighters taking part in the respective military operations was low, rarely more than a few dozen. However, in Karabakh, due to the all-encompassing mobilization of society, the pool of available fighters was quite large, comprising almost the entire male population that were capable of bearing arms.[38] The proportion of men between 20 and 40 amounted to about 40 percent of the population of Karabakh, or around 50,000 men. Hence, it is likely that between 1988 and 1991, the number of fighters in Karabakh was not limited by the size of the recruiting pool but, rather, by the limited supply of weapons available.

In 1998, the number of active fighters was estimated to be around 1,000. Among them were many volunteers from Armenia.[39] As the partisan war increased in intensity, the number of fighters involved in actual military operations also increased. Nevertheless, until 1990, there were rarely more than 200 fighters on each side in engagements between Armenian and Azerbaijani militias. Only as the Karabakh Armenians, in 1991, started to take control over whole Azeri villages and rural areas did the numbers of fighters involved in military actions rise. Thus, for instance, 300 to 400 Karabakh Armenians (and perhaps nearly as many Soviet soldiers of the 366th Motorized Infantry Regiment) participated in the capture of Khojhali. At the capture of Shusha in March 1992, there were around 3,000 men on the Karabakh side, and 6,000 men took part in the capture of Agdam (the largest military action of the war).[40]

The war, as with any other war, produced leaders and heroes, but in the Karabakh conflict two leading figures, Robert Kocharian and Samvel Babayan, are of particular significance because their rise (and fall, in the case of Babayan) are highly symptomatic of many aspects of organized violence in the Caucasus. Kocharian's career is the story of blocked upward social mobility within *nomenklatura* networks but finding a shortcut to power by embracing the national movement;

Babayan's career is the story of a car washer turned warlord—the Caucasian equivalent of the dishwasher turned millionaire.

Robert Kocharian was born in Stepanakert, Nagorny-Karabakh AO. Kocharian's professional career began as an engineer at Stepanakert's electrotechnical plant in 1971. After starting as a turner, he was later promoted to the post of mechanical engineer. In 1982, he graduated from Yerevan Polytechnic Institute's Electro-Technical Department with honors. Throughout the 1980s, he occupied various posts in Nagorny-Karabakh's Communist youth, and made it up to first secretary of the Komsomol, which was quite an important position within the Communist *nomenklatura* of Azerbaijan. By February 1988, Kocharian had become one of the leaders of the Karabakh movement, which strongly opposed the Azerbaijan *nomenklatura*'s rule over Karabakh. According to sociologist Georgi Derluguian, Kocharian's career within the *nomenklatura* in provincial Karabakh is to be explained by the fact that, lacking local patrons, he could not get a job in Armenia. He then returned to Nagorny-Karabakh and worked his way up to first secretary of the Komsomol. Thereafter, however, he could not further crack the Azerbaijani *nomenklatura,* which was dominated by Armenians who owed allegiance to Azeri strongman Heydar Aliyev. Seeing his upward mobility within the *nomenklatura* blocked, Kocharian gladly embraced the new career paths that opened up within the new national movement.[41] He soon became the leader of the *Miatsum* (Unification) organization. In 1991, Kocharian was elected a deputy of the Nagorny-Karabakh Republic's Supreme Soviet of the first convocation. In the course of the war for Nagorny-Karabakh, Kocharian became chairman of the State Defense Committee and the first prime minister of the Nagorny-Karabakh Republic (or NKR). Kocharian was elected its first president on December 24 on the decision of the NKR Supreme Soviet.

On March 20, 1997, Kocharian left his post as president because he was appointed prime minister of Armenia. After Ter-Petrossian's resignation (which he is said to have forced), Kocharian was elected Armenia's second president on March 30, 1998. He is rumored to have been behind the gunning down of several of his opponents on the floor of the parliament in 1999. With Kocharian elected president of Armenia, the takeover of Armenia by the "Karabakh Clan" was complete.

The second strongman of Karabakh was Samvel Babayan. His career is yet another example of the warlord-turned-minister career path, of which the Caucasus between 1989 and 1993 has quite a few examples. The holder of such titles as commander of self-defense forces of Nagorny-Karabakh, minister of defense, and lieutenant general rose to prominence during the early military phase of the war. It was a swift career path for someone whose civilian occupation before 1988 had been as a car mechanic barely out of high school and military service in the Soviet Army. Having joined a paramilitary unit before full-scale war broke out in 1991, he quickly gained in stature, rising to command his own unit and participating in the capture of Shusha in May 1992. When a unified military command was established, Babayan became commander of self-defense forces in 1993, after his predecessor Serzh Sargsian left to become Armenia's defense minister.

After the cease-fire in 1994, Babayan ruled over Karabakh almost unchecked. Allegedly, he had built up—by regional standards—a small fortune during the war, mainly by stripping the occupied Azeri territories of all saleable assets.[42] In peacetime, he appeared to have used his position to acquire land, enterprises, tax and customs privileges, and a monopoly on importing tobacco and alcoholic beverages into Armenia, using army trucks.[43] He is said to be have forced Ter-Petrossian, president of Armenia, to step down in May 1998, to make room for Robert Kocharian. Babayan fell in 2000, when he was accused of having staged an assassination attempt on the president of Karabakh. He was brought to trial and sentenced to 15 years in prison. The trial was interpreted as a showdown between a warlord and the authority of an emerging state and was closely followed in Karabakh and Armenia. The state authorities won, and the national hero, warlord, former defense minister, and entrepreneur of violence was sent to prison. Babayan was pardoned in 2004.

Before 1992, there was no state-organized army in Karabakh; the war was fought by paramilitary groups and self-defense units. The number of fighters active in Karabakh at the beginning of 1992 has been put at 7,000 to 8,000, made up of the local Karabakh militias, as well as volunteers from Armenia. There were another approximately 300 foreign fighters, recruited mostly from the Armenian diaspora in the Near East and in Western Europe.[44] At the end of 1992, the National Defense Council was founded in order to coordinate military efforts.

After 1992, the Karabakh forces were strengthened by around 13,000 soldiers from the newly founded Armenian army. At the end of 1992, therefore, there were more than 21,000 soldiers active in Karabakh; in addition, there were at least the same number of reserves. At this point in time, the Azerbaijani army had around 21,000 soldiers, of whom fewer than half were stationed in Karabakh.[45] In 1994, up to 10,000 soldiers of the Karabakh army, and up to 20,000 of the Armenian army, were involved in the conflict.[46] By this time, the Azerbaijani army had bolstered its forces to around 45,000 men.

As in all post-Soviet conflicts, the weapons were obtained from Soviet stockpiles. From 1989 on, Armenian paramilitary groups procured weapons either through attacks on the arms depots of the Soviet security forces or on the black market. After the collapse of the Soviet Union, automatic weapons from the Soviet arsenals became available in excess, and with the Tashkent Agreement on May 15, 1992, Armenia gained a share of the arsenals of the Soviet Union, including heavy armaments such as tanks, artillery, helicopters, and fighter planes. In Karabakh, a large part of the weaponry of the departing Soviet troops (including tanks) had passed into the possession of the Karabakh Armenians by 1992 at the latest.

There are no reliable data on the funding of the organization of violence in Karabakh. It is clear, however, that the large-scale national mobilization made available a very large pool of recruitable fighters, thus considerably lessening the costs of the organization of violence. In addition, Karabakh received massive support from Armenia in the form of paramilitary troops, weapons, and funding. The support from the diaspora was doubtless also significant, but there are no data on or even estimates of its size. Nevertheless, a former high-ranking official in the Armenian security apparatus said that the war was won with "Russian weapons, Turkish bread, and American money."[47]

Volunteer units to be employed in Karabakh were formed all over Armenia. In the summer of 1990, there were around 50 paramilitary groups.[48] One of the biggest groups was the Azerbaijani National Army, which had approximately 2,000 fighters; in addition, there were numerous small groups with 30 to 40 fighters. On the basis of interviews with commanders and fighters, the total number of available fighters before 1992 can be put at between 6,000 and 10,000.[49] Usually, each of the militias would send 30 to 40 of their fighters to Karabakh, who would then be relieved by the next group after two to three months. Before 1991, these groups were armed mostly with small arms from the plundered arsenals of the Soviet army and police. The militias were often organized by Armenians living in Karabakh. Although neighborhood or kinship ties were usually the organizational basis of these small groups, university institutes and faculties, *kolkhozi,* and industrial plants, as well as criminal networks, also created their own militias, as did the diaspora party, the Armenian Revolutionary Union, or Dashnaktsutiun. The militias were financed chiefly by donations (voluntary and coerced), which came from all classes of Armenian society—ranging from normal people to shadow economy entrepreneurs to the diaspora.

Among these paramilitary groups[50] were "Vardan Mamikonian" under Martun Boyadjian, a professional officer; "David-Bek," under Avo Hakobian, an engineer by training; "Surmalu" under the command of a policeman, Artur Grigorian; "X" under Alexander Tamanian, a physicist and director of the Laboratory of Physics in Yerevan; "Fifth Special Brigade" under Hovsep Hovsepian, a member of the Armenian diaspora in France; "Azatagrakan Banak" (Karabach Army of Liberation) under Leonid Azgaldian, a physicist at the State University of Moscow; and "Nikol Duman" under Albert Bazeyan, an engineer by training who later became parliamentary deputy and the leader of the veterans union Yerkrapah. A famous unit was led by Arkadi "Commandos" Ter-Tadevossian, a professional officer in the Soviet Army; the group "Crusaders" was under Karo Kaikedjian from the Armenian diapora in Syria; and the group of Monte "Avo" Melkonian was from the Armenian diaspora in California.

Melkonian was not the only diaspora commander who rose to the rank of a national hero, but surely his legend outshines the others. Monte Melkonian (1957–1993) was born in California to the family of a self-employed cabinetmaker and an elementary-school teacher. At the age of 15, he left for Japan to study martial arts and the language. From Japan he traveled on his own through southeast Asia, including Vietnam just before the north defeated the south in 1975. This trip exerted a lifelong influence on him. In a videotaped interview in early 1992, he pointed to the Vietnamese national liberation struggle as an inspirational example for the struggle of Nagorny-Karabakh. Returning to the United States, he majored in ancient Asian history and archaeology at the University of California at Berkeley. In 1978 he helped organize an exhibition of Armenian cultural artifacts at one of the university's libraries. The exhibition included the 1915–1919 genocide, the display of which a Turkish consul general tried to prevent.

After graduating from Berkeley in the spring of 1978, Melkonian traveled to Iran, where he taught English and participated in the movement to overthrow the shah. Later, he found his way to Iranian Kurdistan, where Kurdish partisans made a deep impression on him. In the fall of 1978, Melkonian made his way to Beirut, in time to participate in the defense of the Armenian quarter against the right-wing Phalange forces. Melkonian was a member of the Armenian militia in Bourj Hamound for almost two years, when he participated in several street battles against rightist forces. In the spring of 1980, he was inducted into the Armenian Secret Army for the Liberation of Armenia (ASALA). During this time, several Palestinian resistance organizations provided their Armenian comrade with extensive military training. Melkonian carried out terrorist operations in Rome, Athens, and elsewhere, and he helped to plan and train commandos for the "Van Operation" of September 24, 1981, in which four ASALA militants took over the Turkish embassy in Paris. He was arrested in Paris in November 1985 and sentenced to six years in prison for possession of falsified papers and carrying an illegal handgun. He was released in early 1989 and sent from France to South Yemen.

Eventually, he made his way to what was then still Soviet Armenia. Melkonian saw the fate of Karabakh as crucial for the long-term security of the entire Armenian nation. He first joined a volunteer brigade, then the nascent Armed Forces of the Republic of Nagorny-Karabakh where he rose to the rank of lieutenant colonel and commanded a force of as many as 4,000 men. In a year and a half of war, his legend grew among the Armenians of Karabakh, within Armenia proper, and in the diaspora. In April 1993, he was one of the chief military strategists who planned and led the operation to capture the region of Kelbajar, between the Union Republic of Armenia and Karabakh. He was killed in action in 1993. Melkonian was awarded the highest military honors of Nagorny-Karabakh and the Armenian SSR.

Monte Melkonian's biography can be found on many websites dedicated to the heroes of the war in Karabakh; his brother wrote a book titled *My Brother's Road: An American's Fateful Journey to Armenia.* There is a monument to Monte "Avo" Melkonian in the town of Martuni Monteapert, in Nagorny-Karabakh, and in California, and there is the Monte Melkonian Fund, Inc., a nonprofit charity founded in 1995. In a famous quote from his writings on the Armenian question, Melkonian wrote: "It is about time that we loudly repudiate the romantic conceit that 'My pen is my gun.' Pens are pens and guns are guns. There are more than enough 'intellectuals' in the diaspora. What we need are *fighters, soldiers, fedains.*"[51] He was one of those fighters. One can only wonder whether he might have appreciated the irony of the fact that he was fighting in a region in which intellectuals turned president had unleashed nationalist war.

After the collapse of the Soviet Union, the process of incorporating the numerous armed groups in the Armenian territory into a national army under unitary command began. With the Tashkent Agreement of May 15, 1992, in which the division of the Soviet weaponry among the successor states was settled, for the first time the army acquired large amounts of heavy weaponry. Before 1993, the army was able to dispatch around 13,000 soldiers to Karabakh. By 1994, up to 20,000 soldiers were involved in the conflict.[52]

In Azerbaijan, too, military capacities had to be built from scratch. Beginning in late 1989, "self-defense units" had been formed in the Azeri villages and some districts of Stepanakert. As a rule, they were poorly armed, and, until 1991, they only rarely used automatic weapons. These groups were reinforced by volunteer units recruited in Azerbaijan proper, especially in Baku. In the summer of 1989, the Azerbaijani Popular Front was the first to form its own paramilitary units, which sometimes contained Afghanistan veterans and were equipped with weaponry from Soviet arsenals. The recruitment of volunteer fighters was coordinated by the Council of National Defense. Later, other parties besides the Popular Front assembled units. As a rule, these militias were better motivated than the regular state security forces of the Interior Ministry and the KGB but not as well armed. Before the summer of 1992, they comprised almost 3,000 men. In addition, there were around 1,500 mercenaries, including, after 1993, several hundred Afghan Mujaheddins from Hekmatyar's force.[53] The troops from the Azerbaijani Interior Ministry and the Azerbaijani KGB in Karabakh totaled little more than 3,000.[54]

From the winter of 1990 on, they were increasingly, although not systematically, supported by Soviet security forces stationed in Karabakh (army soldiers and special police of the Interior Ministry, altogether around 15,000 men).[55] In October 1991, the Azerbaijani National Army was founded. Recruitment proved to be almost impossible before 1992, however. Thus, between December 1991 and March 1992,

TABLE 6.1
Number of Paramilitary Forces and Armies Deployed to the Karabakh War, 1988–1993

Year	*Azerbaijani Army, Security Forces*	*Azerbaijani Militias*	*Armenian and Karabakh Forces, Paramilitary and Armies*	*Soviet Units*
1988			1,000	15,000
1989			7,275	15,000
1990	3,000	300	10,000	15,000
1991	3,000	2,000	12,000	21,000
1992	23,000	4,900	20,930	2,000
1993	40,000		30,930	
1994	45,000		30,930	

Sources: My estimates and those of Gayane Novikova (2001), "The Institutional Framework of Caucasian and Central Asian Transitional Societies: Armenia and Nagorno-Karabakh," unpublished ms., World Bank DECRG Project on the Economics of Political and Common Violence, Yerevan; Arif Yunusov (1996), Statistics of the Karabakh War (Baku: Institute of Peace and Democracy); and Arif Yunusov (2001), "The Institutional Framework of Caucasian and Central Asian Transitional Societies: Azerbaijan," unpublished ms., World Bank DECRG Project on the Economics of Political and Common Violence, Baku.

Blank spaces indicate no data available.

instead of the planned 20,000 recruits, only 3,614 were mustered.[56] By the end of 1994, the number of soldiers in the army had reached 49,000.[57] Today, the army officially comprises 70,000 soldiers. Table 6.1 gives a breakdown of the deployment figures.

Human Costs of War

There are no official figures on the casualties of the war over Nagorny-Karabakh. Some estimates speak of up to 20,000 soldiers and civilians killed.[58] However, in this conflict as well, the distinction between civilians and fighters is not really meaningful, due to the character of the war. Until the end of 1992, the war between Armenians and Azerbaijanis was conducted by self-defense units and paramilitary groups who were barely distinguishable from civilians. Only after 1992 did state-run armies form on both sides. The dynamics of the proportion of dead civilians to dead fighters is nevertheless clear: between 1988 and 1992, proportionally more civilians died than between 1992 and 1994.[59] After 1992, the forced exchange of populations was completed; the interethnic, local violence, which was directed especially against civilians, lost its raison d'être. Afterward, neither of the warring parties disposed of

TABLE 6.2
Number of Casualties and Number Wounded in the Karabakh Conflict, 1988–1994

	Armenians		Azerbaijanis	
Year	*Dead*	*Wounded*	*Dead*	*Wounded*
1988	32	400	196	600
1989	20	151	51	180
1990	169	400	187	991
1991	270	400	378	496
1992	2,500	10,000	3,300	11,000
1993	1,000	3,000	2,200	6,000
1994	2,000	6,000	4,000	10,000
Total	5,991	20,351	10,312	29,267

Sources: The estimates for Armenian losses are from Gayane Novikova (2001), "The Institutional Framework of Caucasian and Central Asian Transitional Societies: Armenia and Nagorno-Karabakh," unpublished ms., World Bank DECRG Project on the Economics of Political and Common Violence, Yerevan; for Azerbaijanis, from Arif Yunusov (2001), "The Institutional Framework of Caucasian and Central Asian Transitional Societies: Azerbaijan," unpublished ms., World Bank DECRG Project on the Economics of Political and Common Violence, Baku.

the means to attack the civilian population of the other side. Thus, after 1992, fewer civilians died in comparison with other wars, for instance the war in Chechnya.

According to the data of two eminent scholars, Arif Yunusov (for Azerbaijan) and Gayane Novikova (for Armenia), 6,000 fighters and 2,500 civilians died on the Armenian side.[60] The number of casualties on the Azerbaijani side (fighters and civilians) has been put by Yunusov at a total of 10,000 dead and 30,000 injured (Table 6.2).[61]

As of 1995, as a result of the war and of the forced exchange of populations, a total of 204,667 Azeris had left Armenia and 247,000 Armenians had left Azerbaijan. These numbers do not include those migrants not fleeing to their "mother republic" but, instead, to Russia and the West. The number of internally displaced people (including, according to international law, the Azeris driven out of Nagorny-Karabakh to Azerbaijan) totaled 604,000 Azeris and 72,000 Armenians.[62]

Lessons from Karabakh

Karabakh is a showcase of what happens when the central state loses both legitimacy and coercive power. But Karabakh also proves the immense political power that a "hidden transcript" (according to James Scott, as discussed below) can unleash when it suddenly becomes a "public transcript." Moreover, in contrast to Georgia and Chechnya, Karabakh is unique insofar as external threats forged cooperation between incumbent and nationalist oppositional elites, although this cooperation did not prevent the escalation to war but, instead, led to a more effective organization of war.

Karabakh was the first of the Caucasian conflicts to erupt, and, unlike Georgia and Chechnya, it was a Soviet rather than a post-Soviet conflict. Karabakh displayed not only that the Soviet Union had no institutionalized mechanisms to deal with ethnonational conflicts but also the extent to which the Soviet center was quickly losing its coercive capacities. Hence, neither institutions nor policies were available to prevent the region from devolving into war.

Notably, until December 1989, the Karabakh Armenians attempted to handle the question of the territorial transfer in accordance with the Soviet constitution, and they made a formal request to the Soviets of Armenia, Azerbaijan, and the Soviet Union, whose agreement for the change of borders was necessary, according to the constitution. During this phase, the Armenians also pursued a further option—namely, the transfer of Karabakh to Russia. Baku rejected this territorial transfer and left the handling of the conflict to the Soviet center, which repeatedly and decisively ruled against a transfer of territory. Handling the conflict in a constitutional way was thus blocked, and tensions grew. The first violence was widely read by the Armenians as a signal that the Soviet state's monopoly was being eroded. Ill-devised, erratic, and arbitrary employment of force only made things worse. The breaking up of demonstrations at Yerevan airport, the delay in deployment after the pogroms in Sumgait, the bloody crackdown against the Popular Front in Baku in January 1990, the numerous attacks against the population of Karabakh during the period of the Special Administration, and finally Operation *koltso*—each of these activities alienated both sides (Karabakh Armenia and Azerbaijan) from Moscow. In a surprisingly short time, roughly between November 1988 and January 1990, the Soviet center lost its credibility and its coercive power, and the conflict span out of control.

The mishandling of the conflict by the decaying Soviet Union is a crucial factor that explains why the conflict got out of hand; however, it does not explain the underlying factors that caused the conflict. At the core of the conflict lie the mutually exclusive claims of two groups to a single territory. This claim is, on the side of the Armenians, overarched by the unanimously shared conviction that Karabakh and Armenia needed to be united and that the security and even the survival of the nation depended on it. It is a peculiarity of the Karabakh conflict that, due to the historically deeply rooted and omnipresent discourse in Armenian society, the fear of impending Azerbaijani dominance became the fear of the possible recurrence of genocide. The weakening of the Soviet regime provided both a new impetus to this fear and a window of opportunity to remedy the situation. To use James Scott's famous concept, all of sudden, the "hidden transcript" of Armenian society became the "public transcript," and the struggle over Karabakh became the defining core of the Armenians' political life in the transition from Soviet rule to independence.[63]

The Karabakh conflict, precisely because of this ideology, exercised a strong integrative influence. The nationalist challengers and the Communist authorities in Armenia were united in their interpretation of the Karabakh question, as a matter directly pertaining to the physical survival of the nation. There were only differences regarding the tactics to be employed. The more that politics in Armenia centered on a solution to the Karabakh question, the smaller the political differences between nationalist challengers and Communist office-bearers became. Karabakh turned into the real drive for regime change. The pressure from the streets, which had brought the Karabakh Committee to power in the summer of 1990, was chiefly fueled by the mobilization effect of the Karabakh question. But the increasing desovietization and nationalization of the old political elites can also be explained by the dominance of the Karabakh question. Thus, Karabakh both accelerated political transition in Armenia and allowed it to run its course with little confrontation, since, beginning in 1989, the opposition and the regime found themselves in agreement over the most important question. In the summer of 1990, after the elections to the Supreme Soviet, the Armenian National Movement assumed control of the state unspectacularly, and constitutionally, and immediately placed it at the disposal of the war in Karabakh.

By contrast, in Azerbaijan, Karabakh developed far less mobilization potential, and it never became a factor that would bridge the rifts between the Communist regime and the nationalist opposition. Quite the opposite, Karabakh became a political playing field, on which regime and opposition tried to score points off each other. Cleavages between incumbent and oppositional elites hindered an efficient execution of the war and led to military defeats; in turn, every big defeat led to a change of government. The regimes of both Ayaz Mutalibov and Abulfez Elchibey fell as a consequence of military defeats on the Karabakh front. The national mobilization around Karabakh provided the Armenians with a decisive organizational advantage over the Azerbaijanis—by lowering the costs of mobilization, raising the donation-discipline of society, easing recruiting costs, and preventing the inner fragmentation of the elite.

In spite of their much smaller total population, the Armenians thus had a larger pool of recruits, as well as factories, universities, and *kolkhozi,* but they also had rich, shadow-economy entrepreneurs and criminal authorities who were involved in the organization of paramilitary militias. This process may have been helped by substantial donations from the diaspora. Altogether, according to its own estimates, the diaspora provided US $630 million of humanitarian assistance between 1989 and 1999.[64] What share of this support from the diaspora was used directly or indirectly for the war in Karabakh cannot be established. Before the end of 1991, however, financial transactions were massively restricted by the Soviet Union, so that the resources of the diaspora only started to flow to their full capacity after the end of the Soviet Union—at a time when the war over Karabakh was already in first gear.

Karabakh's main contributions to international research into war are that Karabakh poses a challenge to two of the tenets of mainstream conflict theory. Conflict theory predicts that wars are more likely to happen in countries that are mountainous and dependent on natural resources.[65] In the case of Karabakh, the war took place in a mountainous and oil-rich country, yet neither had a role in triggering the violence.

Although Armenia and Nagorny-Karabakh possess no natural resources, Azerbaijan has rich oil deposits and is increasingly dependent on them. In 1992, oil exports accounted for 21.4 percent of the GDP, and in 1999, 70 percent.[66] The analytical narrative, however, shows that there is no causal relationship between natural resource dependency and the outbreak of war in Karabakh. There even seems to be a negative correlation between resource dependence and the duration of war in the case of Nagorny-Karabakh. Azerbaijani warlords and ambitious politicians invested their resources primarily in the power struggle in Baku and not in the war effort in Karabakh, since the "prize"—control over resources—was to be won in the oil fields and not on the battlefields. This contributed crucially to the weakening of the Azerbaijani front and led, in the final analysis, to the military victory of the Armenians.

Likewise, "mountainous terrain" does not offer explanatory power, despite the fact that approximately half of the territory of Nagorny-Karabakh (literally "mountainous Karabakh") is over 950 m above sea level. Karabakh has tall mountain ridges along its northern and western edges, and the south is entirely mountainous. Much of Nagorny-Karabakh is forested. Yet a connection between its physical geography and the secessionist drive is hard to establish. The first phase of the conflict was shaped by the organization or intercommunal, local violence. In these clashes of village against village, or city district against city district, the terrain played no role. When the small-scale war escalated—first to a partisan war against Soviet security forces and then to an interstate war with Azerbaijan—it was initially the Armenian "rebels" who had to capture the strategically important mountain ranges and open up a corridor to Armenia proper. Territory, in the beginning of the war, thus did not favor the rebels, as conflict theory assumes. Terrain has a role inasmuch as the Armenian positions today are very well situated and fortified, so that a recapture would be extraordinarily difficult. For the initial organization of violence, however, terrain has no explanatory power.

As in all other cases of violence in the Caucasus, state weakness was a crucial factor. As described, "state weakness" in the case of Karabakh translates into a lack of conflict-resolving procedures, followed by a rapid delegitimization of the central state, culminating in the loss of coercive capacities. This resulted in a situation that was perceived by the Armenians both as a serious security threat and as a window of opportunity. The drive for secession in Nagorny-Karabakh fueled nationalist mobilization, triggered intercommunal violence, and then led to interstate war.

Also of crucial importance were ethnic settlement patterns and demography. The relevant literature argues that there is a heightened risk of secession and conflict when ethnic groups live relatively compactly in clearly delineated territories[67] and when an ethnic group has a "coethnic big brother" in the neighboring state, who might potentially intervene in its favor. Furthermore, a heightened risk of conflict escalation is predicted for cases where one group has a chance of ethnic dominance.[68] All three conditions are present in Karabakh. Due to the demographic relations (in 1989, the region was made up of 77 percent Armenians and 22 percent Azeris), the possibility of "ethnic dominance," to use Collier and Hoeffler's term was an option for the Armenians within Karabakh.[69] The Armenian majority controlled both the regional parliament and the regional section of the Communist Party—institutions that gained increasing power during perestroika. In 1988 and 1989, the Armenians used these institutions to legitimize their demands for unification with Armenia; as a consequence, the resistance of Moscow and Baku to this legitimate resolution was perceived as an injustice. With the start of the intercommunal violence, the Karabakh Armenians, due to their demographic superiority, had a considerably larger recruitment pool than did the Azerbaijanis, which lessened the costs of the Armenian organization of violence.

In the case of Karabakh, it is difficult to argue (as is in vogue in the social sciences) that histories of wrongs suffered were merely a discourse, exploited or even created by ethnic entrepreneurs. There is a history of violence between Armenians and what is today Azerbaijan over Karabakh, which led to open warfare in both 1905 and in 1918–1920. There is also the history of the Armenian genocide, which, particularly after the pogrom in Sumgait in February 1988, became intrinsically linked to the Karabakh question. In the absence of a power willing to provide credible security guarantees to both sides, violence became unavoidable.

7

Wars That Did Not Happen

Dagestan and Ajaria

Conducting empirically rich case studies of internal wars is one way to enhance knowledge about factors, policies, and institutional settings that explain why and how conflicts spin out of their social embedding and become organized violence. Another way is to conduct case studies on how wars were avoided. The Soviet and post-Soviet Caucasus offers ample opportunity to do both. In the North Caucasus, Chechnya spiraled into war. But its neighbors to the east (Dagestan) and to the west (Ingushetia, Kabardino-Balkaria, and Karachai-Cherkessia) did not. By the same token, in the South Caucasus, out of the three autonomous regions within Georgia, two have sought to break away, whereas the third, Ajaria, has not, thus avoiding a violent conflict within its borders.

In this chapter, two cases of war avoidance are described—Dagestan in the North Caucasus and Ajaria in the South Caucasus. Such an exercise is useful because it helps to highlight factors and policies that have, in these cases, prevented conflict from turning into sustained and organized violence, despite the fact that both Dagestan and Ajaria were considered to be regions with a high risk of war.

Dagestan: Stability against All Odds

In the late 1980s and early 1990s, Dagestan was ranked very high on the list of states at risk of organized violence by many observers of post-Soviet events. Dagestan is a small, mountainous republic in the northeastern Caucasus. It borders, to the east, the Caspian Sea; to the west, Georgia, Chechnya, and Russia; and to the south, Azerbaijan. The northern part of the country and the narrow strip of coast are relatively

flat, while the south and the west are mountainous. With the collapse of the Soviet Union, all preconditions for violent conflict were in place in Dagestan.

The country was no less affected than other post-Soviet polities by the collapse of the Soviet system and the resulting weakening of statehood. Dagestan was very poor, structurally underdeveloped, and, as a recipient of subsidies, especially hard hit by the collapse of the Soviet system; it was also ethnically and linguistically the most heterogeneous region of Russia.[1] More than 30 distinct ethnic groups lived here, potentially providing fertile soil for interethnic tensions and ethnonational mobilization. In addition, three of these ethnic groups—the Lezgins, the Russians, and the Chechens—had an ethnic "big brother" just across the border, a situation which may (and which did in Abkhazia and Ossetia) increase the risk of nationalist mobilization.[2] Moreover, Dagestan was located in a "bad neighborhood" and was threatened by potentially destabilizing overspill effects from conflicts in the area. The violent overthrow of the Soviet regime in Chechnya in 1991 and the tensions between Russia and Chechnya, culminating in a full-scale war in 1994, threatened to destabilize Dagestan. During the first war (1994–1996), hundreds of thousand of Chechens (according to some accounts up to 150,000) found refuge in Dagestan. At the same time, Dagestan suffered sporadic incursions of Chechen fighters and of people from organized cattle rustling and, above all, from organized hostage-taking by bordering wartorn Chechnya.

How real the threat of overspill from Chechnya was became clear in August 1999, when some 1,000 armed fighters from Chechnya, led by Shamil Basayev, made an incursion into Dagestan, with the declared aim of uniting Dagestan with Chechnya to form an Islamist state. Around half of the fighters were Dagestani, who had been trained in Chechen training camps; the other half were Chechen rebels from the ranks of warlords. The immediate objective of Basayev and his fighters was to help local Islamic fundamentalists who were under attack by federal forces in the Dagestani villages of Kadar, Karamakhi, and Chabanmakh. These villages had declared themselves an independent Islamic zone and refused to follow instructions from Makhachkala and Moscow. For the Chechen rebels, the separatist villages were a bridgehead to open up another front against the Russians. The invaders came up against bitter resistance from the Dagestani population, however. Neighborhood self-defense units fought back and were soon supported by Russian troops. On August 24, the invaders retreated to Chechnya. In total, 340 Russian soldiers died in this war, along with about 150 Dagestani and an unknown number of Chechen rebels. This Russian military action, which had the support of the Dagestani population, raised the curtain for the second war in Chechnya. The Russian army capitalized on favorable public opinion and began to bomb Chechen rebel positions from the air and with artillery. After a creeping escalation, the ground offensive in Chechnya began in December 1999.

Dagestan, however, had shown its resistance to destabilizing overspill and refuted the grim predictions of conflict theory. Despite state weakness and political instability at the center, as well as the wide availability of small arms[3] and thousand of unemployed young men, the political elite of Dagestan managed to avoid secessionist politics, came to terms with ethnonational aspirations among some of the largest ethnic groups within Dagestan, proved resistant to overspill from the Chechen war, contained radical Wahhabism, and successfully co-opted potentially oppositional elites. Admittedly, Dagestan is not, and will not soon be, a well-governed accountable polity committed to liberal market reforms. But neither is it "the Lebanon" or "the Balkans" of the Caucasus, as many observers thought it would be. The story of how violent conflict was avoided is one of how micropolitics and the interlocking of formal and informal institutions can defeat structural risks. It also shows the price tag attached to the strategies that produced the kind of stability that Dagestan has reached. Both aspects of the story are embedded in the rise and the fall of the brothers Khachilaev. They could have become patriot-businessmen, assuming a similar role for Dagestan as had Shamil Basaev in Chechnya, Jaba Ioseliani in Georgia, and Samvel Babayan in Karabakh, and indeed their career has striking parallels with these illustrious entrepreneurs of violence. However, it ended on a different note.

The Khachilaev brothers were born into a poor shepherd's family in the Lak region of Dagestan.[4] By the early 1990s, the oldest brother, Magomed, and the second brother, Nadir, had become two of the most powerful men in Dagestan. Their career began, like that of many successful entrepreneurs of violence, with sports and with organized crime in the shadow of the Soviet economy. Magomed was twice karate master of the Soviet Union and five-time karate master of Russia. This earned him and his family enormous prestige throughout Dagestan, which, much like other Caucasian societies, highly values sporting achievements. In the mid 1980s, the brothers became involved in the criminal world of Makhachkala, the capital of Dagestan. Later, Nadir Khachilaev joined Caucasian crime networks in Moscow. At the end of the 1980s, with the opportunities for foreign travel that they enjoyed as sportsmen, the brothers imported computers into Russia and sold them for enormous profits. The proceeds formed the basis of the Khachilaevs' wealth. (Shamil Basaev is also said to have earned his wealth by importing computers.)

At the end of the 1980s, when the tide of nationalism reached Dagestan, many of the various ethnic groups started to form their national movements aimed at preserving and developing traditional culture and language. One of the first was the Tsubarz (New Moon) movement, advocating the national concerns of the Laks, one of the four largest groups in Dagestan. The Laks were engaged in a conflict over land with the Chechens in the Aukhov region. After the Chechens were deported in 1944, the Laks were forcibly resettled onto their lands. After 1991, the Chechens claimed back what they saw as their land. This was when the Khachilaev brothers' political career took off. Being Laks themselves, they soon became patrons of the Lak national movement, and they formed a paramilitary unit of several hundred men, equipping them with weapons and communications gear. Thanks to their new "muscles," the Laks negotiated an agreement with the Chechens that was favorable to the Laks. The Lak movement became the strongest movement in a republic where there were no political parties, and the Lak paramilitary unit was a force that the Dagestani state had to reckon with. Magomed then became the elected leader of the Lak movement. In the meantime, the Khachivalevs continued to amass wealth. According to various sources, the brothers' participation in major scams earned them tens of millions of dollars.[5] They also extended their political links, mainly in Arab countries.

In the meantime, Nadir Khachilaev had obtained a university degree in literature and had become leader of the Russian Union of Muslims. In public speeches, Nadir began calling for the creation of an Islamic state in Dagestan. At this time, he portrayed himself as a religious man who defended the Wahabbites against the followers of traditional Islam. The first Chechen war provided new opportunities for the talents of the Khachilaevs: the brothers are said to have earned another fortune in arms dealing. It is clear that they had indeed forged excellent contacts with Chechen field commanders. In 1996, when the Russian General Lebed sought a peace accord with the Chechen rebels, Nadir Khachilaev was one of the go-betweens. After the war, as Dagestan was plagued by organized kidnappings, the brothers offered their (expensive) services as negotiators between the families of the victims and the kidnappers hiding in Chechnya. Nadir's career peaked in 1996 with his election as a deputy to the Russian parliament. Almost the entire state apparatus of Dagestan had supported his campaign. At that time, his brother Magomed had already been co-opted into the ranks of the Dagestani state elite and had obtained the position of state fishery supervisory authority—one of the most profitable posts in Dagestan, since it includes control over the lucrative caviar trade.

The Khachilaevs had worked their way up through the system. They had started as sportsmen-criminals, accumulating wealth in the shadow economy of the Soviet Union. With the coming of a nationalist tide, they became patrons of a national movement, a move that gained them legitimacy, followers, and the opportunity to form a private militia. Their success and growing influence was "honored" by the Dagestani state elite by co-opting Magomed into the rank of a minister, and Nadir got himself elected to the Russian state parliament, thereby gaining prestige and immunity. Up to this point, the brothers had not directly opposed the ruling elites; rather, they had quite successfully operated in what was the tolerated grey zone (a zone which, in the aftermath of the Soviet collapse, was rather large).

But in 1996 Magomed Khachilaev began opposing the ruling elites in Dagestan, and in May 1998, a public power struggle took place between the Khachilaevs and the state. On May 21, 2000, armed supporters of the brothers occupied the government building in Makhachkala, and this was followed by plundering and wanton destruction. The action had been preceded by a clash between the brothers and a police patrol on May 20, which had turned into a shootout, leaving five police officers dead. Around midday on May 21, the police intervened and attempted to bring the situation in and around the government building under control. At this point, the Khachilaevs tried to give their actions the facade of political protest, by publicly calling for the creation of a presidential regime—a stance they had strictly rejected a few weeks earlier. They similarly attempted to portray the action as an Islamist protest by hoisting the green flag of Islam over the government building. The headline "Green Flag Flies over Makhachkala" reached even the Western media, and the London *Independent* ran a story on May 22, 1998, headlined "Islamic Gunmen Challenge Yeltsin's Rule." After negotiations in which the chairman of the State Council of Dagestan and the Russian interior minister were involved, the tension eased, and the brothers pulled out without bloodshed.

After these events, the Dagestani ruling elite, together with law-enforcement agencies of the Russian Federation, started to put pressure on the Khachilaevs. Magomed was arrested but later released under the condition that he would remain in the mountains in the Lak region and would not appear in Makhachkala or other cities in Dagestan. Nadir Khachilaev sought refuge in Chechnya for a year. In November 1999, he was stripped of his parliamentary immunity and arrested. In 2000, charges were brought against the Khachilaev brothers. Magomed

Khachilaev was sentenced to three years in prison and Nadir to one and a half years. However, immediately after the court reached its decision, the brothers were released under an amnesty dictated by the government in conjunction with the 55th anniversary of victory in World War II. This was the end of the Khachilaevs' career. The state, by means of negotiation, concession, various attempts at co-optation, and, in the end, reliance on force, had prevailed. The factors and the political decisions that enabled this outcome, against the backdrop of the Chechen disaster, are discussed below.

In Chechnya, Soviet state institutions outlived the collapse of the Soviet Union by all of four weeks, and the Communist *nomenklatura* was swiftly replaced by Dudayev's people. In Dagestan, by contrast, Soviet structures, with the exception of the Communist Party, not only survived but also became the core around which Dagestani statehood has been reconstructed. In addition, the Soviet Dagestani elite remained in power and proved to be quite successful at co-opting potential contenders into its ranks. Hence, elite continuity and the capacity to "buy off" contenders rather than to confront them violently explain how Dagestan managed to negotiate its nonviolent transition. Both factors are linked to the largely nonconfrontational relations that Dagestani elites and the Soviet system developed during the 70 years of Soviet rule. In Dagestan, a Dagestani Soviet elite emerged, which saw the Soviet system as an opportunity. Except during the Stalin period, key positions in Dagestan were filled with native cadres, who, as a rule, were recruited from the four largest Dagestani ethnic groups. Thus, after the World War II, all first secretaries of the Communist Party were Dagestani, as were the chairmen of the Council of Ministers and of the Supreme Soviet. When making appointments to these posts, care was taken to ensure that these three officials belonged to different national groups. In addition, the responsible politics of ethnic balancing heightened acceptance of the Soviet system and strengthened the Dagestani Soviet elite.

Chechnya lacked this experience. Correspondingly, a Soviet Chechen elite identifying their interests with the Soviet Union never emerged. What is more, access to Soviet career opportunities was highly restricted for Chechens. Cadre positions were usually filled with Russians, and access to education and to military careers was made difficult. With the collapsing Soviet system, new nationalist elites under Dudayev dismantled the old system. In Dagestan, the old Soviet elite not only stayed in power but also successfully defused the inevitable challenge coming from a newly emerged class of successful "entrepreneurs" by letting these challengers share in power—and thus turning them into stakeholders. The co-optation of new, economically successful elites into the old *nomenklatura* system is a further factor that helps explain the astonishing stability of Dagestan.[6] However, the co-optation strategy had its price; sociologist Enver Kisriev estimates that the bureaucracy has doubled since 1991.[7]

Furthermore, in Dagestan, unlike Chechnya, Georgia, and Armenia, the breeding ground for a powerful nationalist movement was limited. When the nationalist tide reached Dagestan, here, too, an independence movement calling for an independent Republic of Dagestan emerged. But, in contrast to the other Soviet republics and autonomous territories, this movement could not be based on one single ethnonational group because Dagestan was home to 30 national groups, the largest one comprising less than 30 percent of the population. Any independence movement thus required the support of several ethnic groups. The emerging Dagestani "independence" movement was therefore more a movement against the Soviet system than a movement advocating a national program of one single national group. The movement quickly collapsed; in April 1991, a total of 15 out of 53 regional soviets voted against the creation of a sovereign republic in Dagestan. Those regional soviets opposing the sovereignization were dominated by ethnic groups who were already dissatisfied with their position in the Dagestani republic. These groups, among them the Kumyks, the Nogai, and the Lezgins, feared that in an independent Dagestan, the dominance of the four largest groups would only strengthen, and for this reason they rejected independence. This was a clear signal to the political elite of Dagestan: the secession of Dagestan from the Russian Federation would greatly heighten the risk that Dagestan would disintegrate.[8] Consequently, the topic of Dagestani independence quickly disappeared from the political agenda.

One reason for this was undoubtedly the fear of possible consequences, which the ethnonationalist go-it-alone aspirations of one group could have for all groups. "Fear of the consequences" by itself, however, is not sufficient to explain the speedy ebbing of ethnonationalist agitation. An additional explanatory factor is that identity in Dagestan is traditionally multilayered. A survey conducted in 2001 revealed that most Dagestani identified first and foremost with being "Dagestani" rather than as a member of an ethnic group ("Dagestan" refers to a territory, there is no ethnic group of Dagestani).[9] Members of all national groups were asked to choose with which group they identified primarily. They were given five options: "Dagestan," "Russia," "my own ethnic group," "religion," and "community." More than 75 percent of respondents answered that "Dagestan" was the most important reference point for their own identity; a mere 10.5 percent responded that their own ethnic group was the most important source of identity.[10] Hence, Dagestani identity refers to a multiethnic state within the framework of the Russian Federation, with ethnicity playing only a minor role. On such grounds, when civic nationalism trumps ethnic nationalism, the organization of a secessionist nationalist movement becomes difficult.

However, Dagestan might still have fallen victim to intercommunal violence were it not for the interlocking of institutions that, together, made ethnonational mobilization difficult. More specifically, the inherited Soviet practices of ethnic power sharing, a new constitution that provided elements of a consociational democracy, and a traditional societal organization based on territorially defined (rather than ethnically defined) communities made mobilization across ethnic lines difficult and thus enabled Dagestani society to preserve its ethnic balance.

Enver Kisriev, a sociologist from Dagestan, has described how the collapse of Soviet state structures actually strengthened traditional societal organizations. In the rubble of the Soviet system, the institution of the *jamaat* thrived.[11] In Dagestan, this term of Arabic origin denotes a territorialized political community with its own traditional constitution, customary law, and leadership.[12] Usually a *jamaat* is confined to a single large village or two to three smaller villages. Each *jamaat* encompasses several, sometimes up to a dozen, extended families. The heads of these extended families make up the *jamaat*'s council of elders. For centuries, the Dagestani *jamaat*s were factually autonomous communities, governed by a corporatist elite and made up of different extended families. Russian travelers of the 19th century often described the *jamaat*s as independent republics. These polities were structured by customary law (*adat*), which, in some cases, was even written down. *Adat* governed the political, economic, and sociocultural concerns of the community. Since the *jamaat* was based on extended families and territoriality, ethnicity played only a minor role as a structuring feature of Dagestani society. A *jamaat* can be dominated by one ethnic group, with most or all members belonging to the same group, but this is by no means always the case. *Jamaats* can equally well consist of members from several ethnic groups. *Jamaats* constitute solidarity groups, with a binding set of rules, which facilitate collective action. The "national group," by contrast, is an abstract construction with primarily discursive significance for the individual.

As Robert Ware and Enver Kisriev argue, the fact that the *jamaat* is the basic organizational unit in post-Soviet Dagestan strengthens the ethnic balance.[13] Because the relevant political organizational unit in Dagestan is smaller than the respective ethnic groups, they argue, interest representation takes place through and for these local and regional units, not for ethnonational groups. The salience of the *jamaat* hence cross-cuts ethnic identity. Edward Walker describes Dagestani society as follows:

> Dagestani society is thus characterized by a complex set of mostly nested cleavages. Unlike, for example, most of the cleavages separating Armenians from Azeris, they are not coterminous. Other than the relatively weak identity of being a citizen of multinational Dagestan, or the even weaker identity of being a citizen of the Russian Federation, few cleavages intersect ethnic, jamaat, or family loyalties in ways that would unite, for example, a highlander Avar from a particular jamaat with a lowlander Kumyk, let alone an urban Russian. Instead, salient cleavages are generally nested one within the other, like a Russian matrioshka doll —for example, Muslim, highlander, Avar or sub-nationality, jamaat, clan, village, and family. Moreover, identities and political loyalties tend to intensify as the unit of identification gets smaller, with most political activity organized around jamaaty.[14]

Cross-cutting ties and "nested cleavages," in the parlance of rational choice, make the organization of nationalist mobilization more expensive. In addition, the Dagestani elite were careful to continue the Soviet practice of informal policies of ethnic power sharing. Although there are more than 30 national groups in Dagestan, the republic's multiethnic system is dominated by four groups. The Avars, the Dargins, the Kumyks, and the Lezgins make up almost 70 percent of the population and traditionally occupy the most important posts in state and economy. The elites of the other national groups help to balance ethnic relations by entering into temporary alliances with one of more of the four large groups, when the ethnic balance is under threat.[15] Soviet authorities had followed a quota system when filling cadre positions, whereby the three most important offices in the republic were filled by members of different nationalities, and the cadre policy was aimed at ethnic proportional representation in the Supreme Soviet.

After the collapse of the Soviet system, Dagestan continued to ensure its ethnic balance through a set of informal and formal rules and practices. Key positions in the government and the bureaucracy are filled as proportionally as possible. If a key position is vacant, and then filled with a representative of another nationality, the balance is upset. To avoid this, several top positions are simultaneously reshuffled, so that the balance between the nationalities is maintained. Ware and Kisriev call this procedure a "packet replacement."[16]

On July 26, 1994, the first post-Soviet Dagestani constitution was passed, after three years of engaged public debates and tough negotiations behind the scenes between politicians, constitutional lawyers, representatives of the various national groups, and large swathes of the population. The Dagestani constitution was designed to ensure the representation of all national groups and to hinder the emergence of ethnic frontlines in political competition. According to the new constitution, the State Council (*gossovet*), comprising 14 members, was to be the highest executive body of state power. According to Article 88 of the constitution, any one national group can only have one representative in the State Council. This is guaranteed by a complicated electoral procedure laid down in the constitution.

The State Council is convened by a special electoral body, the Constitutional Assembly, whose only role is the election of the council. The Constitutional Assembly comprises all parliamentary deputies, as well as numerous representatives elected on the communal level. The parliament comprises 121 directly elected deputies. Article 72 of the Constitution guarantees the representation of all ethnic groups in Dagestan. This is achieved by a complex electoral law: out of 121 single-member constituencies, 55 are ethnically homogenous. These constituencies are mainly situated in the mountain regions populated by Avars, Dargins, and Lezgins. Since there are no ethnically defined minorities in these constituencies, no special procedures are necessary to handle the ethnic tensions that may be sparked by political competition. The remaining 66 constituencies are ethnically mixed. To prevent ethnic tensions arising in such constituencies, only one ethnic group enjoys passive voting rights. All nationalities, however, enjoy active voting rights. In this way, in such constituencies all national groups elect one representative from a predefined national group.

To secure proportional representation, out of the 66 heterogeneous constituencies, 12 each were assigned to the Avars and Kumyks, 10 to the Russians, 7 to the Dargins, 5 each to the Tabasarans and the Azeris, 4 each to the Chechens and the Lezgins, 3 to the Laks, 2 to the Tats, and 1 each to the Nogai and the Tskhurs. To protect this system from arbitrary changes, each deputy has a right of veto for draft laws affecting his national group. The overturning of the veto requires a two-thirds majority. This complex constituency-geometry works remarkably well. In the parliamentary elections of 1995 and 1999, the national composition of the parliament accurately reflected the national composition of the republic's population.

This electoral system also prevents ethnic rivalries from arising at the regional or local level. In the mixed constituencies, the national group from which the deputy will be elected is fixed from the beginning. Candidates are dependent not only on the votes of their own group to be elected but also on votes from other national groups. This leads to candidates with a narrow, nationalistic agenda mostly failing to get elected. Only those candidates who are able to attract voters from all ethnic groups are successful. Some observers, impressed by how well this system works at hindering the emergence of cleavages across ethnic lines, proposed a similar system for Afghanistan.[17]

But perhaps the most significant reason for the efficiency of the constitution lies in the fact that it strengthens the traditional authority of the *jamaat*. All deputies are elected in single-member constituencies by a majority vote. This means that political competition takes place in the regions, and the emergence of ethnic-nationalist frontlines at the level of the republic is avoided. At the local level, the electoral law prevents two candidates of different nationality from competing against each other. These conditions made for the *jamaat* thus becoming a useful political organizational structure accepted by political entrepreneurs. In this sense, the constitution contributes to the strengthening of the *jamaat* and thereby to the perpetuation of a system, which, in the past, was successful in guaranteeing a (dynamic) ethnic balance. Hence, as Ware and Kisriev conclude:

> The 1994 constitution echoes traditions of the *jamaat* insofar as it provides a codified framework for transcending kinship structures through

> the cooperative interactions of elites. Dagestan's ethnic diversity is the defining feature of its political system, which conforms with consociational models at a number of different points.[18]

A final factor contributing to the Dagestani "stability in spite of everything" is the massive material support from Russia. Especially since the attack by Chechen rebels in the summer of 1999, Russia has transferred considerable resources to Dagestan. In view of the strategic importance of Dagestan's location, this material support is a good investment. In 2000, Dagestan received 6.3 billion rubles to subsidize its budget.[19] This amounted to almost 80 percent of the entire budget. In the same year, Moscow raised the salaries of Dagestani officials by 50 percent. In Dagestan, salaries and pensions from the central Russian budget are paid out punctually. It is these Russian subsidies that make the Dagestani state, as it is often said in Dagestan, a cow that no one wants to kill—the elites have an interest in the continuation of subsidies and thus an interest in the continued existence of the state. The high level of corruption that goes hand in hand with this arrangement is probably the price paid for stability.

Lessons from Dagestan

Various factors combine to explain why Dagestan avoided the Chechen scenario, but Dagestan's major contribution to conflict theory is that it lends support and adds causal explanation to Collier and Hoeffler's argument that ethnically highly fragmented societies are actually less vulnerable to internal wars than are less-fragmented societies.[20] Collier and Hoeffler posit two mechanisms for their argument: first, in highly fragmented societies, the aspirations of individual groups can be blocked by an alliance among other groups; second, there is a relatively smaller pool of ethnic recruits in a highly fragmented society. Both mechanisms increase the costs of violence and thus lessen the risk of conflict. Ethnic fractionalization, therefore, can exert a stabilizing effect. As the case of Dagestan shows, the necessary condition for this is that procedures for coalition formation and consensus finding are present and rehearsed: in other words, institutionalized.

At the core of Dagestan's stability are two interlocking institutions: the traditional, informal system of the *jamaat*s (cross-ethnic communities based on neighborhood), and the formal institution of the 1994 Dagestan Constitution. Traditionally the *jamaat* is the basic social unit in Dagestani society. The unmaking of the Soviet system actually reinforced the social importance of this community-based social unit. The *jamaat* system can be described as consisting of a large number of territorialized political entities. They compete with each other at regional and local levels for scarce resources (land or votes). Such a system nurtures stability for two reasons. The *jamaat* constitute small, flexible "particles" in the political system, which can rapidly form coalitions if the ethnic balance is threatened. In addition, *jamaat*s dominated by the same ethnic group often compete with each other. In this way, the emergence of monoethnic coalitions is prevented. Both mechanisms, the built-in "balancing capacity" and the built-in competition within an ethnic group, increase the costs for the mobilization of an ethnic group.

The benevolent effects of the (informal) *jamaat* system were demonstrated in 1994, when Dagestan adopted its new constitution, which strengthened the position of the *jamaat* as an important social unit by institutionalizing a strong regionalization of politics. Furthermore, the constitution guaranteed a proportional representation of the major ethnic groups in the State Council (the republic's highest executive authority), and informal agreements (continuing a Soviet practice) guaranteed ethnic proportional representation in the higher echelons of state bureaucracy. Taken together, elements of consociational democracy, regionalization of politics, cross-cutting (rather than additive) cleavages, and a tradition of interethnic balancing combined to produce Dagestan's resistance to destabilization.

Other factors also helped, such as the solid embedding and the high binding power of Soviet institutions. In contrast to Chechnya, Soviet institutions did not collapse with the breakup of the Soviet Union but became the core around which statehood could be reconstructed. The importance of these accepted political institutions was shown in 1991, when one-third of the regional soviets voted against the creation of a sovereign republic of Dagestan. These surviving Soviet institutions gave a voice to a significant social group and signaled to the state elite that the possible consequences of secession from the Russian Federation would be heightened interethnic tension within Dagestan.

Furthermore, the Soviet Dagestani elite, which had developed a nonconfrontational relationship with the Soviet center, survived the transformation relatively intact. The high level of elite continuity added stability during transition. When potential oppositional elites emerged —some surfing on the tide of ethnic mobilization, others just willing to transform their newly acquired wealth into political power—most of them were co-opted by the old elite. In this way, the formation of state-bearing elite (comprising the old *nomenklatura* and the new *biznes-meny*) succeeded, and this elite subsequently began to centralize the revenues from the few profitable branches of the economy (oil, fisheries, alcohol, and subsidies from Moscow). Thus, potential challengers were blocked from accessing the resources necessary for the organization of violence. The downside of this successful incorporation of elites, however, wascorruption, embezzlement, and patronage networks.

The final factor contributing to stability in Dagestan is the considerable resource base that Russia has transferred to the republic. These resources filled the kitty, which the elites then divided up among themselves, and thus they made participation in the existing state rewarding.

Ajaria: A Gentleman's Agreement, and Why It Was Honored

After South Ossetia and Abkhazia, Ajaria was the third autonomous territory within the Georgian Soviet Republic. Ajaristan, as it was then called, was annexed by Russia from the Ottoman Empire in 1878 which had ruled the territory from the 16th century. As was the case elsewhere in the empire, Ottoman authorities had ruled via millets, the state-sponsored system of religious communities. Religion was thus the main determinant of group status and the foundation of socioeconomic organization. Ajars are confessionally Muslims but ethnically Georgians. They speak the Gurian dialect of Georgian, which contains many Turkic words. In the chaotic period that followed the Russian Revolution, the political status of Ajaria was contested. Independent Azerbaijan insisted that Ajaria, being a Muslim Caucasian territory, should become its enclave on the Black Sea. British occupying authorities in 1919 favored free port status for Batumi. Both Ottoman and Kemalist Turks claimed it as their own, as did independent Georgia. In turn, Ajars tended to associate with the "Turks" rather than the "Georgians." This became evident in popular attitudes during the chaotic period of 1917–1921, when Ajaria's Muslims aided advancing Turkish forces by waging a guerrilla war against both Russian and Georgian forces. But by 1921, the Bolshevik regime had installed itself firmly in the South Caucasus, and Ajaria's future—together with the future of Armenia, Karabakh, Georgia, and Azerbaijan—was now dependent on the strategic reasoning of the new masters. In order not to rebuke Turkey, which was at that time one of the few allies of the Bolsheviks, Moscow agreed to grant autonomy to the Muslim population of Ajaristan in the Kars treaty. On June 16, 1921, Ajaria was incorporated into the Soviet Union as an ASSR within the Georgian SSR.

In 1989, the all-Soviet census stated that Ajaria had a population of 392,000, of whom 86 percent were Georgians, 8 percent Russians, and 4 percent Armenians. There were no Ajars. What had happened to them? Unlike other Caucasian ethnic groups, they had not been deported but had instead fallen victim to the Soviet criteria for classifying ethnic groups. Language was regarded as an indicator of ethnicity, whereas religions were not. Hence, the Muslim Ajars, speaking a version of Georgian, were not qualified as a distinct ethnic group. Soviet passports reported ethnicity but not religious affiliation. Forthwith, the vast majority of all Ajars were recorded as ethnic Georgians, and there are no precise data for their numbers in Soviet statistics. The Georgian political scientist Gia Tarkhan-Mouravi estimated the size of the Ajari population in 1989 at around 250,000 (67 percent of the overall population of Ajaria).[21]

The fact that Soviet ideology did not allow religion to be an indicator of ethnic difference meant that the Georgian Communist *nomenklatura* could pursue a course of aggressive Georgianization which met with considerable success. Ideologically Ajaria's Islam was an embarrassment to a Georgia that had constructed its national myth on resistance to Turkish encroachment. The assimilation of the Ajars was arguably among the greatest successes of the Georgian national project. By the 1980s, virtually all Ajars knew Georgian.[22] No titular nationality was established in Ajaria, and Georgians won the battle over language. Due to the Soviet politics of secularization, Ajars and Georgians were brought into closer cultural alliance, although Ajars continued to preserve many aspects of traditional, pre-Turkish and pre-Soviet culture, and Muslim-Christian marriages remained rare. By the late 1980s, the ruling elite of Ajaria consisted of a Communist *nomenklatura* mainly recruited from local Ajar notables that ran locally well established networks of patronage, but avoided by and large the ethnic flavor that similar networks had acquired in Abkhazia.

By 1989, the nationalist tide in Georgia had reached its peak, and the nationalist opposition to the Communist *nomenklatura* aggressively played the ethnic card. Tension between the Ossets and the Abkhaz rose to dangerous levels. In Ajaria, too, all the preconditions for ethnic tensions and violence were in place.

Although Georgians and Ajars had lived without conflict between them for the better part of the 70 years of Soviet rule, they had nevertheless a troubled history. In the chaotic time between 1917 and 1921, Ajars sided with Turkey rather than with Georgia or with the Bolsheviks, and Ajari partisans had fought both. During the Soviet period, Ajaria had enjoyed territorial autonomy, but because Ajars were not considered a titular nation, they were denied the privileges that such a status would have entitled them to within the system of Soviet ethnofederalism. Above all, they were denied the right to publicly exercise what distinguished them most from Georgians: their Islamic belief. Furthermore, Ajaria had all the trappings of statehood which, in the cases of South Ossetia and Abkhazia, had facilitated mobilization: a supreme council, with a presidium, 12 ministries and 11 departments, a tax inspectorate, and a supreme court. The Ajars were the majority within their republic, which, according to conflict theory increases the risk for secessionist movements and ethnic violence. It had access to the sea with a strategically important port in Batumi and borders with Turkey, and hence it would have been much more viable than landlocked South Ossetia to become an independent state.

Georgian nationalism threatened not only South Ossetia and Abkhazia but also Ajaria. The leader of the Georgian national movement, Zviad Gamsakhurdia, openly announced that he wanted to abolish Ajaria's autonomy altogether. In 1990, the first free elections were held in Georgia, and the nationalist opposition swept away the Communist Party. In Ajaria, however, the elections kept the Communist Party in power. The Communists won 56 percent of the vote against 24 percent for the Round Table–Free Georgia bloc. This must have been a blow to Georgia's dogmatic new leader, Gamsakhurdia, who saw Georgia's main threat stemming from Communist collaborators within the country. Protesting the chauvinist and ultranationalist turn in Georgia, many Ajars reasserted their distinctiveness from Georgians by means of the very same Marxist ideology (notoriously hostile to nationalism of any sort), as when they used to publicly pray on May Day under the Soviet red banners accompanied by the Soviet anthem.

When Gamsakhurdia voiced his intention of abolishing Ajaria's autonomy, Ajars rose up in protest, and tensions with Georgia escalated dangerously. As in other republics across the Soviet Union hit by the nationalist tide, protestors flocked to the main square, remaining enthusiastically at the square for long hours, often for days. Many of them carried red banners, and workers' bands played the anthems of the Soviet Union and the Georgian SSR. Similar to the early stages of mobilization in Abkhazia and Karabakh, the anti-Soviet nationalist mobilization of the mother republic had triggered a pro-Soviet, ethnic mobilization. Fights broke out with supporters of Gamsakhurdia, and these soon escalated into a riot.

The mobilization of Ajars was facilitated, if not initiated, by the executive of Ajaria's Supreme Council, presided over by Aslan Abashidze. In fact, Gamsakhurdia had helped by persuading the deputies to elect Abashidze, a long-serving member of the *nomenklatura,* as chairman, hoping that the latter would assist in canceling the autonomous status of the region. Abashidze's election was not uncontested. In April, a group of demonstrators, mostly from the mountainous regions, occupied the building of the Council of Ministers of Ajaria and attempted to install their own candidate, Iosif Khimshiashvili, as chairman of the Supreme Soviet because they felt that Abashidze was too soft on Georgian nationalism. It was not successful. A week later, the leader of the Round Table bloc in Ajaria, Nodar Imnadze, a close ally of Gamsakhurdia and a supporter of abolishing Ajaria's autonomy, burst into the building of Ajaria's Supreme Soviet and shot at Abashidze, wounding him. Abashidze's bodyguards (and reportedly Abashidze himself) then shot Imnadze dead.

Abashidze called Ajars, especially the Muslims of the region, to rise in protest. Tensions with central Georgian authorities ensued. On April 22, 1991, pro-Abashidze protesters stormed administrative buildings in central Batumi, demanding the immediate resignation of several officials. The protests were effectively used by Abashidze to establish his own powerbase in the region. Gamsakhurdia, facing serious internal problems already in Tbilisi, preferred not to interfere in these events. Abashidze had thus successfully defended Ajaria's autonomy against Georgia and his personal rule against nationalist Ajari contenders. After this, Aslan Abashidze ruled Ajaria as a personal fiefdom, convincingly taking the role as a guarantor that civil strife would not emerge from within (from a nationalist opposition) or from without (from Georgia which was increasingly plagued by ultranationalism and private militia groups). Abashidze made it very clear that he would not tolerate armed Mkhedrionis' entering Ajaria. Abashidze's militias guarded the internal "border" with Georgia, and the police were granted special powers to combat crime.[23]

Aslan Abashidze was born in 1938 into a renowned Muslim Ajarian family that had been influential since 1463. His grandfather, Memed Abashidze, was a Muslim aristocrat who achieved fame as a writer and member of the Parliament of the Democratic Republic of Georgia between 1918 and 1921; he was shot on Stalin's orders in 1937. Abashidze's father was sent to the Gulag for ten years but survived. Abashidze obtained degrees in history and philology at Batumi University (1962) and in economics at Tbilisi State University (1984). As a member of a prominent local notable family, with good ties to the *nomenklatura* in Georgia, he quickly climbed the Soviet career ladder. He directed several technical service institutes, but was soon appointed minister of community service in Batumi. Later, he was promoted again and transferred to the capital in Tbilisi where he served as first deputy minister of community service. Both positions offered excellent opportunities for forging lucrative networks, as well as for personnel enrichment.

After Gamsakhurdia's overthrow in January 1992, Abashidze declared a state of emergency in Ajaria, closed the borders, refused to allow the newly elected Supreme Soviet to sit, and established his own ruling party, the Union for the Revival of Ajaria. He took control over the customs division, the Batumi seaport, and other strategic objects; created his own semiofficial armed units; and had full control over the Batumi-based 25th Brigade of Georgia's Defense Ministry. When war between Georgia and Abkhazia broke out, Abashidze used it as a pretext for consolidating power. During the summer of 1992, he began to rule through a seven-strong Presidium of the Supreme Soviet, which was composed mostly of his supporters. He ruled by decree, had full monopoly on military force, and enjoyed support from common people for keeping warlordism in check. He even gave weapons to common people and boasted military support from 35 percent of adult males in Ajaria. Most top positions of political and economic power were assigned to the Abashidze, Bakuridze, Bladadze, and Gogitidze families, who were relatives of Abashidze and his wife. Abashidze's son Georgi was put in charge of the family firm "Aghordzineba-N," which produced barges, pleasure vessels, and goods from glass and reinforced plastic. Georgi was also mayor of Batumi.

After Shevardazde's rise to power in 1993, relations between Georgia and Ajaria remained strained but stable. Shevardnadze visited the region several times during his first year in power to attempt reconciliation with Abashidze. They reached a kind of gentlemen's agreement, according to which Abashidze refrained from pushing for secession, lent his support to Shevardnadze's party (Union of Citizens of Georgia), and, in turn, stayed in power and was allowed to exploit the tax and trade revenues of Ajaria at the expense of the central state budget. These revenues were considerable: in 1988, Moscow had to permit cross-border passage trade, and Ajaria had become an important hub for "shuttle" traders from all over Caucasia and southern Russia importing goods from Turkey.

By all accounts, Abashidze's highly personal reign over Ajaria was supported by a consensus among Ajaria's population of managerial elites, the urban middle classes, workers and peasants—both Muslim and Christian Georgians—and national minorities weary of rabid Georgian nationalism and financed by the revenues that an uncontrolled Black Sea port and border trade with Turkey offered. His reign came to an end after the 2003 Rose Revolution in Georgia which swept away Shevardnadze. Georgia's new president, Mikheil Saakashvili, was not willing to honor the gentlemen's agreement but sought to impose central control over all of Georgia's breakaway regions. On March 14, 2004, the central Georgian officials took advantage of Abashidze's being in Moscow and headed to Ajaria to campaign for parliamentary elections scheduled on March 28. However, pro-Abashidze armed groups blocked the administrative border of Ajaria and prevented Saakashvili and other members of the government to travel to the autonomous republic. In retaliation, Georgia's central authorities imposed partial economic sanctions against its defiant region. On March 16, Saakashvili and Abashidze struck a deal that allowed for economic sanctions against Ajaria to be lifted. However, Abashidze refused to disarm his paramilitary forces. Georgia ratcheted up the pressure, and in Batumi an opposition to Abashidze's neopatrimonial regime emerged. On May 4, a large opposition protest rally was attacked by the local security forces in Batumi. Dozens of protesters were reportedly injured. But the violent breakup of a peaceful demonstration proved a catalyst for even larger protests later on the same day. Tens of thousands from all over Ajaria headed for Batumi to demand Abashidze's resignation. Abashidze's position became untenable when local protesters took control of the central part of the city of Batumi and Georgian Special Forces entered the region and started to disarm pro-Abashizde militants. Later on the same day, Secretary of the Russian Security Council Igor Ivanov arrived in Batumi. Abashidze stepped down after overnight talks with Ivanov and left for Moscow, where he was granted a comfortable political asylum.

Lessons from Ajaria

Why did Ajaria not follow the path of South Ossetia and Abkhazia, despite the fact that the prerequisites for secessionist violence were all in place? Approximately 70 percent of the population were Ajars; Ajaria had all the political institutions that had proved to be instrumental for mobilization in South Ossetia and Abkhazia; Ajars and Georgians have a troubled past, much more so than Georgians and Ossets, as most Ajars are Muslims, whereas for Georgian national identity being Christian (and not a "Turk") is central; the Ajar leadership had enough resources, followers, and arms to equip its own armed formations; and Georgian nationalism indeed threatened Ajaria's autonomy.

One could put forward a null hypothesis and claim that violent conflict was avoided because Ajars did not consider themselves ethnically different from Georgians but saw themselves as part of the Georgian nation, and Ajaria as part of the Georgian state. This is indeed the key argument of Monica Toft.[24] In her view, conflict was avoided because there was not enough cultural difference between Georgians and Ajars to propel Ajaria to seek independence. The reason Ajaria was not willing to secede from Georgia is ultimately the same as the reason St. Petersburg, in spite of its privileged access to the sea, highly developed industry, and Westernized architecture did not secede from Russia. Toft quotes Aslan Abashidze as saying: "We have never had, and never can have, any territorial claims against Georgia. . . . Ajaria is historically a part of Georgia, and there has never been any instance in history in which Ajaria has created problems for its motherland."[25]

Georgi Derluguian ultimately supports this argument but adds explanatory depth by identifying the mechanism by which Abkhaz identity was ethnicized, whereas Ajar identity was not.[26] He claims that while the Soviet Union under Stalin initially shored up Abkhazian political power in order to create an ally against opposing political forces in Georgia, it suppressed early moves toward Ajar autonomy, permitting

Georgia to pursue assimilationist policies there. Moscow thus largely created the political relevance of Abkhaz cultural identity while simultaneously preventing Ajar cultural identity from becoming politically relevant.

But Derluguian's intimate knowledge of the region prohibits him from attributing Ajaria's war avoidance exclusively to a monocausal structural explanation. In addition to the fact that Ajar identity was not politicized, the escalation of violence in Ajaria was prevented by a historical contingency when Nodar Imnadze, a prominent adherent to Georgian nationalism favoring the abolition of Ajaria's autonomy, was killed by Abashidze's bodyguards. This instance, he argues, averted the escalation of Georgian nationalism in Ajaria and prevented it from becoming another Bosnia and Gamsakhurdia from becoming another Milosevic.[27] Derluguian also grants the Russian military contingent in Ajaria the role of peacekeepers, which Abashidze flattered on a yearly basis by sending flowers to all the wives of Russian officers stationed in Ajaria on International Women's Day (March 8).

These arguments go a long way in explaining Ajaria's stability. Yet, there are numerous examples of how, in times of crisis and threat, ethnic identities are reconfigured and politicized. One could easily imagine an Ajar ethnic entrepreneur, surfing a nationalist tide and capitalizing on religious difference between Georgians and Ajars. Aslan Abashidzde, as it turned out, was a political entrepreneur who did not consider the ethnic card his trump. The "system of Abashizde" played an important part in the avoidance of war; hence, the factors that account for the success of this system also contributed to avoiding violence. In marked contrast to Georgia, in Ajaria the old *nomenklatura* stayed in power. In the election of 1990 the Communists prevailed. When Abashidze was elected chairman of the Supreme Soviet, he took over a well-established system of networks and patronage to which he was no stranger (having worked as minister in Ajaria and Georgia). The high degree of elite continuity allowed Abashizde to preserve that system and to shield it from oppositional contenders (which were, in Ajaria, loosely organized and lacked a popular base). Abashidze used the revenues from trade and smuggling that the privileged geographic position of Ajaria offered to consolidate his power, and he successfully installed a patrimonial, authoritarian regime that enjoyed support from the population, from managerial elites, and from urban middle classes. He reached a gentlemen's agreement with Shevardnadze, trading support for Shevardnadze and loyalty to Georgia's territorial integrity for a free hand in his small and lucrative fiefdom. Finally, luck and the benefits of time may also have helped the system of Abashidze to survive. In spring 1990, when tensions grew, Gamsakhurdia, who already faced challenges from separatist South Ossetia and from opposition within his own movement, wanted to avoid another front. Likewise, Shevardnadze, fighting a civil war against supporters of Gamsakhurdia, facing an open conflict with secessionist Abkhazia and being under constant threat of removal by the warlords who merely tolerated him, wanted to avoid a conflict with Ajaria. Under such circumstances, the system of Abashidze proved to be the best option for all involved actors.

In the final analysis, Ajaria remained stable, not only because of the nonpoliticized nature of the cultural differences between Ajars and Georgians but also thanks to a regime that was based on high elite continuity, had well-established networks of patronage, and was supported by an informal power and revenue-sharing agreement between the patron of Ajaria and the patron of Georgia.

8

Conclusion

Post-Soviet Wars and Theories of Internal Wars

> It is not that structure does not matter in the production of violence. Different structural elements may contribute to violent outcomes in individual situations but still not leave a systematic trace across multiple cases. . . . Thus, although the conflict out of which violence emerges may be heavily structured by the past, the specific outcome of violence is not.[1]

From Risks to Violence: The Post-Soviet Script

Scholars of internal wars are not only interested in identifying causal links between structural factors, processes, and the occurrence of wars. They are also interested in constructing a general and plausible "script" of organized violence—that is, a metanarrative that integrates different aspects of organized violence into one story that is sufficiently consistent to make sense. Typically, the findings of studies of internal wars lean toward one of three competing scripts. These scripts are not mutually exclusive, but their differences are substantial and have very different policy implications.

The first is the *perception script.* This script assumes that conflicting groups have mutually negative perceptions and that manipulation of hostile images, negative stereotypes, and stories of wrongs suffered is instrumental for internal wars. It is further assumed that a large cultural distance (caused by ethnic, ethnolinguistic, religious, or general worldview differences) between groups increases the potential for conflict, especially if, within a group, narratives of wrongs suffered and the other group's perceived negative or threatening characteristics are deeply rooted. According to this script, conflicts between competing identity groups are particularly prone to violent escalation, and once war breaks out, ethnic identities and negative stereotypes are reinforced in ways that make cooperation between groups highly unlikely.[2]

The second is the *grievance script,* which emphasizes political, economic, and cultural discrimination against groups. This script is based on the assumption that groups embark on the organization of violence as a reaction against their objective or perceived disadvantaging or oppression by the state or another group. In attempting to demonstrate this mechanism, the highlighted factors include the extent of economic inequality, of political rights, of state repression, and of cultural discrimination. The grievance script figures most prominently in the discourse and the self-representation of rebellion movements, since the existence of grievances is portrayed as legitimizing contestations and even rebellion.

The third is the *opportunity script.* Here, a major role is attributed to factors related to the costs of and anticipated profits from the organization of violence. This script proceeds from the basic assumption that rebellions, whatever their political and cultural motivation, only occur if the opportunity is given and can only be sustained if funding and recruitment can be secured. Such an approach generally looks for factors that reduce the real and opportunity costs of rebellion. The opportunity script pays special attention to the existence of lootable resources such as gems, drugs, and oil that may help in financing a rebellion.[3] Atypically low costs for recruiting fighters due to, for example, high unemployment and poverty among young males are also considered.

Based on the case studies presented in this book, the script of organized violence in the post-Soviet Union can now be reconstructed by incorporating propositions from different strands of conflict theory and the cultural, economic, and political characteristics of the post-Soviet Caucasus into a consistent narrative that singles out the nodal points of "thickened history."

Starting in 1987, in the Soviet Union, the tide of nationalist mobilization began to swell into a flood of protest, and by 1989 challenges to the incumbent Communist regime had proliferated all over the Soviet Empire. The Baltic republics (Estonia, Latvia, and Lithuania) took the lead, but nationalist mobilization soon spilled over into other republics. On February 22, 1988, on Theater Square in Yerevan, the capital of Armenia, 30,000 demonstrators rallied. Three days later, on February 25, there were around 1 million demonstrators on the streets of Yerevan—

about a quarter of the total population. By November 1988, in Georgia, the nationalist opposition mobilized up to 200,000 demonstrators and in Azerbaijan, there were as many as half a million demonstrators on Lenin Square in central Baku. These mass rallies continued, with different rhythms, in all three Caucasian republics until the end of the Soviet Union, or until the new states had gained enough strength to channel politics away from the streets and back into political institutions.

Campaigning for elections to the republican parliaments, which were to be held in the beginning of 1990, led to a new surge of mobilization. In Georgia, Armenia, Azerbaijan, Chechnya, and Dagestan, the incumbent elites faced growing pressure from political challengers, who had become organized in mass movements named Popular Fronts or National Congresses, thus displaying their roots in the "nation" or the "people." Surfing on the wave of nationalist mobilization, oppositional elites in Armenia and Georgia won the elections and took over the state; in Azerbaijan, the old Communist regime only hung onto power because it manipulated the elections, but it eventually collapsed in 1992 under intense pressure from the nationalist opposition, which carried the protest back onto the streets and made the country de facto ungovernable.

The elections to the republican parliaments infused these institutions with a degree of legitimacy they never had during the Soviet period. As the central institutions of the Soviet Union unraveled, as a result of the political reforms at the center and of the pressure from oppositional elites, these parliaments became the locus of political power within the republics, which were now rapidly moving toward independence. In the midst of the collapsing Soviet Union, the political arena had shrunk, and so, too, had the time horizon for actors. Strategic interaction now mainly took place within the republic or within the autonomous region and was largely determined by local actor constellations and local political aspirations, as well as by the perception that the window of opportunity was wide open. All the new elites had instrumentalized ethnic and national passions as their key resource in the struggle against the established authorities. Ambitious political entrepreneurs invariably turned into ethnic entrepreneurs because the national aspirations of different ethnic groups proved to be the best available resource in the struggle against the incumbent Soviet elites.

In August 1991, after the failed coup of Communist hardliners against President Mikhail Gorbachev, the Soviet Union ceased, for all practical purposes, to exist. Independence was now no longer an option, it was a necessity. Georgia, Armenia, and Azerbaijan, along with the other union republics, became independent states.

Some groups saw it as an opportunity, but others as a threat. The latter was particularly true for ethnic groups within those newly independent states that the Soviet ethnofederal system had vested with a territorial unit below the federal unit. Karabakh Armenians within Azerbaijan, Ossets and Abkhaz within Georgia, and Chechens within Russia all had their own territorial units, and the Soviet system had guaranteed them (in many cases disproportionate) representation and access to positions within the administration. With their "mother" republics becoming independent, these groups saw their status threatened. They feared that the leadership of the new states, which were still riding the nationalist wave, would not be willing or able to guarantee the status quo to its minorities. They also assumed that being an ethnic minority group within the federal Soviet Empire, with its numerous ethnic groups, was fundamentally different from being the sole minority within a nationalizing, unitary state. Consequently, some of these groups resented the move toward independence of their mother republics, and they advocated staying within the Soviet Union. Once the Soviet Union unraveled, they gradually shifted toward secession from their mother republics. Thus, the move of the union republics toward secession from the Soviet Union was countered by the move of the autonomous republics and regions toward secession from the union republics. A spiral of competing ethnonationalisms gained momentum.

These developments were intrinsically linked to the Soviet-style ethnofederalisms that had ascribed borders and territories vested with different status and differing degrees of autonomy to these groups. Once the center (Moscow) grew weaker and finally broke away, this system proved to be a "subversive institution" (according to Valerie Bunce), predetermining the cleavage structures that, in some cases, led eventually to organized violence. The Soviet ethnofederal institutions proved to be a powerful organizational resource that made mobilization along predetermined ethnic lines easier. The political institutions of the Soviet Union thus created a path dependency for fragmentation along ethnic lines.[4]

The nationalist mobilization and the growing tension between competing ethnic groups was accompanied and exacerbated by a devaluation of state capacities. The disruptive regime transitions from 1988 onward paralyzed Soviet (central) state institutions, while the young successor states of the Soviet Union were not yet capable of effectively carrying out key state functions. Many accounts of the unmaking of the Soviet Union and the emergence of the successor states focus predominantly on the processes of liberalization and democratization that spilled over from the center to the republics, eventually enabling the "national revolutions" in Georgia, Armenia, Chechnya, Azerbaijan, and Russia, but they tend to underrate the impact of the sudden loss in state capacities that all successor polities experienced.

Imagine a state that has no army and no defense ministry, no internal security forces, no working communication lines, and no tax revenues. Moreover, in this state an intense competition between incumbent and challenging elites is continuing over the future of this state and, especially, over the crafting of its political institutions, and the population is highly mobilized and carries politics onto the streets and the squares of the capital. This, in a nutshell, is how the successor states of the Soviet Union looked between around 1989 and 1992. They were, in the words of Venelin Ganev, "infrastructurally weak states, lacking functional bureaucracies, hopelessly ensnared in losing battles with predatory rent-seekers ravaging [their] resources, powerless to monitor lower state officials, unable to extract resources from the population, and operating in a social milieu that renders the rapid regeneration of state structures largely impossible."[5]

Perhaps most affected by the collapse of the Soviet Union were those institutions that exercised coercive capacities. Defense and internal security were the prerogative of the federal center, and its collapse left the successor states without any meaningful institutions that could have claimed the monopoly of violence.

By 1990, the Caucasus was caught by a double state weakness; the weakness of the old, dying Soviet state was paralleled by the weakness of the new, emerging independent states. The double state weakness opened wide a window of opportunity: it offered oppositional elites the chance to challenge the Communist incumbent elites, and it offered those ethnic groups that were dissatisfied with their current or anticipated future status the opportunity to better their circumstances. But the double state weakness not only provided ample opportunity to capture the state; it also gave rise to serious commitment problems. The new independent states that the new national elites tried to form out of the old union republics lacked meaningful state capacities and were therefore not able to deal with rising tensions within their territories or with their neighbors.

Both conflicts over Abkhazia and Karabakh exemplify the nature of the commitment problem. The secessionist aspirations of the Armenian population of Nagorny-Karabakh, expressed openly from the end of the 1980s on, could possibly have been defused by credible guarantees from the Soviet state of the Karabakh Armenians' safety, but in view of the political situation during the transition of 1988–1991, this was impossible. By 1989, the Soviet Union was seen as too weak and unwilling to commit itself, and the nationalizing state of Azerbaijan was seen, quite rightly, as extremely hostile to a change of status. Consequently, Karabakh Armenians ratcheted up the conflict by unilaterally opting for secession. Similarly, the Abkhaz had good reason to believe that Georgia would not be able to stick to an agreement over the future status of Abkhazia—a perception that proved to be justified. Consequently, both Karabakh and Abkhazia pushed for secession and the conflict spiraled into war.

The first interethnic clashes occurred between Armenians and Azeris in November 1987. Soon after, in November 1987, intercommunal violence on a much larger scale broke out in southern Armenia.[6] The forced population exchange between Azerbaijan and Armenia gained momentum, and by 1993, both countries had expelled their minorities.

Within Georgia, the first interethnic clashes between Ossets and Georgians took place in May 1989 and between Georgians and Abkhaz in June 1989. In both cases, violence flared up but did not yet escalate into large-scale, organized violence. As with intercommunal violence in Armenia and Azerbaijan, fragments of the local authorities actively took part in the organization of violence, together with private entrepreneurs of violence. This collaboration between local security organs and private entrepreneurs of violence is a recurring feature of the early stages of organized violence in the Caucasus.

Perhaps surprisingly, intercommunal violence did not occur between Russians and Chechens within Chechnya. The tide of national mobilization reached Chechnya quite late, but in August 1991, in perhaps the most revolutionary way of any regime changes in the former Soviet Union, popular protest had swept away the Soviet regime, and the National Congress of the Chechen People assumed power under the leadership of an ex-general of the Soviet army, Dzokhar Dudayev. Nevertheless, the large Russian community within Chechnya was not harassed.

Even when war broke out between Russia and the self-declared independent Chechen Republic, intercommunal violence was a rare occurrence.

Small-scale violence can occur spontaneously and can be inflicted by very small groups with few or no weapons. However, large-scale, sustained violence requires planning, investment, organization, and a certain number of organized fighters. In the literature on civil war, it is common to assume that "states" command far higher capacities than "rebels" to organize violence. Rebels then need to overcome this huge power asymmetry in order to challenge the state. For violent conflicts in the Caucasus, this dichotomy does not hold. Both the state and the rebels had to build their organizational capacities from scratch. They were similar to two start-up firms competing for the same market. In this way, for example, until 1992, the war between the "rebels" in Karabakh and the Azerbaijani "state" was waged by private militias on both sides. Only in 1992 did the government of the newly independent Azerbaijan and the government of the newly independent, albeit unrecognized, Karabakh start to organize the war. Likewise, the "troops" of the Georgian "state," which fought against the Ossets and later the Abkhaz "rebels," comprised volunteer militias and brigades under the command of and funded by private violent entrepreneurs (even if the Georgian state at times bestowed state office on these violent entrepreneurs) and were indistinguishable from the militias of the Ossets and Abkhaz. Moreover, the "rebels" in Chechnya, Karabakh, Ossetia, and Abkhazia laid claims to independence and began constructing statehood in the same manner as the mother state they wished to leave.

Since statehood was a project still to be achieved, the boundaries between the public/state and the private organization of violence were blurred and shifting on both sides. The only significant difference between state and rebels was the fact that the states (i.e., the former union republics) were awarded the status of sovereign, independent states after 1991, and the rebels were not. Volunteer militias, self-defense units, part-time and weekend fighters, and various groups of mercenaries fought on all sides, and they were barely subordinated to political control. There was little coordination between the numerous units, shared integrated command structures were nonexistent, and military discipline was often low. Criminal and military activities were barely distinguishable, and often profit-oriented activities such as looting, extortion, and hostage-taking took priority over military actions.

However, despite the chaotic array of various entrepreneurs of violence, be they state or private or politically or economically motivated, there was always a certain structural path-dependence behind the organization of sustained violence. Not all movements were able to overcome the threshold that separates spontaneous flare-ups of violence from sustained and organized violence.

In the beginning, the organization of violence in all conflict theaters relied on small volunteer units. These units were based on various, quite different, and relatively small scale social networks. It was a common pattern across the Caucasus that the organization of violence did not initially rely on an "impersonal" state bureaucracy but, rather, on densely knit, small-scale networks of interaction that facilitated trust and cohesion among their members. Some of these units were based on kinship, others on communal ties (villages and urban neighborhoods) or place of residence (the so called *zemlyachestvo*—people of common regional origin). Still others were formed around socioprofessional networks—research institutes, factories, or even schools formed their units.[7] With regard to the early stages of organized violence in Karabakh, the journalist Varten Hovanisian recalls: "A village formed its own unit, or two people met in courtyards, got in a car and just went. One person found a weapon, another hunting rifle. The weapons were absolutely extraordinary; people made their own do-it-yourself weapons and blew themselves up."[8]

Among the best-organized and best-equipped units in the early stages were paramilitary groups that had been formed by criminal organizations. They brought in an expertise in organizing violence, substantial financial means "earned" in the highly lucrative shadow economy of the Soviet Union, and quite often also a taste for fighting in the name of the nation. Tom de Waal reports an interview with an Azerbaijani volunteer who stated: "Criminals are often very big patriots. War is a very good place for criminals. You can do whatever you want. You can stab and kill. An educated person never goes to war. Criminals go to war. And at that time our army was commanded by criminals."[9]

This pattern holds not only for Azerbaijan. Paramilitary units with a background in organized crime also played a crucial role in Chechnya, Georgia, and Armenia, and similar patterns are reported for Kosovo and Serbia.[10]

The various armed groups and movements relied on different sources of funding. These differences were shaped both by preexisting structural conditions and by the trajectories of the conflicts that rearranged the options of accumulation. Sources of funding included sacrifices by the population (both as material donations and as volunteer labor in military units), donations from diaspora or ideologically motivated sponsors of violence, extraction of mineral resources, informal taxing of economic activities, and profits from criminal economic activities such as smuggling and extracting ransoms.

In the beginning, weapons procurement was a problem since the Soviet Union was arguably a state that exercised very tight control over the availability of small arms. The first automatic weapons were stolen from local police stations. In 1989, police units in Armenia and in Georgia reported mass thefts of stockpiled weapons, but it is highly plausible that many of these "thefts" were indeed a camouflage for criminal deals. With tension between different groups growing, local security forces also started to actively support private organizers of violence. They handed out weapons to nationalist paramilitaries, or they transformed themselves into military units. Small weapons became available on a large scale in the summer of 1991, when the Soviet army was in disarray and started to trade weapons, flooding local arms markets with cheap Kalashnikovs. In the spring of 1991, an AK-47 would have cost about US $600 in the central market in Grozny, Chechnya. In 1996, the price had fallen to US $100.[11] After May 1992, under the Tashkent Agreement, Soviet heavy weaponry was divided among the CIS states, and the level of violence reached a new high.

Gradually, the governments of the emerging states tried to gain more control over the various paramilitary groups and to foster coordination among them. The success of these efforts differed across the various theaters of conflict. Undoubtedly, the Armenians were the most successful. The leadership of Armenia and Nagorny-Karabakh, while de jure being two different entities, was highly successful in coordinating their joint war efforts against Azerbaijan. Soon after Armenia's declaration of independence on September 21, 1991, the National Army of Armenia was formed on the basis of various volunteer armed groups, which were created in 1988 for the defense of Nagorny-Karabakh; in Karabakh proper, the army of the Republic of Nagorny-Karabakh was formed. The two armies were highly integrated; its separation was largely a fiction. Armenian success on the battlefield was not least due to the high level of coordination between the newly emerging state structures and private entrepreneurs. However, even in Armenia, the subordination of pirate organizers of violence under the state's authority proved too difficult and repeatedly brought Armenia to the brink of state collapse.

In Abkhazia and South Ossetia, from the early stages of the conflicts, there was also a quite successful coordination between state and private entrepreneurs of violence. Arguably, as in the case of Armenia, the high threat perception vis-à-vis an enemy which was seen as clearly outnumbering the "rebel" forces facilitated this integration.

By contrast, in Chechnya and Georgia, the emerging state structures proved themselves unable to co-opt the private entrepreneurs of violence, which they had actually actively encouraged and supported. As a result, private entrepreneurs of violence hijacked the state, thereby perpetuating the conditions for organized violence. As a result, Chechnya lapsed into another war with Russia, and Georgia lapsed into civil war.

The situation in Azerbaijan fell somewhere between the situation in Armenia on the one side and in Chechnya and Georgia on the other. Clearly, the state failed to coordinate war efforts against Armenia; efforts were largely left to private entrepreneurs. In contrast, Azerbaijan avoided, although in extremis, outright civil war, and private entrepreneurs of violence did not capture the state. Instead, it was Heydar Aliyev, former KGB boss and first party secretary of Azerbaijan, who "stabilized" the state by imposing an authoritarian patronage system. By that time, however, the war was long lost.

In sum, the Caucasian script reads like this: exogenous institutional change increased the incentives for both state capture by nationalist elites and nationalist secession; the institutional legacy of Soviet ethnofederalism provided the structure for ethnic ties and cleavages, leading to a spiral of ethnonational competition. The dramatic lack of administrative capacities in the newly emerging states led to serious commitment problems, exacerbating ethnonational competitions and increasing incentives for secession. All organizers of violence initially relied on small, voluntary units which, in many cases, had their roots in organized crime, and the new states not only tolerated but actively sponsored these private entrepreneurs of violence. Not all states were successful in gradually imposing state control over entrepreneurs of violence; the hijacking of the state by private entrepreneurs negatively affected the consolidation of the new states, which, in turn, changed the trajectories of the conflicts and paved the way for new waves of violence. The sources of financing differed between the cases and changed over time; a common pattern, however, was that all violent movements relied on both donations from the community and criminal economic activities. Finally, with the collapse of the Soviet Union, small weapons and, after 1992, also heavy weaponry from the stockpile of the Soviet Union became widely available, which led to an escalation of violence.

Such a script, then, does not exclusively subscribe to the perception, the grievance, or the opportunity script. Wrongs suffered, ancient hatred, and perceived political, economic, and cultural discrimination were indeed often links in the causal chain leading to escalated organized violence, but they were by no means indispensable in this respect. These aspects contributed above all to the lowering of the costs of mobilization and recruitment, thus accelerating the escalation of conflict into organized violence. In this way, for instance, the general discourse of the Karabakh Armenians on their economic discrimination in the Azerbaijan SSR had a mobilizational effect, and the Armenian interpretive routine, according to which any conflict with Azerbaijan counted as posing a threat to their very existence, brought about rapid escalation. In Chechnya as well, the discourse of wrongs suffered was deep rooted. In particular, the deportation by Stalin and the topos of the eternal war against Soviet or Russian repression contributed greatly to the rapid mobilization of the Chechens. But more powerful even than perceived existing discrimination was the fear of discrimination to come in mobilizing groups. Because Armenians in Karabakh, Ossets and Abkhaz in Georgia, and some of the smaller groups in Dagestan feared that their status would deteriorate in the wake of sovereignization of their "mother republics," and of the simultaneous weakening of the center operating as guarantor of minority rights, they mobilized as soon as it was permitted by the new political freedoms brought by Gorbachev's glasnost. In multiethnic polities, this led to a countermobilization of other ethnic groups.

What Can Conflict Theory Learn from the Caucasus?

The wars in the post-Soviet Union and in the former Yugoslavia account for 30 percent of all internal wars since 1989, for 12 percent of all wars outside the least-developed countries since 1945, and for 64 percent of all wars within Europe since 1945.[12] If one accepts that the wars in the former Soviet Union and the former Yugoslavia have many similarities, then the sample presented in this book represent an important and sufficiently large "subclass" of cases to deserve the attention of general theories.

The lessons from the cases presented in this book speak to the following topics. First, and perhaps most surprising, the post-Soviet wars do not support two of the statistically most established claims of general conflict theory, the association between mountainous terrain and the advent of civil war, and the association between a low level of economic development and the advent of war. Second, the study of the post-Soviet wars offers valuable insights into the causal mechanisms that link newly independent states, state weakness, and the occurrence of internal wars. All Caucasian polities suffered from a sudden loss of state capacities, but some were able to reconfigure statehood and avoid violence. The explanation for success or failure is found in the cleavage structure of elites and in the degree of internal fragmentation of the new nationalist elites. Third, the cases support the importance of ethnic demography and offer insights into the circumstances in which ethnic demography increases the risk of internal wars. Fourth, the post-Soviet wars in the Caucasus hold some unexpected lessons with regard to the financing (and hence the feasibility) of rebel organizations. Rebel movements in the Caucasus financed themselves by different means, and the support of the population in what were, in the beginning, popular wars, played a significant role. But all the organizers of violence actually accumulated their start-up capital in the shadow and criminal economy of the Soviet Union.

To summarize, as discussed in chapter 3, perhaps the statistically most robust finding emerging from cross-national time-series datasets is that there is an association between a low level of development and an increased risk of internal wars. Based on these findings, the World Bank has installed a special program called LICUS (Low Income Countries under Stress) that seeks to specifically address the needs of these fragile states which are either on the brink of violence or recovering from recent wars. These most vulnerable countries typically have a GDP per capita level of below US $1,000, they suffer from very high child mortality, large parts of the population lack access to improved water and sanitation and other basic government services, and the administrative capacities of the state are very low. Although it is difficult to gauge the level of economic development and institutional capacity of the Soviet Caucasian Republics in the late 1980s (due to the notorious unreliability of Soviet statistics, and to the high levels of the unaccounted economic activity), it is clear that the polities in the Caucasus were by no means anything close to low-income countries under stress. They were, in global perspective, lower- to middle-income countries, with a relatively high degree of urbanization, very high levels of education, a good health care system, and high administrative capacities. Hence, from a global comparative perspective, the Caucasian counties cannot be qualified as poor and less developed countries.

However, there is also little evidence that a low level of development had an effect on the emergence of internal war when comparing across the Soviet Union: the Caucasus was neither the most "well off" region in the Soviet Union (the most affluent were the few urban centers in Russia and the Baltic Republics) nor the worst off (those were the Central Asian Republics). The well-to-do Baltic Republics rebelled but avoided violence. The poor Central Asian Republics, which wanted to preserve the Soviet Union, avoided violence, with the exception of Tajikistan, which fell victim to a bloody internal war that claimed as many as 50,000 lives between 1992 and 1997. Clearly, a comparison across the Soviet Union does not reveal a systematic association between violence and level of development.

Finally, within the Caucasus region, some secessionist groups did refer to economic discrimination to legitimize their secessionist claims. The Karabakh Armenians and the Abkhazians, in particular, complained that they were economically disadvantaged by the unloved republican centers. It is difficult to find substantial evidence to support such claims, however. Abkhazia was a rather affluent region within Georgia, mainly because of its privileged position as an all-Soviet *kurort* and its flourishing export trade in tea and citrus fruits. Karabakh was certainly an economically backward region, compared with urban centers such as Baku and Yerevan; but, according to most economic indicators, it was more prosperous than most other regions in Azerbaijan. In sum, there is no visible evidence that a low level of development (in absolute or in relative terms) played a significant role in the occurrence of internal wars in the post-Soviet Caucasus.

The second, allegedly robust finding of global conflict theory which events in the Caucasus do not support is the association of mountainous territory and war. This comes as a surprise, and at first it seems paradoxical since, indeed, the Caucasian cases have ideal topographies to sustain guerrilla warfare. However, the case studies do not reveal any convincing causal mechanism between mountainous terrain and risk of conflict. The decisive battles in Chechnya and Abkhazia took place on the plains, and mostly in an urban environment. In Karabakh, the rebels initially had the terrain against them, as did the Ossets in the conflict with the Georgians. Furthermore, no rebel movement had its origins in rural elites opposing urban elites. On the contrary, all rebel movements were initiated and led by the provincial urban intelligentsia, which formed alliances with entrepreneurs of violence with a background in the Soviet shadow economy. Hence, events in the Caucasus do not lend support to the claim that mountainous terrain advantaged rebels over governments and thus lowered the threshold for organizing wars.

Nevertheless, there is at least indirect evidence that "terrain" may be a proxy that has picked up the effect of two other factors. First, it could be argued that mountainous terrain made it more difficult for the central state to penetrate the remote mountainous regions; hence, mountainous regions remained peripheral, only loosely connected to the administrative center of the imperial power. A weakening of the central power (Moscow) then led to centrifugal reactions in such peripheral regions. Although this argument clearly finds support in the history of the Russian colonization of the North Caucasus, it is more difficult to sustain in the South Caucasus. Certainly, one could argue that Karabakh, Ossetia, and Ajaria were peripheral regions only loosely connected to their mother republics.

Second, "mountains" may be a proxy for untypical low costs associated with mobilizing young men as fighters. Many of the fighting units in Chechnya, Abkhazia, Ossetia, and Karabakh were filled by rural youth, recruited on the basis of village communities and family ties. Once the rebellions gained momentum and needed "muscles," the rural, mountainous regions provided recruits: family ties and village communities were preserved and often facilitated collective action, traditional values of honor were held in high esteem, and unemployment among young men was high. All helped to mobilize recruits. Indeed, many witnesses of the surges of violence that hit the Caucasus associated this previously unimaginable rupture of their way of life with the rural mob invading the urban centers. There is certainly an element of truth in this perception; however, it is important to note that most leaders of the rebellions came from the urban provincial intelligentsia, and most entrepreneurs of violence from the urban underworld.

In sum, mountains may be a proxy for peripheral regions with inbuilt centrifugal tendencies or for atypically low mobilization costs. Taken together, these two explanations go further toward explaining the intrinsic risks of mountainous terrain than the classical argument of guerrillas hiding in the mountains from government troops.

With regard to ethnic demography, the evidence from the case studies supports the main propositions of conflict theory. In particular, theory predicts a heightened risk of secessionism when ethnic groups inhabit relatively compact and clearly bordered territories and when they have an ethnic "big brother" or are backed by a diaspora community. In the Caucasus, this constellation came together for the Abkhaz, Ossets, Karabakh Armenians, and Chechens. A heightened risk of escalation also exists, when a group is potentially capable of assuming a dominant position within "its" territory at the expense of other groups, in order to secure privileged access to resources and key bureaucratic positions. In South Ossetia, Chechnya, and Nagorny-Karabakh, the titular nation constituted an absolute majority of the population and hence dominated the public sphere and the parliaments (soviets) brought to life by Gorbachev's reforms. Due to their demographic superiority, Chechens, Karabakh Armenians, and Ossets could put through resolutions and constitutional changes in "their" parliaments with the aim of extending their own sovereignty at the expense of the host republic. This demographic predominance undoubtedly increased their readiness for violence or military engagement, since ethnic numerical superiority lessened the costs of recruitment relative to the opponent. However, as the example of Abkhazia shows, admittedly, groups clearly in the minority (in 1989, at 17 percent) in "their" republic can also embark on violence escalation if they fear the loss of their privileged status.

The case studies showed, furthermore, that, once having broken out, violence in areas of high ethnic diversity quickly spreads and only ceases when ethnic cleansing has been completed. This was the case in Karabakh in particular, as well as in Abkhazia, West Georgia, and South Ossetia, but it is remarkable how long interethnic relations stayed free of violence in South Ossetia and Abkhazia. In both cases, it only came to massive, organized, violence after entrepreneurs from Georgia exported violence to South Ossetia and Abkhazia. Contrary to what might be expected, the local ethnic framework proved itself to be quite resistant to stress. Local ethnic mediating structures failed only when massive external breakdowns occurred. The case of Karabakh, admittedly, is structured differently; here, intercommunal violence began on the local level, long before the conflict escalated into an international war.

If the "ethnic dominance" factor can aggravate risks, then high ethnic fractionalization reduces risks. In the case study on Dagestan, it was shown that high ethnic fractionalization lowered the risk of conflict. This confirmed Collier and Hoeffler's thesis, according to which highly fractionalized societies are more stable than homogenous ones, since in ethnically highly fractionalized societies, the costs of organizing violence are higher than in less-fractionalized ones.[13] In highly segmented societies, the aspirations of an ethnic group can be blocked by a political alliance of other groups, and if the organization of violence nevertheless takes place, the recruitment pool for "ethnic rebels" in societies comprising many small groups, is, for each single group, small. Both mechanisms raise the costs of violence and hence lower the risk of conflict so that ethnic fractionalization can stabilize. This, however, requires that mechanisms for coalition formation and the achievement of consensus exist and are well rehearsed—in other words, are institutionalized. In the case study on Dagestan, it was described how the traditional institution of the *jamaat* and the Dagestani constitution, especially the electoral law, interlock in such a way as to ensure this stability.

Clearly, Soviet ethnic federalism decisively shaped the way ethnic cleavages emerged. Ethnic settlement patterns and demography, or the extent of ethnic fractionalization, depend on political, hence socially construed, borders. It is the drawing of borders and the endowment of a polity with political institutions that turns an identity group into an "ethnic minority" that aspires to change its status, or into a titular nation that is afraid of losing its privileges. Soviet ethnofederalism guaranteed the titular nations of the autonomous regions privileged access to resources and, especially in Abkhazia, a disproportionate representation in cadres. The elites of the titular nations saw in the moves toward independence of the union republics they belonged to a threat to their privileged status, and hence they opted for secession from the host republic. Mobilization and moves toward secession in Karabakh, Abkhazia, South Ossetia, and Chechnya led to an escalation of violence. The political institutions of the ethnofederal units proved essential for the mobilizing of ethnic groups, and they provided a measure of legitimacy to the national aspirations. In the secessionist regions (with the exception of Chechnya), a key role was played by local soviets, which attained a high degree of legitimacy with the free elections of 1989.

Not all forms of violent societal contestation transform into rebel organizations. For this to happen, rebel organizations need to mobilize material and social capital that makes the organization of violence feasible and sustainable. Organizers of violence may generate profits from the extraction of natural resources such as oil or diamonds;[14] from donations from the diaspora;[15] from taxing the population; from control over segments of the legal, illicit, or illegal economy; or from sponsors abroad. Material resources must be backed up by social capital, which is needed to overcome collective action problems. Organizers of violence hence also depend on mechanisms of social trust and social control that exist within certain segments of society, and which make the coordination of collective action possible. It is these small but dense networks that stem from communal ties, kinship, and socioprofessional interaction that bring agency to groups.

As was shown in the case studies, the organization of violence in the Caucasus relied on various sources of income and support. The wars in Chechnya, Karabakh, and Abkhazia were initially popular wars, seen by large segments of the population as legitimate self-defense. The social capital available within the society was therefore readily put at the service of organizing violence. Community and village ties, family bonds, and professional networks were used to mobilize recruits, and the population supported the rebels with donations. In marked contrast to Karabakh and Chechnya, popular support for the war in Azerbaijan never translated into a willingness to put the available social capital into the service of war. Azerbaijan, the resource richest of all Caucasian polities, was therefore the least prepared to sustain a war.

Conflict theory states that one important source of financing for rebellions stems from the extraction of natural resources. In the Caucasus, natural resources played a minor and ambiguous role. Only Chechnya and Azerbaijan possess significant natural resources, in both cases oil. In Chechnya, revenues from illegal and decentralized oil extraction doubtless contributed to the prolonging of the war. A direct causal connection between oil and the start of organized violence cannot be established, however. In Azerbaijan, too, there was no causality between the outbreak of conflict and the presence of oil. There is even a negative correlation between oil reserves and the length of war in the case of Karabakh as Azerbaijani strong men gave priority to investing in the power struggle in Baku and not in the war against Armenia. This crucially weakened the Azerbaijani front and led to the battleground victory of the Armenians.

As an alternative source of financing for the organization of violence, in all cases of war covered in this book, the diaspora provided material support and also fighters. However, this support was not decisive for either the onset of war or for the outcome on the battlefield. Despite the differences between the various rebel organizations, all of them (to various extents) initially relied on war capital accumulated in the shadow and criminal economy of the Soviet Union. Many of the key figures of the various rebel movements made their first career steps as entrepreneurs in the shadow economy, such as Shamil Basayev, or they were members of the criminal world, like Jaba Ioseliani, the leader of the Georgian Mkhedrioni. In Chechnya, the Dudaev regime was mainly financed by semilegal or outright criminal operations, such as the trade in nontaxed goods or the profits made from exporting cheap Russian oil to international markets. Entrepreneurs in the Soviet shadow economy made huge profits, using de facto independent Chechnya as a hub for their transactions. These entrepreneurs had a vested interest in a weak Chechen state, out of the reach of the Russian state but with access to Russian resources and to the world market. Georgia was dominated between 1989 and 1993 by two de facto private militia groups: one, the Mkhedrioni, originated in organized crime; the other, the National Guard, was quick to finance itself by criminal activities. It is one of the peculiarities of the Caucasian wars that many of these entrepreneurs of violence invested in the "national cause," obviously not without reaping benefits. Such alliances between patriot-businessmen and intellectual nationalists dominated politics after the political tide turned in 1990. They did not outlast the wars, but they arguably were instrumental in starting them, by combining material and social capital.

Access to weapons is an indispensable condition for the organization of violence. None of the groups in the Caucasus experienced problems in procuring weaponry. In the final analysis, all weapons originated in the stockpiles of the Soviet army and security forces, but different methods of procurement at different stages can be detected. The first wave of available weapons came from the militia and the security forces of the Interior Ministry, undergoing voluntary "nationalization" as a result of the weakness of the Soviet central state, and putting their weapons, and often their labor, at the service of the sovereignizing polities. In addition, groups in all polities systematically attacked the weapons depots of the security forces or purchased weapons from them (often such illegal weapons sales were simply declared to be robbery by the sellers, to distract from their lucrative and illegal arms dealing). After 1991, enormous quantities of light weaponry (including automatic guns, machine-guns, mortars, antitank rocket launchers, and multiple-rocket launchers) from the arsenal of the disbanding Soviet army came into the hands of the security forces of the successor polities, and after 1992, a part of the heavy weaponry of Soviet army arsenals was handed over to the now-independent former union republics. The conflicts in the former Soviet Union after 1991 caused a flourishing weapons trade to emerge, mostly in weapons of Russian manufacture. The most important retail outlet was the Russian army itself, especially in the very conflicts in which it was involved.

The study of post-Soviet wars also offers insights into the causal mechanisms that link newly independent states, state weakness, and the occurrence of internal wars. These insights are relevant beyond the Caucasus. At least 12 percent of the new states admitted to the United Nations after 1945 fell into internal war within two years of independence. Of the Soviet and Yugoslav successor states, roughly 33 percent descended into hostilities in the first decade after independence. Hence, the association between being a newly independent state and state weakness is statistically well documented.

The collapse of the Soviet Union was an unprecedented historical event; this book has not sought to explain the historical conditions and political events that caused the end of the Soviet Empire. Instead, by treating the unmaking of the Soviet system as an independent variable, the focus has been on its consequences in the post-Soviet successor states: the regime change and the subsequent state-building processes that were necessitated by the unraveling of the Soviet central state. Regime change and state building are necessarily highly conflict-prone processes. The post-Soviet Caucasian polities were open to violent conflicts because they were caught in power struggles between old and new elites, engaged by mobilizing ethnic groups, seriously restricted in their capacities to provide public goods, and lacking an established monopoly on the legitimate means of violence. But while some Caucasian societies evaded violent escalation, others did not. This is not to argue that there is a clear and unambiguous pattern to be observed that convincingly explains this variance. The emergence of violence is too complicated a process, contingent on a multitude of factors, of which some are highly idiosyncratic. Yet there are some broad lessons to be learned from the post-Soviet wars in the Caucasus.

First, the evidence from the Caucasus prompts us to expand the notion of state weakness. The last years of the Soviet Union were not only marked by a creeping loss of legitimacy, dwindling administrative capacities, and, ultimately, the loss of the monopoly over the means of violence. These years were also marked by booming opportunities in the shadow and criminal economies. As the case studies show, all successful organizers of violence had access to the profits generated in the Soviet shadow economy, or at least they formed coalitions with shadow entrepreneurs. It was a peculiarity of the Soviet Caucasus that much of these profits were allocated to the nationalist cause, but the general lesson remains valid: state weakness opens up opportunities in the shadow and criminal economies, the profits of which may turn into a source of funding for rebel organizations. In the cases reported in this book, this source proved to be more important than the sources which, in the literature, are primarily associated with funding rebel activities: exploitation of oil, timber, gemstones, and narcotics.

Second, whether a polity sailed through the storms of state weakness by and large unharmed, or perished in it, depended to a large extent on the structure of elite ties and cleavages. Two broad patterns characterize the outcome of the transitions in different union republics. In the Baltic states, nationalist elites and the reformist *nomenklatura* formed a broad coalition that greatly outnumbered the small die-hard Communist *nomenklatura*. The new nationalized elite then took control of the existing political institutions and turned them into instruments for the achievement of independence. The "revolution" ran its course essentially "legalistically," within the relevant political institutions, based on a broad elite consensus, supported by the overwhelming majority of the population, and somewhat tamed by the lure of membership in the European Union, which helped to soften extreme nationalist and exclusionist polices that threatened interethnic stability. The other pattern can be found in its "pure" form in the Central Asian republics and in Azerbaijan before 1992, where a powerful rump of the *nomenklatura* adopted some nationalist rhetoric but essentially stayed in power and kept the Soviet system in place.

Notably, the Caucasian polities that fell victim to internal wars differed from both patterns. In Chechnya, the so-called Chechen revolution swept away the old *nomenklatura*. The old Soviet elite was completely replaced, but the new nationalist elite was highly fragmented and soon engulfed in fractional struggles. A similar pattern was observed in Georgia, where the nationalist elite took over (other than in Chechnya, by means of elections), but this new elite was neither willing to open its ranks and compromise with the old *nomenklatura* nor capable of controlling mavericks within its own ranks. As a result, the Georgian national movement was not only radicalized and internally fragmented; it was also unable to engage in any (if only tactical) compromise with the old elites. Politics in Georgia became even more deinstitutionalized. Deprived of any meaningful tools for ruling, the new Georgian elites relied on their only resource—nationalist populism.

In Chechnya and in Georgia, private violent entrepreneurialism, usually linked to the most lucrative segments of the shadow and criminal economies, flourished. The "state"—at that time, little more than a name—actually called for the services of these private entrepreneurs of violence because it needed military muscle. This symbiosis was made official by the appointment of violent entrepreneurs as defense or prime ministers. As a result, far from claiming the monopoly of violence, the state became, to a certain extent, a free rider on the private organization of violence—which it was never able to control. The private entrepreneurs of violence had little inclination to invest in state building since a strong state would not tolerate their lucrative business activities. In this way, a downward spiral leading to further erosion of statehood was set in motion.

Azerbaijan initially seemed to follow the Central Asian pattern. Until 1992, the old Communist *nomenklatura* stayed in power, although the nationalist opposition, in contrast to Central Asia, was powerful and able to fill the streets of Baku with hundreds of thousand of demonstrators. In summer 1992, the old regime fell because it was losing in the war against Karabakh and Armenia. The new nationalist elite stayed in power for only 15 months. It proved to be too fragmented internally, it lacked the support of the bureaucratic cadres, it did not do better on the battlefield than its predecessor, and it could never control the entrepreneurs of violence that had formed private militias for use at the front in Karabakh and, as it turned out, at home.

Armenia, once more, is a paradox. Here, the mode of transition resembled entirely the Baltic mode—the new nationalist elites, after having campaigned successfully on the Karabakh issue, took over the state but then formed a broad coalition with the old *nomenklatura*. Hence, old and new Armenian elites avoided fragmentation. But whereas in the Baltic states this broadly supported elite consensus helped steer the countries peacefully through transition and toward entrance in the

European Union, in the case of Armenia the elite coalition was instrumental in organizing the war over Karabakh. Hence, the Armenian elites' closing rank did not just help manage the transitions, it helped to successfully organize a national war.

Finally, in Dagestan, it was the conjuncture of a near complete elite continuity, the capacity to co-opt potentially oppositional elites, and the preservation of formal and informal power-sharing mechanisms that allowed Dagestan to be steered unharmed through the calamities of post-Soviet transition.

In conclusion, the successful recovering of statehood after the shock of the Soviet collapse is attributable to three factors: a high level of elite continuity, the capability of new elites to form coalitions with significant parts of the old *nomenklatura,* and the degree of internal fractionalization of new elites. These factors, in turn, were shaped by highly idiosyncratic social and cultural constellations, which can be described, as in this book, but which resist any further generalization.

Notes

NOTES TO CHAPTER 1

1. According to some estimates, only 4.4 percent, or 2 out of 45, potential cases of conflict escalated into enduring violent conflicts. See Fearon and Laitin, 1996.

2. For a good overview of the numerous small conflicts, see Tishkov, 1997.

3. The database compiled under the leadership of Mark Beissinger, "Non-Violent Demonstrations and Mass Violent Events in the Former USSR, 1987–1992," registers a total of 2,177 occurrences of mass violence for the entire Soviet Union between January 1986 and December 1992. At least 80 percent of these took place in the Caucasus (Beissinger, 1992a; Beissinger, 1992b; Beissinger, 2002).

4. Among the most influential are Collier and Hoeffler, 2004a; Doyle and Sambanis, 2000; Fearon and Laitin, 2003; Hegre et al., 2001.

5. Collier and Hoeffler, 2004a.

6. Fearon and Laitin, 2003.

7. Ross, 2004.

NOTES TO CHAPTER 2

1. This is the title of a seminal essay of Valery Tishkov, 2000, in which he argues against a substantive conceptualization of nation and ethnos in the context of the former Soviet Union.

2. In this summary of Caucasian history, I rely on the following studies, among others: Gammer, 1994; Baddeley, 1908; Broxup, 1992; Suny, 1989; Suny, 1993; Goldenberg, 1994; Lieven, 1998; Khodarkovsky, 2002; Tishkov, 1997.

3. On the social organization of the Vainakh, see Zelkina, 1996.

4. See chapter 10 (" 'We Are Free and Equal Like Wolves': Social and Cultural Roots of the Chechen Victory") of Anatol Lieven's 1998 book on the Chechen War.

5. Reynolds, 2000.

6. Suny, 1993, p. 3.

7. A concept of Freud's, which Michael Ignatieff, 1998, applies for the contemporary Balkans.

8. Goldenberg, 1994, p. 26.

9. On this, see Hill, 1995, p. 12; Sheehy, 1991, pp. 63–78; Zlapotol'skii, 1960.

10. The category "Dagestani," which surfaces in some censuses, does not refer to an ethnic group but to the multiethnic population of the Dagestan ASSR.

11. Bugaj, 1995.

12. Of the altogether over 100 "official" ethnic groups, 35 were allocated their own territory (Bremmer, 1997, p. 8).

13. Law 15, Article 13, Paragraph 252 (Zakon o poryadke resheniya voprosov, svyazannikh s vykhodom soyuznoy respubliki iz SSSR) stipulates that in case of secession of a SSR that "za narodami avtonomnykh respublik i avtonomnykh obrazovanij sokhranyaetsya pravo na samostoyatel'no reshenie voporosov o prebyvanii v SSSR ili v vykhodyashchei respublike, a takzhe na postanovku voprosa o svoem gosudarstvennom pravovom statuse." [The peoples of the Autonomous Republics and Autonomous Units retain the right to independently decide whether they remain in the USSR or in the seceding republic, but also on the question of their legal status.]

14. See Holton, 1998, chapter 6: "Nationalism and Ethnicity: Obsolete Relicts, Anti-global Trends or Key Component of the Global Field?"

15. The "Triumph of the Nations" as concept enjoyed both wide circulation and intellectual respectability (Carrere D'encausse, 1993; see also Fowkes, 1997).

16. Zürn and Brozus, 1996; Huntington, 1993.

17. Gumilev, 1989.

18. Bromley, 1973; Bromley, 1981; Bromley, 1983.

19. Gumilev, 1989.

20. Brubaker, 1996.

NOTES TO CHAPTER 3

1. Brown et al., 1997, p. 4.

2. Sandole, 1999, p. 17.

3. Most studies use data from the seminal Correlates of War Project (COW) and apply its definition of civil war. The COW definition of civil war requires that there is organized military action that results in at least 1,000 battle deaths; that the national government at the time is actively involved as a party to the conflict; and that, in order to distinguish wars from genocide, massacres, and pogroms, there is effective resistance—therefore, at least 5 percent of the deaths must have been inflicted by the weaker party. Other datasets have reduced the number of battle deaths to capture internal wars with lower levels of violence and to better differentiate between levels of violence. The dataset compiled by Gleditsch et al., 2002, for example, codes three levels of violence: minor con-

flicts produce more than 25 battle-related deaths per year; intermediate conflicts produce more than 25 battle-related deaths per year, with a total conflict history of more than 1,000 battle-related deaths; and wars are conflicts that result in more than 1,000 battle-related deaths per year.

4. Among the most influential studies, of which the results are reported here, are Collier and Hoeffler, 2004a; Fearon, 2004; Fearon and Laitin, 2003; Hegre et al., 2001; Sambanis, 2001; Sambanis and Elbadawi, 2002.

5. Collier et al., 2003a.

6. Fearon and Laitin, 2003.

7. Hegre et al., 2001.

8. Fearon and Laitin, 2003.

9. Horowitz, 1985.

10. Fearon and Laitin, 2003. Instability is coded as a change of three or more on the Polity IV scale in any of the three years, preceding the country year in question. Transition periods and interruptions, coded as 77 and 99 in the Polity IV dataset, are also taken as an indicator of instability. The measure of instability is lagged in order to avoid the tautological finding that instability equals internal war.

11. Hegre et al., 2001.

12. Collier and Hoeffler, 2001; Collier and Hoeffler, 2004a; Fearon and Laitin, 2003.

13. These are called, in the Polity IV dataset terminology, anocracies. A regime is coded as an anocracy when its polity score is between −5 and +5. A full democracy has a score of +10, a full autocracy a score of −10 (Jaggers and Gurr, 1995).

14. Hegre et al., 2001; Goldstone et al., 2005. The same argument is made by Snyder, 2000, and, for external wars, by Mansfield and Snyder, 2002.

15. Fearon, 1995; Fearon, 1998; Walter and Snyder, 1999.

16. Ross, 2004b.

17. Collier, 2001; Collier and Hoeffler, 2004a; Fearon and Laitin, 2003; Ross, 2004b.

18. For a discussion of possible causal mechanisms, see Humphreys, 2005.

19. Collier and Hoeffler, 2004b.

20. Humphreys, 2005.

21. Collier and Hoeffler, 2004a.

22. Collier et al., 2003a. The same argument is supported by Walter, 2004.

23. Walter, 2004.

24. Elbadawi and Sambanis, 2002; Fearon and Laitin, 2003; Collier and Hoeffler, 2004a—all reach this conclusion.

25. Collier and Hoeffler, 2004a; Hegre et al., 2001. This finding is not supported by Fearon and Laitin, 2003.

26. Fearon and Laitin, 2003.

27. De Rouen and Sobek, 2004; Elbadawi and Sambanis, 2002; Zürcher, Baev, and Koehler, 2005.

28. Gurr, 2000. Problems with the classification of ethnic groups in the Minorities at Risk Project are discussed below, but for a critical discussion of the entire Minorities at Risk Project, see Tishkov, 1999.

29. Gurr and Harff, 1995. A similar argument is made by Horowitz, 1985.

30. Examples include the case studies on Peru and Colombia in Sherman, 2001.

31. Collier and Hoeffler, 2004a; Fearon and Laitin, 2003. Fearon and Laitin claim to control for group level discrimination by including a measure of democracy. They reason that "other things being equal, political democracy should be associated with less discrimination and repression along cultural or other lines, since democracy endows citizens with a political power (the vote) they do not have in dictatorships" (p. 79). This argument is not convincing. From the viewpoint of a minority, the shift to democracy may actually lead to greater discrimination, since the majority could use its numerical dominance at the ballots to vote to abolish specific minority protection rights. Democracy is thus not necessarily a good indicator for nondiscriminatory arrangements.

32. Tishkov, 1999a, 572.

33. Griffin, 2003.

34. Olson, 1965.

35. Nevertheless, some authors argue that motivation is the key factor; see, for example, Gurr, 1993.

36. Weinstein, 2005.

37. Collier and Hoeffler, 2004b; De Soysa, 2000; Ross, 2001; Ross, 2003.

38. According to Collier and Hoeffler, 2004a, this is a determining factor.

39. For example, Putnam, Leonardi, and Nanetti, 1993.

40. These are the elements of social capital, according to Onyx, 2000.

41. Wall, Ferazzi, and Schryer, 1998.

42. Woolcock and Naranyan, 2001.

43. Elwert, 1997; Elwert, 2003.

44. There are now numerous excellent studies of economies of internal wars. For example, Kaldor, 1999; Elwert, Feuchtwang, and Neubert, 1999; Elwert, 2003; Elwert, 1997; Jean and Rufin, 1999; Keen, 1998; Keen, 2000; Collier and Hoeffler, 1999a; Collier and Hoeffler, 1999b; Collier and Hoeffler, 2001; Collier, 2000a; Collier, 2000b; Collier, 2000c; Reno, 1999; Reno, 2000; Duffield, 2000.

45. Elwert, 2003.

46. McAdam, Tarrow, and Tilly, 2001, p. 194.

47. Mayntz and Scharpf, 1995; Scharpf, 1997.

48. Brinton and Nee, 2001; Powell and Dimaggio, 1991.

49. North, 1990, p. 3.

50. There are very few accounts of the the post-Soviet turmoils centering on an empirical analysis of formal and informal institutions. Among those that do provide such an analysis are Koehler and Zürcher, 2003; Zürcher and Koehler, 2001.

51. A number of studies on regime change do focus on institutional factors and occasionally also touch on the causes of ethnopolitical violence. For example, Bratton and Walle, 1996; Snyder, 2000, particularly p. 48, "Building Nationalist Institutions"; Bunce, 1999; Rubin and Snyder, 1998.

52. There may be different reasons for this striking observation. Perhaps most important, the dominant strand of conflict research, large-*n* quantitative statistical approaches, is not well suited to integrating institutionalist approaches into its research agenda because social institutions cannot easily be quantified, proxied, or measured. For attempts to integrate an institutional approach into conflict analysis, see Koehler and Zürcher, 2003; Zürcher, 2002; Zürcher, 2004; Zürcher and Koehler, 2001.

53. Lijphart, 1975; Lijphart, 1985.

54. Derluguian, 1998.

55. Admittedly, this was not true for Russians, who held key positions in all republics to act as the arbiter between the groups.

56. Arguably, this is the case for post-Soviet Armenia, Georgia, and Azerbaijan (Koehler and Zürcher, 2004; Easter, 1996). The same can be claimed for post-Soviet Central Asia and many states in Southeast Asia and Africa. For African states, see, for example, Easter, 1996; Elwert, 2001; Reno, 2000.

57. Steinmo, Thelen, and Longstreth, 1992.

NOTES TO CHAPTER 4

1. Vasil'eva, 1994, p. 58.
2. Lieven, 1998, p. 57.
3. Holoboff, 1995a.
4. Gall and De Waal, 1997, p. 127.
5. Gammer, 2002.
6. Hill, 1995, p. 44.
7. Schrepfer-Proskurjakov, 2006.
8. Interview with author, Chechnya, September 1996.
9. Zürcher, 1999.
10. Bennigsen and Wimbush, 1986; see also the discussion in Blandy, 2003, pp. 40–47.
11. Lieven, 1998.
12. Derluguian, 2005, p. 49; Sorkirianskaia, 2005.
13. Sokirianskaia, 2005.
14. Sokirianskaia, 2005, p. 461.

15. Text published in Abdulatipov, Boltenkova, and Yarov, 1993, pp. 22–25.

16. Halbach, 1994; Halbach, 1995.

17. Pain and Popov, 1995; Segbers, 1994; Halbach, 1994; Halbach, 1995; Zürcher, 1997; Zürcher, 1998; Dunlop, 1998; Gall and De Waal, 1997.

18. According to Sergei Yushenko, chairman of the Duma Committee for Defense, these are the words of Oleg Lobov, then secretary of the National Security Council (Gall and De Waal, 1997, p. 161).

19. In November 1994, this included A. Korzhakov, Yeltsin's chief bodyguard; N. Egorov, former minister of Nationalities and special representative in Chechnya; V. Ilyushin, head of the presidential chancellery; Oleg Lobov, secretary of the Security Council; P. Grachev, minister of Defense; O. Soskovets, vice-premier; and V. Stepashin, head of the Federal Security Service. With the exception of Ilyushin and Korzhakov, all these men belonged to the National Security Council, which formalized the decision to go to war on November 29, 1994. Apart from the president and the head of his chancellery, ex officio the heads of the power ministries (Defense Ministry, Interior Ministry, and the foreign and domestic intelligence services), the foreign minister and the head of the government belong to the Security Council.

20. For an overview of alleged Russian strategic interests, see "Geostrategische Motive Rußlands in Tschetschenien-Krieg?" 1995.

21. See Holoboff, 1995; Götz, 1995.

22. Kovalyev et al., 1995; Orlov and Cherkassov, 1998; Orlov, Cherkasov, and Sirotkin, 1995.

23. Kovalyev et al., 1995.

24. Kisriev, 2004, p. 178.

25. Yusupov, 1998.

26. "Chechnya: Parliament, Sharia Court Likely to End Conflict," 1998.

27. Arabic for "consultation." In early Islamic history, Shura denoted an electoral college, which the second Kalif Umar I (634–644) convened to choose his successor. Later, "Shura" in Islamic states denoted a state council, a consultative body, a parliament, or a court, before which subjects could bring their complaints about the government. The word "Shura" is also the title of the 42nd chapter of the Koran, in which the faithful are called on to settle their affairs through consultation.

28. Isayev, 1998.

29. Quoted in Balburov, 1999, p. 7; my translation.

30. "Dual Power in Chechnya?" 1999.

31. "Moscow Grozny Seek to Contain Latest Crisis," 1999.

32. Yusupov, 1998.

33. Yusupov, 1998.

34. Quoted in Balburov, 1999, p. 7; my translation.

35. Kisriev, 2004, p. 172.

36. Yusupov, 1998.

37. Interior Minister Kazbek Makashev, interview with the author, Grozny, October 6, 1996.

38. "New Government of Chechnya to Start Functioning No Later Than 20 January," 1997.

39. "The Time the Chechen Authorities Gave the Illegal Armed Formations to Cease Their Activity Has Run Out," 1998.

40. Putin, 1999.

41. Zürcher, 2000.

42. International Helsinki Federation for Human Rights et al., 2005.

43. International Helsinki Federation for Human Rights et al., 2005, p. 6.

44. Sapozhnikov, 2003.

45. During the first war, no statistics on the internally displaced were kept. The figures come from Russian news reports and the human rights organization Memorial (A. Orlov, interviews by the author, Moscow and Grozny, September 1996).

46. Lambroschini, 2000; Bunich, 1995; Gall and De Waal, 1997, p. 129.

47. Gall and De Waal, 1997, p. 131.

48. Gall and De Waal, 1997, p. 127.

49. Some sources speak of up to 9 billion petrodollars. This number is surely exaggerated. Other estimates speak of US $800–900 million as illegal profits from oil export in 1993 (Kolokloceva, 1995; Russian Information Centre and R. I. A. Novosti, 2001).

50. Gall and De Waal, 1997, p. 127.

51. "Put' Djokhara—kuda on privel?" 1998.

52. Taysumov, 1997.

53. "Over Half of Oil Produced in Chechnya in 1998 Stolen," 1999.

54. Decree No. 199 of June 21, 1999, "On Incentives for Staff of State-Run Bodies Engaged in Implementing Decree of President No. 131, April 28, 1999" (quoted in Russian Information Centre and R. I. A. Novosti, 2001).

55. For comparison: in Russia, there were 823 kidnappings in 1996; 1,140 in 1997; and 1,415 in 1998 (Dzhambulayev, 2000).

56. Memo from Russia's Interior Ministry, "On the State of Struggle against Kidnapping and Hostage Taking in the North Caucasian Region," (quoted in Russian Information Centre and R. I. A. Novosti, 2001).

57. Borisov, 2001.

58. Memo from Russia's Interior Ministry.

59. Borisov, 2001. In Kazakhstan, the figure is apparently 10 percent of regular income.

60. Fairbanks, 2002.

61. *Izvestia,* January 6, 1995, p. 2, quoted in Tishkov, 2004, p. 67.

62. Makarenko, 2001.

63. For example, www.quoqaz.com. After September 11, the site was no longer accessible.

64. Gall and De Waal, 1997, p. 207.

65. Gall and De Waal, 1997, p. 208.

66. Felgenhauer, 1995.

67. Lambroschini, 2000; Bunich, 1995; Gall and De Waal, 1997.

68. Gall and De Waal, 1997, p. 113.

69. Author's notes, Grozny, September 1996. See also Lagnado, 2000. Gall and De Waal, 1997, p. 192, put the price of an AK-74 on the market in Grozny at U.S. $600 before the war and U.S. $200 during the war. For the arms sales of the Russian army, see Gall and De Waal, 1997, p. 240.

70. Tishkov, 2004, pp. 35–48.

71. Lapidus, 1998.

NOTES TO CHAPTER 5

Parts of this chapter originally appeared in the volume *Statehood and Security: Georgia after the Rose Revolution,* edited by Bruno Coppieters and Robert Legvold (Cambridge, MA: MIT Press, 2006), copyright American Academy of Arts and Sciences. Reprinted with permission.

1. This is an estimate by Georgian political scientist Gia Tarkhan-Mouravi. There are no precise figures for Adzharia. Ajars differ from Georgians chiefly in that they are Muslim. This was barely reflected in Soviet statistics, and when it was, then incorrectly.

2. Even later Western estimates do not capture the extent of the upswing. World Bank data indicate GDP growth per capita of just over 7.5 percent between 1980 and 1985. These data are cited in Zürcher, Baev, and Koehler, 2005.

3. Soviet and Georgian statistical data, cited in Baev, 2003.

4. Wheatley, 2005, pp. 41–42.

5. Gerber, 1997.

6. These data come from the *1989 USSR Population Census: The Final and Most Comprehensive Population Census of the Former Soviet Union Ever Conducted* (Goskomstat, 1996). The figures need to be treated with caution, since this census was less than accurate and not free of political manipulation. Demography is a hotly disputed issue between Georgians and Abkhazians.

7. For example, Slider, 1997, p. 170.

8. Much of this population movement was instigated by the Soviet authorities for political reasons (Derluguian, 1998).

9. Suny, 1994, p. 323.

10. Wheatley, 2005, p. 45.

11. Goskomstat, 1996.

12. Zverev, 1996.

13. Adamon Nykhas (People's Assembly) was the South Ossetian popular movement created as a political platform for advancing the claim for more autonomy.

14. Gachechiladze, 1995, pp. 14, 41; Nodia, 1988.

15. An additional explanation of the nonmobilization of the Armenians in Georgia draws on Armenians' self-policing capacities. The political leaders of Armenia proper, together with the leaders of the Armenian community in Georgia, were able to contain the community's mobilization. Any such mobilization was seen as clearly undesirable by Armenia, which was already engaged in the conflict over Nagorny-Karabakh. This explanation is not often mentioned in the literature, but decision makers in the region repeatedly put it forward in conversations with the author in July 2002.

16. Derluguian, 1998, p. 262.

17. Jones, 1993; Suny, 1995; Wheatley, 2005.

18. Nodia, 1995.

19. Wheatley, 2005.

20. Baev, 1996.

21. Nizharadze, 2001.

22. Slider, 1997. See also Fuller, 1993; Jones, 1995.

23. The organization changed its name in October 1992 and became the Confederation of the Peoples of the Caucasus (CPC).

24. Nizharadze, 2001.

25. Nizharadze, 2001. See also Gleditsch et al., 2002.

26. Nizharadze, 2001.

27. Damoisel and Genté, 2004. Other sources speak of around 2,500 battle-related deaths (Gleditsch et al., 2002).

28. Nizharadze, 2001; Baev, 2003.

29. Beissinger, 2002.

30. This is also the main argument of Suny, 1995.

31. Zürcher, Baev, and Koehler, 2005.

32. Zürcher, Baev, and Koehler, 2005.

33. Data according to Zürcher, Baev, and Koehler, 2005.

34. Alkhazashvili, 2004.

NOTES TO CHAPTER 6

1. Suny, 1993, p. 194; Jacoby, 1998a, p. 229.

2. The relatively strong negotiating position of the Azerbaijani Party leader Narimanov, who could use control of the Azerbaijani oil production as a bargaining chip, certainly played a part here. In addition, the creation of an auton-

omous region with an Armenian majority on Azerbaijani territory weakened both republics and thus benefited the central authorities: the Armenians in Karabakh needed a guarantee of security from Moscow to exercise their right to autonomy, and the Azerbaijanis required the support of the central power to exercise control over Karabakh. Both factors strengthened the role of the Moscow center as arbitrator. In addition, the assignment of Karabakh to Azerbaijan and the creation of an Azerbaijani exclave Nakhichevan in Armenia also improved relations between the young Soviet Union and the young Turkish Kemalist state, since Turkey now acquired in Nakhichevan a direct border to Azerbaijan.

3. Technically, the AO was initially subordinated to the Transcaucasian Republic, which comprised the Georgian SSR , the Armenian SSR, and the Azerbaijani SSR . This republic was a short-lived paper tiger, however, and was rendered irrelevant with the founding of the USSR in 1924. It was abolished in 1936.

4. Some Armenian authors tend to exaggerate the change in ethnic demography. In actual fact, the proportion of Armenians in Karabakh fell from an estimated 80 to 85 percent in 1924 to 76 percent in 1989.

5. Suny, 1993, p. 195.

6. Goldenberg, 1994; Jacoby, 1998b.

7. Jacoby, 1998a, p. 238; my translation.

8. Libaridian, 1999, p. 88.

9. Luchterhandt, 1993, p. 42.

10. Suny, 1993, p. 198.

11. Members of this first Karabakh Committee were, among others, writer Silva Kaputikyan; chairman of the Academy of Sciences of the Armenian SSR, Viktor Hambarcumyan; economist Igor Muradian; theater director Vyacheslav Sarukhanian; Manvel Sargsian; historian Shahen Mkrtichian; and student Gagik Safarian.

12. Fuller, 1988. On the role of the Azerbaijani refugees, see Laitin and Suny, 1999.

13. Beissinger, 2002; Suny, 1993, p. 199. According to both authors, Azerbaijani refugees from Armenia were involved in the Sumgait pogrom, which implies that by February 1988 an organized forced migration of Azerbaijanis from Armenia had already taken place.

14. Jacoby, 1998a, p. 180.

15. Quoted in Chorbajian, Donabedian, and Mutafian, 1994, p. 89.

16. Novikova, 2001.

17. *Krunk* means "stork." The stork is a symbol of the Armenians' longing for their homeland.

18. Novikova, 2001.

19. Suny, 1993, p. 202.

20. Jacoby, 1998a, p. 165.

21. Goldenberg, 1994, p. 163.

22. De Waal, 2003, p. 67.

23. This congress is comparable with the National Congresses created in 1989 in Estonia and Latvia. These were elected assemblies, from which non-Latvians and non-Estonians, respectively, were excluded, and which rivaled the Supreme Soviet. The National Congresses exerted constant pressure on the Supreme Soviet.

24. Armpress International Service, September 26, 1989, quoted in Croissant, 1998, p. 35.

25. Libaridian, 1999, p. 20.

26. Jacoby, 1998a, speaks of 54 dead and 200 injured.

27. Croissant, 1998, p. 37.

28. Goltz, 1999, p. 114.

29. Yunusov, 2001.

30. Novikova, 2001.

31. Croissant, 1998, p. 41.

32. Formally, on September 2, 1991, Karabakh (together with the district of Shauminan, which did not belong to the NKAO) declared independence from Azerbaijan, not from the Soviet Union. This was supposed to satisfy the demands of Soviet law, especially the already quoted (in Chapter 2, note 13) law of April 1990, on the secession of the union republics, which ruled that, in the case of the secession of an SSR, the AOs and ASSRs had the right to decide for themselves whether they wished to leave the union together with the SSR, or leave the SSR and remain in the union. In September, however, the USSR de facto no longer existed, so that the decision of Karabakh to separate from Azerbaijan and not from the USSR was motivated more by formal, legal reasoning. The referendum of December 10, 1991, on the independence of Karabakh no longer referred to the Soviet Union, which at this point in time only existed on paper. As shown in Chapter 2, the arguments for and against the independence of AOs and ASSRs, with reference to the statute books of the Soviet Union are contradictory, for many reasons. First, with the collapse of the Soviet Union, which preceded the declarations of independence, the frame of reference for the legislation vanished. Second, the law was loosely phrased and did not lay down any procedures on how the decision on status was to be met. Third, ethnic cleansing had preceded the self-determination of the Karabakh Armenians (there was no doubt about their desire not to live in an Azerbaijani state), so there are considerable questions about the legitimacy of the referendum. With the Karabakh declaration of independence, Karabakh and Armenia had silently reversed their unification of December 1989. The Armenian government decided against retaining the unification resolution, with the argument that this had occurred within the framework of the Soviet constitution, which, after the end of the Soviet Union, had no further validity. The newly founded republic of

Armenia recognized the principles of the OSCE Helsinki Convention, which designated irredentist claims as contrary to international law, if all sides were not in agreement over a change of borders. This pragmatic decision saved Armenia from international isolation and did not obstruct it from being a party to the war of Karabakh against Azerbaijan.

33. Goltz, 1999, p. 74.
34. De Waal, 2003.
35. De Waal, 2003, p. 172.
36. Yunusov, 2001; my calculations.
37. Goltz, 1999; Goldenberg, 1994, pp. 345, 357–359, 124–125.
38. Novikova, 2001; Alexanian, 2001.
39. Yunusov, 2001.
40. Yunusov, 2001.
41. Derluguian, 2005.
42. De Waal, 2003.
43. Groong, 2004.
44. *Analiticheskii vestnik agenstva Postfactum* (1992), no. 2, p. 3.
45. Yunusov, 2001, p. 1.
46. Yunusov, 2001, Table 2A.
47. Conversation with the author, Yerevan, July 2001.
48. Novikova, 2001.
49. Novikova, 2001.
50. Information on the paramilitary groupings is provided by Novikova, 2001.
51. Melkonian and Melkonian, 1993, p. 194.
52. Yunusov, 2001.
53. Weisbrode, 2001, p. 29.
54. Arsaly, 1995, pp. 4–18.
55. Yunusov, 2001.
56. Yunusov, 2001, p. 1.
57. Arsaly, 1995, p. 61.
58. For example, Bercovitch and Jackson, 1997.
59. Novikova, 2001.
60. Novikova, 2001.
61. Yunusov, 1996, p. 17, appendix 1; Yunusov, 2001.
62. Yunusov, 1997; Yunusov, 2000.
63. Scott, 1990. The "hidden transcripts" around Karabakh are elaborated in Koehler and Zürcher, 2003.
64. Diaspora Humanitarian Assistance to Armenia in the Last Decade, 1999.
65. Collier et al., 2003a.
66. Yunusov, 2001.
67. Van Evera, 1994; Sandole, 1999.

68. Collier and Hoeffler, 2001.
69. Collier and Hoeffler, 2001.

NOTES TO CHAPTER 7

1. In 1989, the population of Dagestan was 1.77 million. Dagestan is ethnically and linguistically the most heterogeneous region of Russia. More than 30 distinct national groups live here, and linguists have counted over 80 separate languages. The largest group in Dagestan is the Avars, accounting in June 1996 for approximately 540,000 people, or 27 percent of the total population. The second largest group is the Dargins, comprising, in 1996, 15.5 percent of the population (310,000 people). The Laks (100,000 people, or around 5 percent of the total population) live alongside the Dargins in the central highlands of Dagestan. The third of the four largest national groups is the Lezgins (230,000, or 11.5 percent) and their close relatives, the Tabasarans (90,000, or 4.5 percent) and the Rutul (16,000). They populate the coast of the Caspian Sea. On the Caspian plain live the Kumyk, an Altaic Turkic-language group (250,000, or 13 percent). The Nogai (1.5 percent) are another Turkic people. In addition to these groups, around 70,000 Chechens; 80,000 Shiite Azeris; 160,000 Russians; and 10,000 Persian-speaking mountain Jews also live in Dagestan. Figures quoted in Wase and Kiesriev, 2001.
2. Brubaker, 1994; Lake and Rothchild, 1998.
3. Kisriev, 2002.
4. The saga of the Khachilaev brothers is reported by Nabi Abdullaev, a Dagestan-based journalist with the Institute for War and Peace Reporting: Abdullaev, 1998a; Abdullaev, 1998b; Abdullaev, 1998c; Abdullaev, 1998d.
5. Abdullaev, 1999.
6. Kisriev, 2003.
7. Kisriev, 2003.
8. The greatest threat to Dagestani stability was the national movement of the Lezgin, one of the four largest ethnic groups in Dagestan. Since 1991, the area inhabited by the Lezgin has been dissected by the international border between Dagestan and Azerbaijan. Around 200,000 Lezgin live in Dagestan, and around 170,000 in Azerbaijan. During the Soviet period, Azerbaijani and Dagestani Lezgin crossed the purely nominal border without any hindrance. Since June 1992, however, the border is an international border, drastically restricting the mobility of the Lezgin. Although Russia and Azerbaijan have repeatedly agreed to keep the border open, in 1994, Russia closed the border, primarily because Chechen rebels were being supplied through this route. This led to a strong reaction from the Lezgin. In April 1994, in Derbent, clashes between Lezgin, Azerbaijanis, and the police took several lives. In response to these events, Makhachkala sought to incorporate the Lezgin more strongly into the

state. The main concern of the Lezgin is now no longer the improvement of their status in Dagestan—as a rule, this is regarded as being entirely satisfactory—but, rather, the improvement of the situation for the Lezgin in neighboring Azerbaijan. The blame for the strict border regime is placed on Moscow and Baku, not on Makhachkala, which has credibly lent its support to the concerns of the Lezgin—thus defusing a potential secessionist movement.

9. Ware et al., 2001, p. 6.

10. Ethnicity plays a somewhat larger role for the Russians, the Chechens, and the Lezgin—that is, for those groups with an "ethnic big brother" in bordering regions.

11. Ware and Kisriev, 2001; Leonhardt, 1998; Kisriev, 2003.

12. Walker, 2000.

13. Ware and Kisriev, 2001; Ware and Kisriev, 2000.

14. Walker, 2000, p. 18.

15. Ware and Kisriev, 2001; Ware and Kisriev, 2000.

16. Ware and Kisriev, 2001, p. 25.

17. Aleksseev, 2001.

18. Ware and Kisriev, 2001, p. 13.

19. Ware and Kisriev, 2000.

20. Collier and Hoeffler, 2004a.

21. Personal communication, Tbilisi, July 28, 1998.

22. Derluguian, 1998.

23. Derluguian, 1998.

24. Toft, 2001;Toft, 2003.

25. Toft, 2003, p. 113.

26. Derluguian, 1998.

27. Derluguian, 2005.

NOTES TO CHAPTER 8

1. Beissinger, 2002, p. 283.

2. Gurr, 2000.

3. Ross, 2004a; Ross, 2004b.

4. This argument is elaborated by Brubaker, 1994; Bunce, 1999; Hughes and Sasse, 2001a; Hughes and Sasse, 2001b; Hughes and Sasse, 2002; Roeder, 1991; Roeder, 1999; Toft, 2001.

5. Ganev, 2005, p. 428.

6. De Waal, 2003, p. 19.

7. Novikova, 2001.

8. Quoted in De Waal, 2003, p. 163.

9. Quoted in De Waal, 2003, p. 165.

10. Grandits and Leutloff, 2003; Raufer, 2003.

11. Author's observation.
12. Based on the data compiled by Sambanis and Doyle, 2000.
13. Collier and Hoeffler, 2001.
14. Collier and Hoeffler, 2004b; De Soysa, 2000; Ross, 2001; Ross, 2003.
15. According to Collier and Hoeffler, 2004a, this is a determining factor.

Bibliography

Abdulatipov, Ramazan G., Boltenkova, Lubov F., and Yarov, Yuri F. (1993). *Federalizm v Istorii Rossii.* Moscow: lzdatel'stvo Respublika.

Abdullaev, Nabi (1998a). "Dagestan's Ethnic Elites." Institute for East-West Studies (IEWS), *Russian Regional Report* 3(21). Available online at http://se2.isn.ch/serviceengine/FileContent?serviceID=PublishingHouse&fileid=7187CA63-8DA6-390B-B15D-628054DA8B93&lng=en (accessed February 15, 2007).

Abdullaev, Nabi (1998b). "Dagestan Considers Banning Felons from Parliament." Institute for East-West Studies (IEWS), *Russian Regional Report* 3 (44). Available online at http://se2.isn.ch/serviceengine/FileContent?serviceID=PublishingHouse&fileid=7187CA63-8DA6-390B-B15D-628054DA8B93&lng=en (accessed February 15, 2007).

Abdullaev, Nabi (1998c). "Dagestani Leader Reelected with Undemocratic Procedures." Institute for East-West Studies (IEWS), *Russian Regional Report* 3 (26). Available online at http://se2.isn.ch/serviceengine/FileContent?serviceID=RESSpecNet&fileid=9281D91D-8E80-6797-A23E-01ECC3AD4067&lng=en (accessed February 15, 2007).

Abdullaev, Nabi (1998d). "A Personal Account of Chechen Terror: The Most Recent Prisoner of the Caucasus." Institute for East-West Studies (IEWS), *Russian Regional Report* 3(9), Available online at http://se2.isn.ch/serviceengine/FileContent?serviceID=RSSpecNet&fileid=5B227D16-7FB70376C-2D52-9324C14E898C&lng=en (accessed February 15, 2007).

Abdullaev, Nabi (1999). "Nadir and Magomed Khachilaev: Politicians for the New Russia." *Prism* 5(18). Available at http://www.jamestown.org/publications_details.php?volume_id=6&issue_id=402&article_id=3694 (accessed February 15, 2007).

Alexanian, Armine (2001). "The Institutional Framework of Caucasian and Central Asian Transitional Societies: Nagorno-Karabakh." Unpublished ms., prepared for the World Bank Development Economics Research Group Project on the Economics of Political and Common Violence,

Alexseev, Mikhail A. (2001). "Assuaging Ethnic Factionalism: Dagestan's Lessons for Post-Taliban Settlement in Afghanistan." *PONARS Policy Memo* 210. December 2001.

Alkhazashvili, Mark (2004). "South Ossetia's Reliance on Contraband." *Messenger. Georgia's English Language Daily,* July 15, 2004.

"Analiticheskii vestnik agenstua Postfactum" (1992). p. 2.

Arsaly, Dzh (1995). "Armyano-azerbaydzhanskii konflikt: voennyi aspekt." In: Dzh Arsaly (ed.), *Armyano-azerbaydzhanskii konflikt: voennyi aspekt.* Baku: N.p., pp. 4–68.

Baddeley, John F. (1908). *The Russian Conquest of the Caucasus.* London: Longmans, Green.

Baev, Pavel (1996). *The Russian Army in a Time of Troubles.* Thousand Oaks, Calif.: Sage.

Baev, Pavel K. (2003). "Civil Wars in Georgia: Corruption Breeds Violence." In: Jan Koehler and Christoph Zürcher (eds.), *Potentials of Disorder: Explaining Conflict and Stability in the Caucasus and in the Former Yugoslavia.* Manchester: Manchester University Press, pp. 127–145.

Balburov, Dmitry (1999). "Sharia Trial for Aslan Maskhadov." *Moscow News,* April 7, 1999, p. 7.

Beissinger, Mark (1992a). "Codebook for Event Databases: Non-Violent Demonstrations and Mass Violent Events in the Former USSR, 1987–1992." Unpublished ms., University of Wisconsin-Madison.

Beissinger, Mark (1992b). "Event Database Mass Violent Events in the Former USSR, 1987–1992." Unpublished ms., University of Wisconsin-Madison.

Beissinger, Mark R. (2002). *Nationalist Mobilization and the Collapse of the Soviet State.* Cambridge: Cambridge University Press.

Bennigsen, Alexandre, and Wimbush, S. Enders (1986). *Muslims of the Soviet Empire: A Guide.* Bloomington: Indiana University Press.

Bercovitch, Jacob, and Jackson, Richard (1997). *International Conflict: A Chronological Encyclopedia of Conflicts and Their Management 1945–1995.* Washington, D.C.: Congressional Quarterly Press.

Blandy, C. W. (2003). *Chechnya: Normalisation.* Camberley, Surrey: Defence Academy of the United Kingdom, Conflict Studies Research Center.

Borisov, Timofey (2001). "Na chi Dengi voyuyut Chechenskie Boeviki?" *Rossiyskaya Gazeta,* June 16, 2001, p. 7.

Bratton, Michael, and Walle, Nicholas Van Der (1996). *Democratic Experiments in Africa: Regime Transitions in Comparative Perspective.* Cambridge: Cambridge University Press.

Bremmer, Ian (1997). "Post-Soviet Nationalities Theory: Past, Present, and Future." In: Ian Bremmer and Ray Taras (eds.), *New States, new Politics: Building the Post-Soviet Nations.* Cambridge: Cambridge University Press, pp. 3–29.

Brinton, Mary C., and Nee, Victor (2001). *The New Institutionalism in Sociology.* Stanford: Stanford University Press.

Bromley, Yulian V. (1973). *Etnos i etnografiia.* Moscow: Nauka.

Bromley, Yulian V. (1981). *Sovremennye problemy etnografii.* Moscow: Nauka.

Bromley, Yulian V. (1983). *Ocherki teorii etnosa.* Moscow: Nauka.

Brown, Michael E., Coté, Owen R., Lynn-Jones, Sean M., and Miller, Steven E. (1997). *Nationalism and Ethnic Conflict: An International Security Reader.* Cambridge: MIT Press.

Broxup, Marie Benningsen (1992). *The North Caucasus Barrier.* London: C. Hurst.

Brubaker, Rogers (1994). "Nationhood and the National Question in the Soviet Union and Post-Soviet Eurasia: An Institutionalist Account." *Theory and Society* 23(1), pp. 47–78.

Brubaker, Rogers (1996). *Nationalism Reframed: Nationhood and the National Question in the New Europe.* Cambridge: Cambridge University Press.

Bugaj, Nikolai F. (1995). "Die stalinistischen Zwangsumsiedelungen kaukasischer Völker und ihre Konsequenzen." In: Uwe Halloach and Andreas Kappeler (eds.), *Krisenherd Kaukasus.* Baden-Baden: Nomos, pp. 216–244.

Bunce, Valerie (1999). *Subversive Institutions: The Design and the Destruction of Socialism and the State.* Cambridge: Cambridge University Press.

Bunich, Igor (1995). *Khronika chechenskoy voiny: Shest' dnei v Budennovske.* Petersburg: Oblik.

Carrere D'encausse, Helene (1993). *The End of Soviet Empire: The Triumph of Nations.* New York: New Republic.

"Chechnya: Parliament, Sharia Court Likely to End Conflict" (1998). *Itar-Tass,* Grozny, December 29.

Chorbajian, Levon, Donabedian, Patrick, and Mutafian, Claude (1994). *The Caucasian Knot: The History and Geo-politics of Nagorno-Karabakh.* London: Zed Books.

Collier, Paul (2000a). "Doing Well out of War: An Economic Perspective." In: Mats Berdal and David M. Malone (eds.), *Greed and Grievance: Economic Agendas in Civil Wars.* Boulder, Colo.: Lynne Rienner, pp. 91–113.

Collier, Paul (2000b). *Economic Causes of Civil Conflict and Their Implications for Policy.* Available online at http://www.worldbank.org/research/conflict/papers/civilconflict.htm (accessed January 6, 2001).

Collier, Paul (2000c). "Rebellion as a Quasi-Criminal Activity." *Journal of Conflict Resolution* 44(6), pp. 839–853.

Collier, Paul (2001). "Economic Causes of Civil Conflict and Their Implications for Policy." In: Chester A. Crocker, Fen Osler Hampson, and Pamela Aall (eds.), *Turbulent Peace. The Challenges of Managing International Conflict.* Washington, D.C.: U.S. Institute for Peace, pp. 143–163.

Collier, Paul, Elliot, V. L., Hegre, Havard, Hoeffler, Anke, Reynal-Querol, Marta, and Sambanis, Nicholas (2003a). *Breaking the Conflict Trap: Civil War and Development Policy.* New York: Oxford University Press.

Collier, Paul, Elliot, V. L., Hegre, Havard, Hoeffler, Anke, Reynal-Querol,

Marta, and Sambanis, Nicholas (2003b). "What Makes a Country Prone to Civil War?" In: Paul Collier, V. L. Elliot, Havard Hegre, Anke Hoeffler, Marta Reynal-Querol, and Nicholas Sambanis (eds.), *Breaking the Conflict Trap: Civil War and Development Policy.* New York: Oxford University Press, pp. 53–92.

Collier, Paul, and Hoeffler, Anke (1999a). "Justice Seeking and Loot-Seeking in Civil War." Unpublished ms., World Bank, Washington, D.C.

Collier, Paul, and Hoeffler, Anke (1999b). "On the Economic Causes of Civil War." *Oxford Economic Papers* 51(1), pp. 563–573.

Collier, Paul, and Hoeffler, Anke (2001). *Greed and Grievance in Civil War,* Revised Version, October 2001). Available online at http://www.worldbank.org/research/conflict/papers/greedandgrievance.htm (accessed May 14, 2002).

Collier, Paul, and Hoeffler, Anke (2004a). "Greed and Grievance in Civil War." *Oxford Economic Papers* 56(4), pp. 563–595.

Collier, Paul, and Hoeffler, Anke (2004b). "Resource Rents, Governance, and Conflict." *Journal of Conflict Resolution* 49(4), pp. 625–633.

Coppieters, Bruno, and Legvold, Robert (eds.) (2006). *Statehood and Security: Georgia after the Rose Revolution.* Cambridge: MIT Press.

Croissant, Michael P. (1998). *The Armenia-Azerbaijan Conflict: Causes and Implications.* Westport, Conn.: Praeger.

Damoisel, Mathilde, and Genté, Régis (2004). "Abkhazia: Stable but Fragile." *Le Monde Diplomatique* 01. Available online at http://mondediplo.com/2004/01/08abkhazia (accessed February 27, 2007).

Derluguian, Georgi M. (1998). "The Tale of Two Resorts: Abkhazia and Ajaria before and since the Soviet Collapse." In: Beverly Crawford and Ronnie D. Lipschutz (eds.), *The Myth of "Ethnic Conflict": Politics, Economics, and "Cultural" Violence.* Berkeley: University of California Press/University of California International and Area Studies Digital Collection, Edited Volume No. 98, pp. 261–292. Available online at http://repositories.cdlib.org/cgi/viewcontent.cgi?article=1064&context=uciaspubs/research (accessed December 12, 2002).

Derluguian, Georgi M. (2005). *Bourdieu's Secret Admirer in the Caucasus: A World-System Biography.* Chicago: University of Chicago Press.

De Rouen, Karl R., and Sobek, David (2004). "The Dynamics of Civil War Duration and Outcome." *Journal of Peace Research* 41(3), pp. 303–320.

De Soysa, Indra (2000). "The Resource Curse: Are Civil Wars Driven by Rapacity or Paucity?" In: Mats Berdal and David M. Malone (eds.), *Greed and Grievance: Economic Agendas in Civil Wars.* Boulder, Colo.: Lynne Rienner, pp. 113–137.

De Waal, Thomas (2003). *Black Garden: Armenia and Azerbaijan through Peace and War.* New York: New York University Press.

"Diaspora Humanitarian Assistance to Armenia in the Last Decade" (1999).

Paper prepared for Armenia Diaspora Conference, Yerevan, September 22–23, 1999. Available online at http://www.armeniadiaspora.com/conference99/humanitarian.html (accessed November 1, 2002).

Doyle, Michael W., and Sambanis, Nicholas (2000). "International Peacebuilding: A Theoretical and Quantitative Analysis." *American Political Science Review* 94(4), pp. 779–801.

"Dual Power in Chechnya?" (1999). *RFE/RL Caucasus Report* 2(6). Available online at http://rfe.rferl.org/reports/caucasus-report/1999/02/6-100299.asp (accessed February 17, 2007).

Duffield, Mark (2000). "Globalization, Transborder Trade, and War Economies." In: Mats Berdal and David M. Malone (eds.), *Greed and Grievance: Economic Agendas in Civil Wars*. Boulder, Colo.: Lynne Rienner, pp. 69–91.

Dunlop, John P. (1998). *Russia Confronts Chechnya: Roots of a Separatist Conflict*. Cambridge: Cambridge University Press.

Dunlop, John P. (2000). "How Many Soldiers and Civilians Died during the Russo-Chechen War of 1994–1996?" *Central Asian Survey* 19(3–4), pp. 328–338.

Dzhambulayev, D. (2000) "Kidnappers and Victims: A Scientist's Viewpoint." *Dagestanskaya Pravda*, 13 October. E-mail to mailing list AltChechnya@egroups.com, Thursday, October 26.

Easter, Gerald (1996). "Personal Networks and Post-Revolutionary State-Building: Soviet Russia Reexamined." *World Politics* 48, pp. 551–578.

Eilat, Yair, and Zinnes, Clifford (2002). "The Shadow Economy in Transition Countries: Friend or Foe? A Policy Perspective." *World Development* 30(7), pp. 1233–1254.

Elbadawi, Ibrahim, and Sambanis, Nicholas (2002). "How Much War Will We See? Estimating the Prevalence of Civil War in 161 Countries, 1960–1999." *Journal of Conflict Resolution* 46(3), pp. 307–334.

Elwert, Georg (1997). *Gewaltmärkte: Beobachtungen zur Zweckrationalität der Gewalt*. Cologne: Westdeutscher Verlag, pp. 86–101.

Elwert, Georg (2001). "The Command State in Africa: State Deficiency, Clientelism and Power-Locked Economies." In: Stefan Wippel and Inse Cornelssen (eds.), *Entwicklungspolitische Perspektiven im Kontext wachsender Komplexität (Festschrift Dieter Weiß)*. Bonn: Weltforum, pp. 419–452.

Elwert, Georg (2003). "Intervention in Markets of Violence." In: Jan Koehler and Christoph Zürcher (eds.), *Potentials of Disorder: Explaining Conflict and Stability in the Caucasus and in the Former Yugoslavia*. Manchester: Manchester University Press, pp. 219–243.

Elwert, Georg, Feuchtwang, Stephan, and Neubert, Dieter (1999). *Dynamics of Violence: Processes of Escalation and De-Escalation in Violent Group Conflicts*. Berlin: Duncker and Humblot.

Fairbanks, Charles H., Jr. (2002). "Weak States and Private Armies." In: Mark

Beissinger and Crawford Young (eds.), *Beyond State Crisis: Postcolonial Africa and Post-Soviet Eurasia in Comparative Perspective.* Washington, D.C.: Woodrow Wilson Center Press, pp. 129–159.

Fearon, James D. (1995). "Rationalist Explanation for War." *International Organisation* 49(3), pp. 379–414.

Fearon, James D. (1998). "Commitment Problems and the Spread of Ethnic Conflict." In: David Lake and Donald Rothchild (eds.), *The International Spread of Ethnic Conflict: Fear Diffusion, and Escalation.* Princeton: Princeton University Press, pp. 107–127.

Fearon, James D. (2004). "Why Do Some Civil Wars Last So Much Longer Than Others?" *Journal of Peace Research* 41(3), pp. 275–301.

Fearon, James D., and Laitin, David D. (1996). "Explaining Interethnic Co-operation." *American Political Science Review* 90(4), pp. 715–735.

Fearon, James D., and Laitin, David D. (2003). "Ethnicity, Insurgency, and Civil War." *American Political Science Review* 97(1), pp. 75–90.

Felgenhauer, Pavel (1995). "The Chechen Campaign." In: Mikhail Tsypkin (ed.), *War in Chechnya: Implications for Russian Security Policy.* Monterey, Calif.: Naval Postgraduate School.

Fowkes, Ben (1997). *The Disintegration of the Soviet Union: A Study in the Rise and Triumph of Nationalism.* New York: Macmillan.

Fuller, Elizabeth (1988). "Armenian Claims on Nagorno-Karabakh: The Backlash in Azerbaijan." *Radio Liberty* 35, pp. 7–10.

Fuller, Elizabeth (1993). "Paramilitary Forces Dominate Fighting in Transcaucasus." *RFE/RL Research Report* 2, pp. 74–82.

Gachechiladze, Ravaz (1995). *The New Georgia: Space, Society, Politics.* London: University College London Press

Gall, Carlotta, and De Waal, Thomas (1997). *Chechnya: A Small Victorious War.* London: Pan Original.

Gammer, Moshe (1994). *Muslim Resistance to the Tsar: Shamil and the Conquest of Daghestan.* London: Frank Cass.

Gammer, Moshe (2002). "Nationalism and History: Rewriting the Chechen National Past." In: Bruno Coppieters and Michael Huysseune (eds.), *Secession, History and the Social Sciences.* Brussels: VUB Brussels University Press, pp. 117–140.

Ganev, Venelin (2005). "Post-Communism as an Episode of State Building: A Reversed Tillyan Perspective." *Communist and Postcommunist Studies* 38, pp. 425–445.

"Geostrategische Motive Rußlands in Tschetschenien-Krieg?" (1995). *Osteuropa* 47(7), pp. A376–380.

Gerber, Jürgen (1997). *Georgien: Nationale Opposition und kommunistische Herrschaft seit 1965.* Baden-Baden: Nomos.

Gleditsch, Nils-Petter, Wallensteen, Peter, Eriksson, Mikael, Sollenberg, Margareta, and Strand, Havard (2002). "Armed Conflict 1946–2001: A New Dataset." *Journal of Peace Research* 39(5), pp. 615–637.

Goldenberg, Suzanne (1994). *Pride of Small Nations: The Caucasus and Post-Soviet Disorder.* London: Zed Books.

Goldstone, Jack A., Bates, Robert H., Gurr, Ted Robert, Lustik, Michael, Marshall, Monty G., Ulfelder, Jay, and Woodward, Mark (2005). "A Global Forecasting Model of Political Instability." Paper prepared for Annual Meeting of the American Political Science Association, Washington, D.C., September 1–4, 2005.

Goltz, Thomas (1999). *Azerbaijan Diary: A Rogue Reporter's Adventures in an Oil-Rich, War-Torn, Post-Soviet Republic.* New York: M. E. Sharpe.

Goskomstat (1996). *1989 USSR Population Census: The Final and Most Comprehensive Population Census of the Former Soviet Union Ever Conducted = Itogi Vsesoyuznoi perepisi naseleniya 1989 goda.* Minneapolis, Minn.: East View.

Götz, Roland (1995). "Noch ein Krieg ums Öl? Wirtschaftliche Analysen der russischen Invasion in Tschetschenien." *Aktuelle Analyse des BIOst (Bundesinstitut für Ostwissenschaftliche und Internationale Studien)*, 11.

Grandits, Hannes, and Leutloff, Caroline (2003). *Discources, Actors, Violence: The Organisation of War—Escalation in the Krajina Region of Croatia 1990–1991.* In: Jan Koehler and Christoph Zürcher (eds.), *Potentials of Disorder: Explaining Conflict and Stability in the Caucasus and in the Former Yugoslavia.* Manchester: Manchester University Press, pp. 23–46.

Griffin, Nicholas (2003). *Caucasus: Mountain Men and Holy Wars.* New York: St. Martin's.

Groong (2004). *The Rise and Fall of Samvel Babayan.* Armenian News Network/Groong. Available online at http://groong.usc.edu/ro/ro-20041006.html (accessed March 4, 2007).

Gumilev, Lev N. (1989). *Etnogenez i biosfera Zemli.* Moscow: Nauka.

Gurr, Ted R. (1993). "Why Minorities Rebel: A Global Analysis of Communal Mobilization and Conflict since 1945." *International Political Science Review* 14(2), pp. 161–201.

Gurr, Ted R. (2000). *Peoples versus States: Minorities at Risk in the New Century.* Washington, D.C.: U.S. Institute of Peace.

Gurr, Ted R., and Harff, Barbara (1995). "A Framework for Analysis of Ethnopolitical Mobilisation and Conflict." In: Ted R. Gurr and Barbara Harff (eds.), *Ethnic Conflict in World Politics: Order.* Boulder, Colo.: Westview, pp. 77–97.

Halbach, Uwe (1994). "Russlands Auseinandersetzung mit Tschetschenien." *Bericht des BIOst (Bundesinstitut für Ostwissenschaftliche und Internationale Studien)*, 61.

Halbach, Uwe (1995). "Jelzins Krieg im Kaukasus. Part II: Motivation, Rechtfertigungen, Ängste." *Aktuelle Analyse des BIOst (Bundesinstitut für Ostwissenschaftliche und Internationale Studien)*, 2.

Hegre, Havard, Ellingsen, Tanja, Gates, Scott, and Gleditsch, Nils Peter (2001). "Toward a Democratic Peace? Democracy, Political Change, and Civil War, 1816–1992." *American Political Science Review* 95(1), pp. 33–48.

Hill, Fiona (1995). *Russia's Tinderbox: Conflict in the North Caucasus and Its Implications for the Future of the Russian Federation.* Boston: Strengthening Democratic Institutions Project, Harvard University.

Holoboff, Elaine M. (1995). "Oil and the Burning of Grozny." *Jane's Intelligence Review* 7(6), pp. 253–257.

Holton, Robert J. (1998). *Globalization and the Nation State.* New York: St. Martin's.

Horowitz, Donald L. (1985). *Ethnic Groups in Conflict.* Berkeley.: University of California Press.

Hughes, James, and Sasse, Gwendolyn (2001a). "Comparing Regional and Ethnic Conflicts in Post-Soviet Transition States." *Regional and Federal Studies* 11(3), pp. 1–35.

Hughes, James, and Sasse, Gwendolyn (2001b). "Conflict and Accommodation in the Former Soviet Union: The Role of Institutions and Regimes." *Regional and Federal Studies* 11(3), pp. 220–240.

Hughes, James, and Sasse, Gwendolyn (2002). *Ethnicity and Territory in the Former Soviet Union.* London: Frank Cass.

Human Rights Watch (1995). *Russia: Three Months of War in Chechnya.* Helsinki: Human Rights Watch. Available online at http://www.hrw.org/reports/1995/Russia1.htm (accessed March 4, 2007).

Human Rights Watch (1996). *Russia, Chechnya and Daghestan: Caught in the Crossfire. Civilians in Gudermes and Pervomaiskoye.* Helsinki: Human Rights Watch.

Humphreys, Macartan (2005). "Natural Resources, Conflict, and Conflict Resolution." *Journal of Conflict Resolution* 49(4), pp. 508–537.

Huntington, Samuel (1993). "The Clash of Civilizations?" *Foreign Affairs* 72 (3), pp. 23–49.

Ignatieff, Michael (1998). *The Warriors Honor: Ethnic War and the Modern Conscience.* New York: Henry Holt.

International Helsinki Federation for Human Rights (1996). *The International Helsinki Federation for Human Rights Fact Finding Mission to Chechnya: 1–11. October 1996.* Vienna: Report to the Organization for Security and Develoment in Europe (OSCE).

International Helsinki Federation for Human Rights et al. (2005). *In a Climate of Fear: "Political Process" and Parliamentary Elections in Chechnya.* Helsinki: International Helsinki Federation for Human Rights (IHF), International Federation for Human Rights (FIDH), Norwegian Helsinki Committee, Center "Demos," and Human Rights Center "Memorial."

Isayev, Said (1998). "Opposed Chechen MPS to Debate Arsavon's Motion on New Body." *Itar-Tass*, Grozny, December 21.

Jacoby, Volker (1998a). "Geopolitische Zwangslage und nationale Identität: Die Konturen der innenpolitischen Konflikte in Armenien." Ph.D. diss., Johann Wolfgang Goethe-Universität, Frankfurt am Main.

Jacoby, Volker (1998b). "Geschichte und Geschichtsschreibung im Konflikt um Berg-Karabach." *Ethnos-Nation* 6, pp. 63–84.

Jaggers, Keith, and Gurr, Ted R. (1995). "Tracking Democracy's Third Wave with the Polity III Data." *Journal of Peace Research* 32(4), pp. 469–482.

Jean, François, and Rufin, Jean-Christophe (1999). *Ökonomie der Bürgerkriege*. Hamburg: Hamburger Edition.

Jones, Stephen F. (1993). "Georgia: A Failed Democratic Transition." In: Ian Bremmer and Raymond Taras (eds.), *Nation and Politics in the Soviet Successor States*. Cambridge: Cambridge University Press, pp. 288–310.

Jones, Stephen F. (1995). "Adventurers or Commanders? Civil Military Relations in Georgia since Independence." In: Daniel G. Zirker and Constantine P. Danopoulos (eds.), *Civil-Military Relations in the Soviet and Yugoslav Successor States*. Boulder, Colo.: Westview, pp. 35–52.

Kaldor, Mary (1999). *New and Old Wars: Organized Violence in a Global Era*. Stanford, Calif.: Stanford University Press.

Keen, David (1998). *The Economic Functions of Violence in Civil Wars*. London: Oxford University Press.

Keen, David (2000). "Incentives and Disincentives for Violence." In: Mats Berdal and David Malone (eds.), *Greed and Grievances: Economic Agendas in Civil War*. Boulder, Colo.: Lynne Rienner, pp. 19–43.

Khodarkovsky, Michael (2002). *Russia's Steppe Frontier: The Making of a Colonial Empire, 1500–1800*. Bloomington: Indiana University Press.

Kisriev, Enver (2002). "Dagestan: Rasprostranenie legkikh i strelkovykh vooruzhenii, problemy bezopasnosti i gumanitarnye posledstviya." Unpublished ms., Saferworld.

Kisriev, Enver (2003). "Why Is There Stability in Dagestan but Not in Chechnya?" In: Jan Koehler and Christoph Zürcher (eds.), *Potentials of Disorder: Explaining Conflict and Stability in the Caucasus and in the Former Yugoslavia*. Manchester: Manchester University Press, pp. 103–127.

Kisriev, Enver (2004). *Islam i Vlast' v Dagestane*. Moscow: O.G.I.

Koehler, Jan, and Zürcher, Christoph (eds.) (2003). *Potentials of Disorder: Explaining Conflict and Stability in the Caucasus and in the Former Yugoslavia*. Manchester: Manchester University Press.

Koehler, Jan, and Zürcher, Christoph (2004). "Der Staat und sein Schatten: Zur

Institutionalisierung hybrider Staatlichkeit im Süd-Kaukasus." *WeltTrends* 12(45), pp. 84–96.

Kolokloceva, Elena (1995). "Chechnya: Finansovyi Aisberg." *Moskovskie Novosti,* November (78), pp. 12–19.

Kovalyev, Sergei A., Blinushov, Andrei, et al. (1996). *By All Available Means: The Russian Federation Ministry of Internal Affairs Operation in the Village of Samashki.* Moscow: Memorial Human Rights Center.Lagnado, Alice (2000). "Russians Try to Bar Rebels' Escape Route." *Times* (London), January 26, 2000. Available online at http://www.cdi.org/russia/johnson/4069.html (accessed February 22, 2007).

Laitin, David D., and Suny, Robert G. (1999). "Armenia and Azerbaijan: Thinking a Way out of Karabakh." *Middle East Policy.* Available online at http://www.mepc.org/journal/9910_laitinsuny.html (accessed January 6, 2002).

Lake, David A., and Rothchild, Donald (1998). *The International Spread of Ethnic Conflict.* Princeton: Princeton University Press.

Lambroschini, Sophie (2000). "Russia: Journalist Kholodov's Alleged Assassins on Trial in Moscow." RFE/RL. Available online at http://www.rferl.org/nca/features/2000/11/15112000155511.asp (accessed September 14, 2001).

Lapidus, Gail (1998). "Contested Sovereignty: The Tragedy of Chechnya." *International Security* 23(1), pp. 5–49.

Leonhardt, Manuela (1998). "Nation and Nationality in Post-Soviet Daghestan." Paper prepared for the conference Potentials of (Dis-)Order: Former Yugoslavia and Caucasus in Comparison, Institute for East-European Studies, Free University, in Cooperation with the Institute of Ethnology, Berlin, 11–13 June 1999.

Libaridian, Gerard J. (1999). *The Challenge of Statehood: Armenian Political Thinking since Independence.* Watertown, Mass.: Blue Crane.

Lieven, Anatol (1998). *Chechnya: Tombstone of Russian Power.* New Haven, Conn.: Yale University Press.

Lijphart, Arend (1975). *The Politics of Accommodation: Pluralism and Democracy in the Netherlands.* Berkeley: University of California Press.

Lijphart, Arend (1985). *Power-Sharing in South Africa.* Berkeley: Institute of International Studies, University of California.

Luchterhandt, Otto (1993). "Das Recht Berg-Karabaghs auf staatliche Unabhängigkeit aus völkerrechtlicher Sicht." *Archiv des Völkerrecht* 31, pp. 30–81.

Makarenko, Tamara (2001). *The Changing Faces of Terrorism within the Russian Federation.* Caspian Brief No. 18. Stockholm: Cornell Caspian Consulting

Mansfield, Edward, and Snyder, Jack (2002). "Democratic Transitions, Institutional Strength, and War." *International Organization* 56(2), pp. 297–337.

Mayntz, Renate, and Scharpf, Fritz W. (1995). "Der Ansatz des akteurszentrierten Institutionalismus." In: Renate Mayntz and Fritz W. Scharpf (eds.), *Gesellschaftliche Selbstregelung und politische Steuerung.* Frankfurt am Main: Campus, pp. 39–72.

McAdam, Doug, Tarrow, Sidney, and Tilly, Charles (2001). *Dynamics of Contention.* Cambridge: Cambridge University Press.

McAuley, Alastair (ed.) (1991). *Soviet Federalism, Nationalism and Economic Decentralisation.* Leicester: Leicester University Press.

Médecins Sans Frontières (1999). "The Tracking of Civilians: Interviews with Chechen Refugees in Georgia," December 31. Available online at http://www.reliefweb.int/ (accessed March 4, 2007).

Melkonian, Monte, and Melkonian, Markar (1993). *The Right to Struggle: Selected Writings by Monte Melkonian on the Armenian National Question.* San Francisco: Sardarabad Collective.

"Moscow Grozny Seek to Contain Latest Crisis" (1999). *RFE/RL Caucasus Report* 2(11). Available online at http://www.rferl.org/reports/caucasus-report/1999/03/11-170399.asp (accessed February 22, 2007).

"New Government of Chechnya to Start Functioning No Later Than 20 January" (1997). *Ria Novosti, Kometa Tepsayeva,* Grozny, January 4.

Nizharadze, Georgii (2001). "The Institutional Framework of Caucasian and Central Asian Transitional Societies: Georgia, Abkhazia and South-Ossetia." Unpublished ms., World Bank Development Economics Research Group (DECRG) Project on the Economics of Political and Common Violence, Tbilisi.

Nodia, Ghia (1988). "The Conflict in Abkhazia: National Projects and Political Circumstances." In: Bruno Coppieters and Yuri Anchabadze (eds.), *Georgians and Abkhazians: The Search for a Peace Settlement.* Cologne: Bundesinstitut für Ostwissenschaftliche und Internationale Studien, pp. 14–48.

Nodia, Ghia (1995). "Georgia's Identity Crisis." *Journal of Democracy* 6(1), pp. 105–116.

North, Douglas (1990). *Institutions, Institutional Change and Economic Performance.* Cambridge: Cambridge University Press.

Novikova, Gayane (2001). "The Institutional Framework of Caucasian and Central Asian Transitional Societies: Armenia and Nagorno-Karabakh." Unpublished ms., World Bank Development Economics Research Group (DECRG) Project on the Economics of Political and Common Violence, Yerevan.

Olson, Mancus (1965). The Logic of Collective Action: Public Goods and the Theory of Groups. Cambridge: Harvard University Press.

Onyx, J, Bullen, P. (2000). "Measuring Social Capital in Five Communities." *Journal of Applied Behavioral Science* 36(1), pp. 23–42.

Orlov, O. P., and Cherkassov, A. V. (1998). *Rossia–Chechyna: Tsep' oshibok i prestuplenii.* Moscow: Zven'ya, Obshchestvo Memorial.

Orlov, Oleg, Cherkasov, Aleksandr, and Sirotkin, Stepan (1995). *Conditions in Detention Camps in the Chechen Republic Conflict Zone: Treatment of Detainees.* Moscow: Memorial Human Rights Center.

"Over Half of Oil Produced in Chechnya in 1998 Stolen" (1999). *Itar-Tass,* Grozny, March 1.

Pain, Emil A., and Popov, Aleksander (1995). "Chechenskaya Politika Rossii s 1991 do 1994 gg." *Mirovaya Ekonomika i Mezhdunarodnye Otnosheniya* 5, pp. 19–32.

Powell, Walter W., and Dimaggio, Paul (1991). *The New Institutionalism in Organizational Analysis.* Chicago: University of Chicago Press.

"Put' Djokhar—kuda on privel?" (1998) Trud, 8 December.

Putin, Vladimir (1999). Press conference, September 24; quoted at http://en.wikiquote.org/wiki/Vladimir_Putin (accessed 23 February 2007).

Putnam, Robert D., Leonardi, Robert, and Nanetti, Raffaella (1993). *Making Democracy Work: Civic Traditions in Modern Italy.* Princeton, N.J.: Princeton University Press.

Raufer, Xavier (2003). "A Neglected Dimension of Conflict: The Albanian Mafia." In: Jan Koehler and Christoph Zürcher (eds.), *Potentials of Disorder: Explaining Conflict and Stability in the Caucasus and in the Former Yugoslavia.* Manchester: Manchester University Press, pp. 62–75.

Reno, Williams (1999). *Warlord Politics and African States.* Boulder, Colo.: Lynne Rienner.

Reno, William (2000). "Shadow States and the Political Economy of Civil Wars." In: Mats Berdal and David M. Malone (eds.), *Greed and Grievance: Economic Agendas in Civil Wars.* Boulder, Colo.: Lynne Rienner, pp. 43–69.

Reynolds, Michael A. (2000). "Indigenous Attempts at State Building in the North Caucasus." Paper prepared for the Annual Conference of the American Society for the Study of the Nationalities (ASN), Columbia University, New York, April 13–15, 2000.

Roeder, Philip G. (1991). "Soviet Federalism and Ethnic Mobilization." *World Politics* 43(2), pp. 196–232.

Roeder, Philip G. (1999). "Revolutions and States after 1989: The Political Costs of Incomplete National Revolutions." *Slavic Review* 58(4), pp. 743–755.

Ross, Michael (2001). "Natural Resources and Civil Conflict: Evidence from Case Studies." Paper prepared for the World Bank/UC Irvine workshop on Civil Wars and Post-Conflict Transitions, Irvine, Calif., May 18–20, 2001. Available online at http://www.hypatia.ss.uci.edu/gpacs/newpages/Ross1.pdf (accessed April 27, 2002).

Ross, Michael L. (2003). "Oil, Drugs and Diamonds: The Varying Roles of Natural Resources in Civil Wars." In: Karen Ballentine and Jake Sherman (eds.), *The Political Economy of Armed Conflict.* Boulder, Colo.: Lynne Rienner, pp. 47–70.

Ross, Michael L. (2004a). "How Do Natural Resources Influence Civil War? Evidence from Thirteen Cases." *International Organization* 58(1), pp. 35–67.

Ross, Michael L. (2004b). "What Do We Know about Natural Resources and Civil War?" *Journal of Peace Research* 41(3), pp. 337–356.

Rubin, Barnett R., and Snyder, Jack (1998). *Post-Soviet Political Order: Conflict and State Building.* London: Routledge.

"Russian Crackdown in Chechnya Killed 40,000 Civilians," *Agence France Presse,* May 15, 2000.

Russian Information Centre and R. I. A. Novosti (2001). *Chechnya: The White Paper.* Second edition. Russian Information Centre and RIA Novosti, Moscow. Available online at http://www.infocentre.ru/eng_user/index.cfm?page=10 (accessed September 14, 2001).

Sambanis, Nicholas (2001). "Do Ethnic and Non-Ethnic Civil Wars Have the Same Causes? A Theoretical and Empirical Inquiry (Part 1)." *Journal of Conflict Resolution* 45(3), pp. 259–282.

Sambanis, Nicholas, and Doyle, Michael (2000). "International Peacebuilding: A Theoretical and Quantitative Analysis." American Political Science Review 94(4), pp. 779–801.

Sambanis, Nicholas, and Elbadawi, Ibrahim (2002). "How Much War Will We See? Estimating the Prevalence of Civil War in 161 Countries, 1960–1999." *Journal of Conflict Resolution,* 46(3), pp. 307–334.

Sandole, Dennis (1999). *Capturing the Complexity of Conflict: Dealing with Violent Ethnic Conflicts of the Post-Cold War Era.* London: Pinter.

Sapozhnikov, Boris (2003). "Second Chechen Campaign Takes Its Toll." *Gazeta.Ru,* February 18, 2003. Available online at http://www.cdi.org/russia/johnson/7076-8.cfm (accessed February 22, 2007).

Scharpf, Fritz W. (1997). *Games Real Actors Play: Actor-Centered Institutionalism in Policy Research.* Boulder, Colo.: Westview.

Schrepfer-Proskurjakov, Alexander (2006). "Deportation der Tschetschenen. Stalin liess 450 000 Tschetschenen und Inguschen deportieren." *IfT (Information für die Truppe),* April 5, 2006. Available online at http://ifdt.de/0401/Artikel/sp.htm (accessed March 4, 2007).

Scott, James C. (1990). *Domination and the Arts of Resistance: Hidden Transcripts.* New Haven, Conn.: Yale University Press.

Segbers, Klaus (1994). "Danke, Boris! Rußlands desaströse Politik gegenüber Tschetschenien ist Produkt eines kurzatmigen innenpolitischen Kalküls." *Die Tageszeitung* (Berlin), December 31, 1994, p. 10.

Sheehy, Anne (1991). "Ethnographic Developments and the Soviet Federal System." In: Alastair McAuley (ed.), *Soviet Federalism, Nationalism and Economic Decentralisation.* Leicester: Leicester University Press, pp. 33–55.

Sherman, Jake (2001). "The Economies of War: The Intersection of Need,

Creed and Greed." Paper prepared for the conference on the Economics of War, International Peace Academy, Woodrow Wilson International Center for Scholars, Washington, D.C., September 10, 2001.

Slider, Darrell (1997). "Democratization in Georgia." In: Karen Dawisha and Bruce Parrot (eds.), *Conflict, Cleavage and Change in Central Asia and the Caucasus*. Cambridge: Cambridge University Press, pp. 156–200.

Snyder, Jack (2000). *From Voting to Violence: Democratization and Nationalist Conflict*. New York: Norton.

Sokirianskaja, Ekaterina (2005). "Families and Clans in Ingushetia and Chechnya: A Fieldwork Report." *Central Asian Survey* 24(4), pp. 453–467.

Steinmo, Sven, Thelen, Kathleen Ann, and Longstreth, Frank (1992). *Structuring Politics: Historical Institutionalism in Comparative Analysis*. Cambridge: Cambridge University Press.

Suny, Ronald G. (1989). "Return to Ararat: Armenia in the Cold War." *Armenian Review* 42(3/167), pp. 1–19.

Suny, Ronald G. (1993). *Looking toward Ararat: Armenia in Modern History*. Bloomington: Indiana University Press.

Suny, Ronald G. (1994). *The Making of the Modern Georgian Nation*. Bloomington: Indiana University Press.

Suny, Robert G. (1995). "Elite Transformation in Late-Soviet and Post-Soviet Transcaucasia, or: What Happens When the Ruling Class Can't Rule?" In: Timothy J. Colton and Robert C. Tucker (eds.), *Patterns in Post-Soviet Leadership*. Boulder, Colo.: Westview, pp. 141–167.

Taysumov, Bakar (1997). "Nakanune stolknoveniya s metropliyey." *Nezavisimaya Gazeta*, February 21, 1997, p. 5.

"The Time the Chechen Authorities Gave the Illegal Armed Formations to Cease Their Activity Has Run Out" (1998). *Ria Novosti, Kometa Tepsayeva*, Grozny, July 21.

Tishkov, Valerie (1997). *Ethnicity, Nationalism and Conflict in and after the Soviet Union: The Mind Aflame*. London: Sage.

Tishkov, Valery (1999). "Ethnic Conflict in the Former USSR: The Use and Misuse of Typologies and Data." *Journal of Peace Research* 36(5), pp. 571–591.

Tishkov, Valery A. (2000). "Forget the 'Nation': Post-Nationalist Understanding of Nationalism." *Ethnic and Racial Studies* 23(4), pp. 625–650.

Tishkov, Valerii (2004). *Chechnya: Life in a War-Torn Society*. Berkeley: University of California Press.

Toft, Monica Duffy (2001). "Multinationality, Regional Institutions, State-Building and the Failed Transition in Georgia." *Regional and Federal Studies* 11(3), pp. 123–142.

Toft, Monica Duffy (2003). *The Geography of Ethnic Violence: Identity, Interests, and the Indivisibility of Territory*. Princeton, N.J.: Princeton University Press.

Van Evera, Stephan (1994). "Hypotheses on Nationalism and War." *International Security* 18(4), pp. 5–39.

Vasil'eva, Olga Muzaev Timur (1994). *Severnii Kavkaz v posikakh regional'noi ideologii.* Moscow: Progress.

Walker, Edward W. (2000). *Russia's Soft Underbelly: The Stability of Instability in Dagestan.* Working Paper Series. Berkeley: Berkeley Program in Soviet and Post-Soviet Studies, University of California.

Wall, E., Ferazzi, G., and Schryer, F. (1998). "Getting the Goods on Social Capital." *Rural Sociology* 63, pp. 300–322.

Walter, Barbara (2004). "Does Conflict Beget Conflict? Explaining Recurring Civil War." *Journal of Peace Research* 41(3), pp. 371–388.

Walter, Barbara F., and Snyder, Jack (1999). *Civil Wars, Insecurity and Intervention.* New York: Columbia University Press.

Ware, Robert B., and Kisriev, Enver (2000). "Political Stability in Dagestan: Ethnic Parity and Religious Polarization." *Problems of Post-Communism* 47 (2), pp. 23–34.

Ware, Robert B., and Kisriev, Enver (2001). "Ethnic Parity and Political Stability in Dagestan: A Consociational Approach." *Europe and Asia Studies* 53 (1), pp. 105–133.

Ware, Robert B., Kisriev, Enver, Patzelt, Werner J., and Roericht, Ute (2001). "Democratization in Dagestan." Paper prepared for delivery at the Annual Meeting of the American Political Science Association, San Francisco, September 1, 2001.

Weinstein, Jeremy M. (2005). "Resources and the Information Problem in Rebel Recruitment." *Journal of Conflict Resolution* 49(4), pp. 598–624.

Weisbrode, Kenneth (2001). *Central Eurasia: Price or Quicksand? Contending Views of Instability in Karabakh, Ferghana and Afghanistan.* London: International Institute for Strategic Studies.

Wheatley, Jonathan (2005). *Georgia from National Awakening to Rose Revolution: Delayed Transition in the Former Soviet Union.* Aldershot: Ashgate.

Woolcock, Michael, and Naranyan, Deepa (2001). "Social Capital: Implications for Development Theory, Research and Policy." *World Bank Research Observer* 15(2), pp. 225–249.

Yunusov, Arif (1996). *Statistics of the Karabakh War.* Baku: Institute of Peace and Democracy.

Yunusov, Arif (1997). "Azerbaijan in the Post-Soviet Period: Problems and Possible Ways of Development." In: Olga A. Vorkunova and Armen E. Iskandaryan (eds.), *Collection "Northern Caucasus–Transcaucasus": Problems of Stability and Prospects of Development.* Moscow: Company Grif-F, pp. 127–147.

Yunusov, Arif (2000). *Migratsionnye potok: oborotnaya storona nezavisimosti stran Zakavkaz'ya.* Moscow: ZAO Finstatinform, pp. 107–115.

Yunusov, Arif (2001). "The Institutional Framework of Caucasian and Central Asian Transitional Societies: Azerbaijan." Unpublished ms., World Bank DECRG Project on the Economics of Political and Common Violence, Baku.

Yusupov, Musa (1998). *Region Early Warning Report: Chechnya.* FEWER, Forum on Early Warning and Response. Available online at http://www.fewer.org/caucasus/index.htm. (accessed October 4, 2001).

Zelkina, Anna (1996). "Islam and Society in Chechnia: From the Late Eighteenth to the Mid-Nineteenth Century." *Journal of Islamic Studies* 7(2), pp. 241–243.

Zlapotol'skii, D. L. (1960). *Gosudarstvennoe Ustroistvo SSSR.* Moscow: Izd. Yuridicheskoi Literatury.

Zürcher, Christoph (1997). "Krieg und Frieden in Tschetschenien: Ursachen, Symbole, Interessen." Working paper 2, Osteuropa-Institut der Freien Universität, Berlin. Available online at http://userpage.fu-berlin.de/%7Esegbers/downloads/working_papers/AP02.pdf (accessed February 27, 2007).

Zürcher, Christoph (1998). "Der Pyrrhus-Sieg der Republik Itschkeria: Zur Situation in Tschetschenien nach dem Krieg." *Perspektiven* 31(June–July), pp. 16–17.

Zürcher, Christoph (1999). "Multikulturalizm i etnopoliticheskii poryadok v postsovetskoi Rossii: Nekotorye metodologicheskie zamechaniya." *POLIS* 6, pp. 105–118.

Zürcher, Christoph (2000). "In den Kreml via Grozny: Putins Krieg in Tschetschenien." *Berliner Osteuropa-Info* 14, pp. 38–41.

Zürcher, Christoph (2002). "Institutionen und organisierte Gewalt: Konflikt- und Stabilitätsdynamiken im (post-)sowjetischen Raum." Habilitationschrift, Fachbereich Politik- und Sozialwissenschaft der Freien Universität Berlin.

Zürcher, Christoph (2004). "Entbettung: Empirische institutionenzentrierte Konfliktanalyse." In: Julia Eckert (ed.), *Anthropologie der Konflikte: Georg Elwerts konflikttheoretische These in der Diskussion.* Bielefeld: Transcript, pp. 102–121.

Zürcher, Christoph, and Koehler, Jan (2001). "Institutions and Organizing Violence in Post-Socialist Societies." *Berliner Osteuropa Info* 17, pp. 48–52.

Zürcher, Christoph, Baev, Pavel, and Koehler, Jan (2005). "Civil Wars in the Caucasus." In: Paul Collier and Nicholas Sambanis (eds.), *Understanding Civil War: Evidence and Analysis.* Vol. 2: *Europe, Central Asia and Other Regions.* Washington, D.C.: World Bank, pp. 259–299.

Zürn, Michael, and Brozus, Lars (1996). "Kulturelle Konfliktlinien: Ersatz für den Kalten Krieg?" *Internationale Politik* 12, pp. 45–54.

Zverev, Alexei (1996). *Ethnic Conflicts in the Caucasus 1988–1994.* Available online at http://poli.vub.ac.be/publi/ContBorders/eng/ch0101.htm (accessed March 13, 2002).

Index

About the Author

Christoph Zürcher is Professor of Political Science at the Free University in Berlin. He is the editor of *Potentials of Dis/Order: Explaining Violence in the Caucasus and in the Former Yugoslavia.*